International Socialism 138

Spring 2013

Analysis

Economic blues · *Alex Callinicos* · 3

Imperialism and instability in East Asia today · *Ha-young Kim* · 21

The class struggles in Europe · *Joseph Choonara* · 49

Portugal's struggle against austerity · *Catarina Príncipe* · 79

Marxism and women's oppression today · *Sheila McGregor* · 95

Lenin's "Left-Wing" Communism: An Infantile Disorder revisited · *John Rose* · 129

Two in one? · *Leandros Bolaris* · 147

Agriculture, class and capitalism · *Henry Bernstein* · 161

Feedback

Greece, politics and Marxist strategy · *T Kampagiannis* · 173
A reply to Nigel Harris · *Adrian Budd* · 181
Some thoughts on Paul Levi · *Ian Birchall* · 199

Reviews · 209

Marx and nationalism, the pharmaceutical industry, early Christianity, struggle in Botswana, radical black internationalism, youth culture in China
Ben Selwyn, Sophie Williams, Nick Evans, Andy Wynne, Christian Høgsbjerg, Sally Kincaid

Pick of the quarter · 223

Contributors

Henry Bernstein is now retired from teaching at SOAS. He was co-editor with Terry Byres of the *Journal of Peasant Studies* from 1985-2000, and founding editor with Byres of the *Journal of Agrarian Change* in 2001.

Ian Birchall has just edited an issue of *Revolutionary History* devoted to solidarity action with the Algerian liberation struggle by European revolutionaries, and is currently working on a book about internationalism and the French left.

Leandros Bolaris is a member of the Greek Socialist Workers Party (SEK).

Adrian Budd teaches politics at London South Bank University, where he is UCU branch secretary. His book *Class, States and International Relations: A Critical Appraisal of Robert Cox and Neo-Gramscian Theory* is published in Spring 2013.

Joseph Choonara is a regular contributor to *International Socialism* and the author of *Unravelling Capitalism: A Guide to Marxist Political Economy*.

Nick Evans is a postgraduate student and activist at the University of Oxford.

Christian Høgsbjerg is editor of a special edition of CLR James's 1934 play about the Haitian Revolution, *Toussaint Louverture: The Story of the Only Successful Slave Revolt in History*.

Thanasis Kampagiannis is a lawyer in Athens and a member the editorial board of *Sosialismos Apo ta Kato* (Socialism From Below), the magazine of SEK in Greece.

Ha-young Kim is a member of All Together and co-editor of *Marx 21* in South Korea.

Sally Kincaid is a teacher and activist in the NUT in Leeds.

Sheila McGregor is a long time socialist activist and trade unionist, and occasional contributor to *International Socialism*.

Catarina Príncipe is a member of the Portuguese Bloco and the anti-precarity organisation Precários Inflexíveis. She now lives in Berlin.

John Rose is the author of *Myths of Zionism*.

Ben Selwyn teaches at the University of Sussex and is the author of *Workers, State and Development in Brazil: Powers of Labour, Chains of Value*.

Sophie Williams is a postgraduate researcher and activist at the University of Oxford.

Andy Wynne is a socialist activist in Leicester.

Economic blues

Alex Callinicos

It will soon be six years since the credit crunch that developed in the summer of 2007 announced the onset of the present global economic and financial crisis. But the core regions of advanced capitalism remain mired in depression—that is, a long period when economies expand below their growth rate in the years before the crisis. To quote the Marxist economist Michael Roberts: "The world economy crawls along, with the US and China leading the way and Japan and Europe struggling along behind".[1]

The *Financial Times* recently reported the findings of a new real-time growth index:

> In one of the weakest recoveries from recession on record, the pattern of economic data posted has struggled to remain above par in the US, the eurozone, Japan or the UK since the depths of the financial and economic crisis four years ago.

> Persistent weak growth has dashed the hopes of governments and economists and cast doubt on the ability of rich economies to grow at anything like the 2 percent plus annual rates enjoyed before the crisis...

> The research, for example, suggests that US economic news has been no better than normal and the country's recovery has been characterised by

---

1:   Roberts, 2013d.

mini-cycles of moderately good, then bad, data since 2010. The growth figures subsequently published by official sources corroborate that account.

Allesandro Beber, professor of finance at Cass Business School, said: "Since the crisis, the US has been chugging along around zero. Each time the recovery looks like it's picking up, it then falls back."

If the US has struggled to achieve a recovery, with better than normal growth, from recession, it is a miracle economy compared with the eurozone.[2]

Indeed, what has become most visible recently is that the eurozone crisis hasn't gone away. This reality has been masked by the impact of the announcement last July by Mario Draghi, president of the European Central Bank (ECB), that "the ECB is ready to do whatever it takes to preserve the euro". The implicit promise that the ECB would use its unlimited power to create money to prevent the eurozone from disintegrating was followed up with a bizarrely named new programme, Outright Monetary Transactions (OMT). Under this the ECB undertook to intervene in secondary bond markets to buy the debt of eurozone governments that in exchange implemented austerity measures under the surveillance of the troika of the bank itself, the European Commission and the International Monetary Fund (IMF).

No member state has taken up this enticing offer, but Draghi's demarche was sufficient to reassure financial markets. The spreads on government debt for states such as Ireland, Italy, Portugal, and Spain—ie the difference between the interest rate that the governments of these countries need to pay to borrow money and that on ultra-safe German Bunds—narrowed significantly, and investors started buying bank and corporate bonds in the so-called eurozone "periphery". It looked as if the economic situation in the eurozone was beginning to return to what counts as "normality" for the financial markets, even if tens of millions of people were being driven by austerity into conditions of great misery.

The gap between this perception and economic reality was exposed by the outcome of the Italian general election on 24-25 February. The Italian economy has been hit hard by austerity, implemented by Mario Monti, the "technocratic" prime minister installed after his predecessor, Silvio Berlusconi, had been effectively sacked by the German chancellor, Angela Merkel, and the then French president, Nicolas Sarkozy, in November 2011. According to Roberts, "Italy is entering a second year of

---

2:   Giles, 2013.

real GDP contraction since the 'recovery' from the Great Recession" of 2008-9. Monti's measures exacerbated the long-term difficulties of Italian capitalism: the rate of profit has fallen by 20 percent since 2000 and real average earnings are now 2 percent below their 2004 level.[3] In January the unemployment rate rose to 11.7 percent, the highest level for 21 years.[4] Meanwhile, industrial output is 25 percent below the pre-crisis level.

The election was therefore a referendum against austerity. Monti, the Troika's man, was humiliated with 10.56 percent of the vote. The big winners were Beppe Grillo's populist Five-Star Movement (M5S, 25.5 percent), which is, rhetorically at least, against austerity and for an Italian exit from the eurozone, and the right wing coalition headed by Berlusconi (29.18 percent): he managed to clamber out of the political grave by campaigning against Monti's economic policies. The big loser was the social liberal Democratic Party (PD) headed by Pier Luigi Bersani, who sought to demonstrate his moderation by aligning himself with Monti. Although PD and its allies squeaked narrowly into first place with 29.54 percent of the vote, the majority they secured in the Chamber of Deputies thanks to the rule that gives the first party extra seats isn't enough to form a stable government because they lack a majority in the upper house of parliament.

Grillo's ambiguous politics combines denunciations of Italy's deeply corrupt establishment with much more reactionary themes (for example, opposition to the children of immigrants getting Italian citizenship, and hostility to the trade unions). The M5S's anti-elite rhetoric and identification with protest movements against high-speed rail lines and the privatisation of water attracted the votes of workers and young people disillusioned with the PD and the radical left. Grillo, who describes his role as that of "social containment", preventing discontent turning violent, seems intent on acting as a spoiler in the cabinet games now being played out in Rome, presumably in the hope of winning the next election outright.

Political instability in Italy sent a shiver through the markets reminding them of the economic weakness underlying the recovery in confidence since Draghi's intervention last summer. Spreads on Italian and Spanish government debt widened. Elsewhere in southern Europe the picture also looks grim: Greece's central bank predicts that the economy will shrink another 5 percent in 2013 (the sixth straight year of a 1930s style slump) and the government is resisting the Troika's demand that it sack 25,000 civil servants.[5]

3: Roberts, 2013c.
4: www.tradingeconomics.com/italy/unemployment-rate
5: Hope and Spiegel, 2013.

But these problems have been overshadowed by a development that underlines the scale of the crisis that the financialised capitalism of the neoliberal era is facing. In mid-March southern Cyprus became the fourth eurozone member (after Greece, Ireland and Portugal) to be bailed out by the troika. The Greek Cypriot banking system has been used by Russian oligarchs to launder money then employed to finance property speculation all over Europe. Southern Cyprus banks, which were hit hard by the Greek crisis, held €68 billion in deposits (an estimated €25 billion of these Russian) at the end of January, compared to a GDP of only €17.31 billion.[6] The €10 billion "rescue" would have been larger if the IMF and German finance minister Wolfgang Schäuble hadn't in an astonishingly inept move forced Nicosia to seize €5.8 billion from depositors to help pay for their banks' failed gambles and to protect the holders of Cyprus government bonds.

Faced with the imminent collapse of the second biggest bank, Laiki, and with threats by the ECB to withdraw its programme of Emergency Liquidity Assistance from all the island's banks, the newly elected right wing president Nicos Anastasiades caved in and imposed a 6.75 percent tax on deposits of up to €100,000. In hitting small savers he was trying to keep the tax on the bigger fish below 10 percent and thereby to preserve southern Cyprus's role as an offshore banking centre. Instead he provoked a domestic political storm and furious attacks from Russia. We go to press after the Cypriot parliament had rejected the deal: with the finance minister visiting Moscow cap in hand, the ECB threatened to pull out the liquidity plug unless Nicosia accepted the Troika's terms.[7]

As the economic commentator Wolfgang Münchau points out, the deal "effectively defaults on" the national guarantees of bank deposits up to €100,000 introduced by European governments introduced at the height of the financial panic in the autumn of 2008: "If one wanted to feed the political mood of insurrection in southern Europe, this was the way to do it. The long-term political damage of this agreement is going to be huge. In the short term, the danger consists of a generalised bank run, not just in Cyprus".[8] Marc Ostwald of Monument Securities said the bailout "highlights how post 2007 efforts to resuscitate and rescue Western economies have continued to favour the vested interests of the financial sector, while treating the 'population at large' with disdain and contempt—this sort of attitude is still a seedbed for social revolution, as has been witnessed above

---

6:    Hope, Clover and Steen, 2013.
7:    Spiegel, 2013a and 2013b.
8:    Munchau, 2013.

all in the Arab Spring".[9] What looks to be the final deal protects small savers, while bailing the bigger ones into the brutal restructuring of the two biggest banks demanded by the Troika. But the after-effects will make themselves felt well beyond Cyprus for some time to come.

Even before the Cypriot debacle Ian Kelson at T Rowe Price International told the *Financial Times*: "We've now moved from 'crisis contained' to 'crisis not solved'. Growth is still weak, especially in Spain and Italy, and the politics are becoming noisier".[10] There is, however, no sign of any retreat from austerity. In the eurozone it is locked into place by the fiscal treaty signed at German insistence by most European Union (EU) member states. "Much of the fiscal adjustment Italy went through will continue going on on automatic-pilot," Draghi smugly told a recent press conference: so much for the electoral revolt against austerity.[11] The German government has increased the pressure on the rest of the eurozone by announcing it intends to bring the budget into balance in 2015, a year earlier than it is required to under a constitutional amendment passed in 2009 (the new treaty makes signatories write a similar commitment to balanced budgets into their constitutions).

Britain stayed out of the pact, but its Conservative-Liberal coalition continues to press ahead with more cuts in public spending, despite the fact that it is presiding over a shrinking economy. Prime minister David Cameron echoed Margaret Thatcher when he announced before the budget on 20 March: "This month's budget will be about sticking to the course because there is no alternative that will secure our country's future".[12] Across the Atlantic the US economy is also on fiscal autopilot. The standoff between Barack Obama and the Republicans in Congress meant that the sequester agreed on to end the debt crisis in July 2011 came into force at the beginning of March. The cuts it mandates will take $3.5 trillion off federal government spending over the next decade, amounting to nearly 5 percent of national income in 2010-14.[13]

Draghi's prominence in managing the eurozone crisis highlights the other side to the fiscal squeeze on public spending: the central banks are exercising great discretion in seeking to keep the financial system—and the world economy—afloat. The main traditional tool of monetary policy—setting interest rates—is ineffective: even though rates are at record

9:   Quoted in Elliott, 2013.
10: Watkins, 2013.
11: http://blogs.ft.com/money-supply/liveblogs/2013-03-07-2/
12: www.number10.gov.uk/news/economy-speech-cameron-yorkshire. See Wolf, 2013, for a damning critique of this speech.
13: Davies, 2013.

lows, banks are refusing to lend. So central banks are resorting to more unorthodox methods. Draghi's OMT is one example, as is the quantitative easing—creating money to buy government and corporate bonds—used by the US Federal Reserve Board and the Bank of England.

But these haven't kick-started growth, and both Draghi and Paul Tucker of the Bank of England have speculated about introducing negative interest rates—that is, charging banks for the reserves they hold in the central bank as a way of forcing them to lend. Mark Carney, who takes over as governor of the Bank of England in July, has said central banks may have to stop rigidly targeting a low inflation rate (the orthodoxy of the past 20 years) to get economic growth going again. He is being encouraged in this course by Tory chancellor of the exchequer George Osborne, who sees "monetary activism" as the necessary complement to continuing fiscal austerity.[14] In the budget Osborne gave the bank more flexibility to take into account growth in meeting its 2 percent inflation target.

All the cheap money that the central banks have been pumping into the financial system has helped to push the markets upwards. As the Dow Industrial Average reached record levels in early March, the *Financial Times* complained: "Financial markets eye new peaks, yet output is everywhere decelerating or shrinking".[15] Or, as Kit Juckes of Société Générale put it, "despite spending cuts in the US, a lack of any kind of political resolution in Italy and weaker data in Asia, we just can't get a proper 'risk-off' mood going...as mad money trumps every other concern".[16]

"Mad money" also acts as a means through which states can devalue their currencies and, through thereby boosting the competitiveness of their exports, get their economies growing again. One of the most significant political developments of the past few months has been the return to office of the historic party of post-war Japanese capitalism, the Liberal Democratic Party (LDP), thanks to its sweeping victory in the general election last December. The new prime minister, Shinzō Abe, is a right wing nationalist who, as Kim Ha-young shows elsewhere in this issue, is stoking up the growing geopolitical tensions in North East Asia. In February he went to Washington to announce that "Japan is back" and told the *Washington Post* that, "in order to gain natural resources for their economy, China is taking action by coercion or intimidation, both in the South China Sea and the East China Sea".[17]

14: Parker and Giles, 2013.
15: *Financial Times*, 2013.
16: Rodrigues, 2013.
17: *Washington Post*, 2013.

But Abe also has an important domestic agenda. The Japanese economy has been caught in a vicious cycle of deflation and stagnation ever since the collapse of a huge property bubble in the early 1990s. In the past five years it has contracted at a rate of 0.2 percent a year.[18] Abe, while campaigning for the premiership, denounced the orthodox monetary policies of the Bank of Japan (BoJ) under its outgoing governor, Masaaki Shirakawa. He forced the BoJ to adopt in January a target of achieving a rate of inflation of 2 percent, which, since prices continue to fall in Japan, requires the bank to create large amounts of money. Haruhiko Kuroda, Abe's candidate to replace Shirakawa, is pledged to implement this ambitious policy shift. "No other advanced economy has ever tried anything like this", one Japanese economist commented.[19]

A key feature of "Abenomics" is forcing down the yen on the foreign exchange markets and thereby boosting Japan's crucial export industries. Abe said in December that Japan must print more money because "it makes a big difference whether the yen is at 80 to the dollar or 90 to the dollar".[20] By early February the yen had fallen to its lowest rate for the dollar for the past three years. This revived the fears of "an international currency war" first articulated by Guido Mantega, the Brazilian finance minister, in 2010.[21]

Mantega's target was American quantitative easing, which was flooding Brazil and other "emerging market" economies with hot money and therefore pushing their currencies up against the dollar. But now it is Washington that is complaining about Abe's efforts to talk down the yen. In February a senior US Treasury official called on members of the G20 leading economic powers to "refrain from competitive devaluation".[22]

Meetings of G7 and G20 finance ministers papered over the cracks, but it's clear that Japan isn't the only state seeking devaluation as a means of boosting growth. Mervyn King, the outgoing governor of the Bank of England, has encouraged the pound fall by nearly 6 percent against the currencies of Britain's main trade partners so far in 2013. The Chinese commerce minister, Chen Deming, recently warned "about inflation, about competitive currency depreciation and about the negative spillover effects of excessive issuance of the main currencies".[23]

Behind the denunciations of currency wars is the fear that a cycle

---

18: Roberts, 2013a.
19: McLannahan, 2013.
20: Harding, 2013.
21: Wheatley and Garnham, 2010.
22: Steen, Barker and Harding, 2013.
23: Hook and Rabinovitch, 2013.

of competitive devaluations might precipitate another global slump. The example of the 1930s is often cited, although the evidence suggests the devaluations that followed Britain abandoning the gold standard in September 1931 liberated those governments that went off gold to pursue reflationary policies boosting growth.[24] Nevertheless, austerity, by squeezing domestic demand, does push states to seek growth by exporting.

Here economic competition can fuse with geopolitical rivalries. Abe's attempt to revive Japanese capitalism by devaluing the yen and using a language of confrontation with China is one example. Cyprus is another. Anastasiades is effectively caught between two imperialist powers—a German-dominated eurozone that is seeking to liquidate the bloated southern Cypriot banking system and Russia, for which that system is an important financial outlet and whose energy industry is eyeing the island's gas reserves. The tenth anniversary of the invasion of Iraq by the US and Britain is a reminder of the historic defeat American imperialism has suffered in the "war on terror". But Western intervention in the Middle East and its environs continues, as the French military expedition to Mali and the debate over arming the Syrian resistance show. More importantly, imperialism in the broader sense of a system of capitalist rivalries is very much alive and kicking.[25]

From a more narrowly economic point of view, the increasingly desperate monetary experimentation being practised from Tokyo to London reveals the impasse official policy has reached four years after the world economy started to recover from the depths of the Great Recession. The crucial question is whether the continuing stagnation is simply a consequence of austerity, as Keynesian and post-Keynesian economists such as Paul Krugman argue.[26] Because the present crisis originated in a financial bubble made possible by floods of cheap credit, many companies and households are loaded down with debt. The result is a process of "deleveraging" in which economic actors concentrate on repaying their debts. This has particularly affected the banks in both Europe and the US. A recent study illustrates the negative impact this process may be having on financial globalisation:

> Global cross-border capital flows have shrunk more than 60 percent from their pre-crisis peak, with the UK seeing the biggest decline, highlighting the retrenchment in global finance and pressures on the world's banks.

24: Eichengreen, 1992, makes this case strongly.
25: Callinicos, 2009.
26: For example, Krugman, 2012.

Loans and investment flows between countries were worth $4.6 trillion last year—down from $11.8 trillion in 2007, show calculations by McKinsey.[27]

But deleveraging has a broader negative impact. To repay their debts households and firms must save rather than spend on consumption and investment, reducing aggregate effective demand for goods and services. Unless counterbalanced by spending by the public sector, paying down private debt on a sufficiently large scale will cause the economy to contract.[28] Keynesians argue that austerity, by reducing public expenditure, is kicking away the prop that has been holding the advanced capitalist economies up since the financial crash in 2008. But this argument, while undoubtedly valid, doesn't go deep enough.[29] Both Marx and Keynes identified the critical role played by investment in driving capitalist economies. Roberts argues there is what he calls an "investment strike" in the US, where corporate profits have soared to record levels as a share of national income but investment is still below its pre-crisis peak.[30]

Krugman himself has acknowledged that "the level of corporate

27: Atkins, 2013.

28: See Koo, 2008, for an analysis of this process at work during the Great Depression of the 1930s and the Japanese slump of the past twenty years.

29: Outstanding though the economic analysis that Roberts offers in his blog is, he has a tendency in criticising Keynesians to echo neoliberal arguments that the higher public spending and borrowing they advocate will "crowd out" productive investment. For example: "the increase in government spending begins to encroach on the private sector's ability to make profit, both through increased taxation and also through competing with the private sector in various areas of investment. Of course, pro-capitalist governments bend over backwards to reduce that burden through cutting corporate taxes (and shifting the burden of taxation onto households and to any spending by households). Indeed, during the Great Recession, most large corporations paid little tax as they claimed their losses against future tax charges. But even so, over the long term, if government debt keeps rising or does not fall, it will become an albatross around the capitalist sector, reducing its ability or willingness to invest. That is why debt matters, contrary to the view of the Keynesians, who see government spending (through borrowing or not) as the way out of recession"—Roberts, 2011. But, while in the abstract this may be true, it is hardly relevant when the major economies are operating at well below full employment, particularly since, as Roberts repeatedly points out, companies are sitting on huge cash mountains of profits they are refusing to invest. Nevertheless, Roberts and Guglielmo Carchedi are of course right in their fundamental criticism of Keynesianism—that the main determinant of the accumulation process is profitability, and not, as Keynesians argue, spending (whether consumption or investment: thus Hyman Minsky argues that "financed investment determines aggregate income, its distribution between wages and profits, and the aggregate mark-ups that are realised"—Minsky, 2008, p163). See especially Carchedi, 2012.

30: For example, Roberts, 2012.

profits…is arguably serving as a kind of sinkhole for purchasing power".[31] But the Keynesian explanation for this state of affairs is likely to be that the political uncertainty created by the eurozone crisis and the fiscal battle between Obama and Congress is dampening capitalists' "animal spirits" and discouraging them from investing. Rather than rely on this kind of psychological explanation, Marx argues that the rate of capital accumulation is determined primarily by the rate of profit—that is, by the mass of surplus value relative to the total capital invested. We have consistently argued in this journal that behind the financial bubble and crash that precipitated the present crisis lie the chronic problems of profitability with which the advanced capitalist economies have been struggling since the late 1960s.[32]

For Marx, the devaluation of capital—the reduction in the value of the means of production, which is a trend inherent in capitalist development because of the constant increases in productivity forced on firms by competition—counteracts the tendency of the rate of profit to fall:

> The periodic devaluation of the existing capital, which is a means, immanent to the capitalist mode of production, for delaying the fall in the profit rate and accelerating the accumulation of capital value by the formation of new capital, disturbs the given conditions in which the circulation and reproduction process of capital takes place, and is therefore accompanied by sudden stoppages and crises in the production process.[33]

Economic crises therefore have the function of destroying surplus capital and thereby permitting the resumption of profitable capital accumulation. One can think of the deleveraging as one form taken by this process. The credit bubble of the mid-2000s involved an immense expansion of what Marx called "fictitious capital"—assets created in order to give the holder a claim on the surplus value created in production. Repaying debt involves the liquidation of assets represented by the loans that are being redeemed. Roberts has tried to estimate the amount of deleveraging required by studying:

> global liquidity as measured by the amount of bank loans, securitised debt and derivatives in the world. Global liquidity as a share of world GDP took off in the great credit bubble that began in the mid-1990s. After the credit crunch and the Great Recession, liquidating all that fictitious capital…various

---

31: Krugman, 2013.
32: See most recently Choonara, 2011 and 2012.
33: Marx, 1981, p358.

studies…suggest there is still some way to go…global liquidity to GDP… remains some 11 percent above the pre-credit bubble trend line. At current rates, to get rid of the remaining fictitious capital will take at least until 2015— and then it may only be achieved by a new global slump in production.[34]

So deleveraging is necessary to restore profitability but has a depressing effect on economic output. It is this dilemma that underlies the debates between austerians and Keynesians: austerity may accelerate the destruction of capital but fear of economic collapse leads central banks to create money and pump it into the financial system, thereby slowing down the necessary liquidation of fictitious capital. The Great Recession allowed employers to squeeze their workers harder and thereby to force up the rate of exploitation. As a result the *mass* of profits increased, but by 2012 the *rate* of profit (that is profits relative to the capital invested) was falling again in all the major economic regions.[35]

This analysis has focused on the advanced capitalist economies. But, of course, as Kim shows, China's rise has unbalanced the global economic and geopolitical equations. Beijing responded to the 2008 crash with a huge fiscal stimulus; a flood of loans from the state banks funded a surge of investment that revived the economies of China and its major suppliers. The Chinese government responded to a surge in inflation and signs of a developing credit bubble by engineering an economic slowdown in 2012. Despite much talk of a "rebalancing" of the Chinese economy away from investments and exports and towards domestic consumption, little fundamentally seems to have changed. Unicredit recently commented:

The recent data from the second-largest world economy paint a picture of an overall modest, uneven and still fragile economic recovery that may even peak over the next few months… State-mandated strong FAI [fixed asset investment] as well as upbeat trade figures (although they seem inflated when confronted with the disappointing production picture and moderate global recovery) imply that exports as well as investment activity are still the key drivers of the Chinese recovery.[36]

Over the longer term the Chinese economy is highly vulnerable to deleveraging in the US and Europe, which will constrain demand for its

---

34: Roberts, 2013b.
35: Roberts, 2013b.
36: Quoted in Wagstyl, 2013.

exports. It may consequently be unable to regain the heady 10 percent annual growth rates of the past 30 years. One authoritative commentator, Michael Pettis, writes: "Beijing so far has been very reluctant to force through an adjustment and rebalancing of its extreme underconsumptionist policies, but rapidly rising debt means that within four or five years it will have no choice. As the economy adjusts, I expect Chinese GDP growth to average 3 percent or less over the decade of adjustment".[37]

None of this means that the US and China, the two most robust major economies, may not enjoy somewhat higher growth rates this year. Global capitalism, however, remains stuck in the doldrums. Austerity is, of course, an attempt to displace the cost onto working people and the poor. It is failing economically, but its political fate remains open. Resistance is growing in Europe, albeit unevenly, as Joseph Choonara and Catarina Príncipe show elsewhere in this journal. The giant Portuguese protests on 2 March—1.5 million people out of a total population of 10.8 million demonstrating against austerity—bear witness to the potential. But, to break the vice the troika is imposing on Europe, opposition will have to generalise and to acquire the muscle that only collective workers' action can provide.

The role of politics here is central. The spectacular rise of Syriza (the Coalition of the Radical Left) in Greece has captured the imagination of people right across Europe and indeed the world. But whether Syriza represents a real break with the reformist mould is a matter of much controversy on the radical and revolutionary left. Thanasis Kampagiannis continues the debate in our present issue. His criticisms of the rightward evolution of Syriza since the last Greek general election in June 2012 are not a case of sectarian nit-picking. One reason why Grillo has been able successfully to pose as an alternative to the Italian political elite is the disillusioning effect of the last centre-left government under Romano Prodi in 2006-8, when it continued Italian participation in the occupation of Afghanistan as well as Berluscolin's neoliberal economic policies. The radical left party Rifondazione Comunista was effectively destroyed by its participation in this government, helping to create a political vacuum that Grillo has been able to fill temporarily.[38] How to build genuine political alternatives to austerity and war will continue to preoccupy this journal in coming issues. The stakes are high.

Thunder on the right

The plight of the British coalition government has continued to worsen

---

37: Pettis, 2013, p189.
38: Harman, 2008.

since we surveyed it in our last issue.[39] Output is still 3 percent lower than its peak in 2008. Fears are growing that the pound's devaluation will, by raising import costs, push the British economy into stagflation, with rising prices continuing to squeeze living standards while output remains depressed. The Office for Budget Responsibility's calculations at the time of the budget on 20 March offered a grim prognosis for growth and for the coalition's own targets for reducing government borrowing. Osborne's response was to stick by his guns while slashing corporation tax to 20 percent in 2015, continuing to cut real wages in the public sector, and seeking to revive the property market and please marginal voters with a programme of publicly guaranteed mortgages. An Opinium/ *Observer* poll in early March found that 58 percent of voters believe austerity is harming the economy, compared to 20 percent who think it is the right medicine for the economy. [40] No wonder Labour is ahead in this and other polls.

The predictable result is both greater friction between the coalition parties—for example, over Lord Leveson's recommendations for preventing future press abuses after the News International scandal—and greater divisions among the Tories themselves, notably between Cameron and Osborne on the one hand, and the Thatcherite right on the other. Amid rumours of an absurd leadership challenge by an obscure millionaire backbencher, the *Guardian* reported at the end of January the view of "members of the government and prominent backbenchers" that:

> enough MPs are prepared to trigger a vote of confidence in the prime minister in the summer of 2014 if the Tories experience a setback in the local elections… The events of the past weeks have also clarified in the minds of senior Tories that George Osborne enjoys negligible support on the Tory benches should he decide to stand [for the leadership].[41]

Cameron hoped to head off his right wing with a much trailed and delayed speech on the EU finally given on 23 January. Here he promised that if the Tories won the next general election he would seek to renegotiate Britain's membership, with the aim of "repatriating" powers from Brussels to Westminster, and put the resulting deal to a referendum offering voters the choice of staying in or out of the EU. But whatever political capital this gave him was wiped out by the results of the Eastleigh

39: Callinicos, 2013.
40: Helm and Boffey, 2013.
41: Watt, 2013.

by-election on 28 February. The Liberal Democrats, reeling from multiple scandals, managed to hang onto the seat, while the Tories were shoved into third place, behind the UK Independence Party.

Eastleigh followed a run of good results for UKIP, which was put at 17 percent in the same Opinium/*Observer* poll cited earlier.[42] UKIP's unifying theme is xenophobia—often more effective at the doorsteps when directed at migrants rather than at Brussels. Given that the next general election is barely a couple of years away, the most important effect of Eastleigh will be to encourage the Tories and Labour to engage in a Dutch auction over which party is tougher on immigration. For example, the BBC reports that Cameron is considering limiting British citizens' entitlements to benefits in order to deny these to immigrants from Bulgaria and Romania when restrictions on the latters' access to Britain are scrapped later this year.[43] Labour responded with its own proposals, for example, to ban new migrants from receiving the jobseeker's allowance, as part of what shadow home secretary Yvette Cooper calls a "one nation immigration policy".[44]

What we see at work here is the political logic that Paul Foot so brilliantly analysed back in the 1960s, for example, in Enoch Powell's intervention against Commonwealth immigration: racist demands from the extreme right are taken up and legitimised by establishment politicians, which simply strengthens the far right and increases the pressure on the mainstream parties to accommodate.[45] The fascist organisations—the British National Party and the English Defence League—are down, thanks especially to the campaigning of Unite against Fascism, but not out. We can see elsewhere in Europe, above all in Greece, how the suffering and dislocation caused by the crisis can benefit the extreme right. Vigilance against the Nazis is essential, but it must be linked to effective struggle against austerity and to political opposition to immigration controls.

Debates inside the Socialist Workers Party

International Socialism is relatively unusual among Marxist theoretical journals these days in being the journal of a political organisation—the Socialist Workers Party (SWP), as it was of its predecessors (the Socialist Review group and the International Socialists). We have, therefore, inevitably been affected by the intense internal debates the SWP has experienced

---

42: Helm and Boffey, 2013.
43: www.bbc.co.uk/news/uk-politics-21663825
44: Travis, 2013.
45: Foot, 1969.

over the past six months. These originated in disagreements over how the party handled serious sexual allegations against a leading member, but have broadened out into much wider political arguments.[46]

A special conference of the SWP met on 10 March and sought to resolve the original controversy by setting up a committee to examine the party's disciplinary procedures. But the main resolution passed by a large majority of delegates also stated:

> We believe that underlying many of the recent debates in and around the party lie a series of vital political questions where we need to seek urgently to assert, develop and win our political tradition. Some of the key debates include:
>
> a) The changing nature of the working class.
> b) Lenin's conception of the party and its relevance in the 21st century.
> c) Oppression and capitalism.
> d) The trade union bureaucracy and the rank and file.
> e) The radical left, the united front and the SWP.
> f) The role of students and intellectuals in revolutionary struggle.
> g) The value of new electronic media in the ideological and organisational work of a revolutionary party.

The pages of this journal are an obvious venue for these debates, and we intend to make sure they happen here. Sheila McGregor's article in the present issue on Marxism and women's oppression today represents a start but there will be others, expressing a variety of standpoints. All these debates matter, and not simply for those who share the politics of the SWP.

46: See the material collected at www.swp.org.uk/replies-to-attacks

References

Atkins, Ralph, 2013, "Global Capital Flows Plunge 68 Percent", *Financial Times* (28 February), www.ft.com/cms/s/0/aee926b8-80f6-11e2-9908-00144feabdc0.html

Callinicos, Alex, 2009, *Imperialism and Global Political Economy* (Polity).

Callinicos, Alex, 2013, "British Sounds", *International Socialism 137* (winter), www.isj.org.uk/?id=863

Carchedi, Guglielmo, 2012, "Could Keynes End the Slump? Introducing the Marxist Multiplier", *International Socialism 136* (autumn), www.isj.org.uk/?id=849 Choonara, Joseph, 2011,"Once More (with Feeling) on Marxist Accounts of the Crisis", *International Socialism 132* (autumn), www.isj.org.uk/?id=762

Choonara, Joseph, 2012, "A Reply to David McNally", *International Socialism 135* (summer), www.isj.org.uk/?id=829

Davies, Gavyn, 2013, "The US Economy after Sequestration" (3 March), http://blogs.ft.com/gavyndavies/2013/03/03/the-us-economy-after-sequestration/

Eichengreen, Barry, 1992, *Golden Fetters: the Gold Standard and the Great Depression, 1919-1939* (Oxford University Press).

Elliott, Larry, 2013, "Cyprus Bailout Shows European Policy Elite has Learned Nothing from Crisis", *Guardian* (18 March), www.guardian.co.uk/world/2013/mar/18/cyprus-bailout-eurozone-crisis-larry-elliot

Financial Times, 2013, "Stock Markets Defy Economic Woes" (6 March), www.ft.com/cms/s/0/2fc682aa-8659-11e2-ad73-00144feabdc0.html

Foot, Paul, 1969, *The Rise of Enoch Powell* (Penguin).

Giles, Chris, 2013, "Little Recovery in Advanced Economies", *Financial Times* (5 March), www.ft.com/cms/s/0/28d398c0-85af-11e2-bed4-00144feabdc0.html

Harding, Robin, 2013, "Currency Farce Reveals US-Japan Dispute", *Financial Times* (13 February), www.ft.com/cms/s/0/982990b0-75fd-11e2-9891-00144feabdc0.html

Harman, Chris, 2008, "Italian Lessons", *International Socialism 119* (summer), www.isj.org.uk/?id=452

Helm, Toby, and Daniel Boffey, 2013, "Britons Have Lost Faith in George Osborne's Austerity Plan", *Observer* (9 March), www.guardian.co.uk/politics/2013/mar/09/britons-george-osborne-opinion-poll

Hook, Leslie, and Simon Rabinovitch, "China Warns over Fresh Currency Tensions", *Financial Times* (8 March), www.ft.com/cms/s/0/930f90e6-87ca-11e2-b011-00144feabdc0.html

Hope, Kerin, Charles Clover, and Michael Steen, 2013, "Russia Joins Locals as Aig Cyprus Losers", *Financial Times* (17 March), www.ft.com/cms/s/0/33b7d382-8f2d-11e2-a39b-00144feabdc0.html

Hope, Kerin, and Peter Spiegel, 2013, "Greece and Lenders Fall Out over Firings", *Financial Times* (14 March), www.ft.com/cms/s/0/3df71c6c-8c8b-11e2-aed2-00144feabdc0.html

Koo, Richard, 2008, *The Holy Grail of Macroeconomics: Lessons from Japan's Great Recession* (Wiley).

Krugman, Paul, 2012, *End this Depression Now!* (W W Norton & Co).

Krugman, 2013, "Profits and Business Investment" (9 February), http://krugman.blogs.nytimes.com/2013/02/09/profits-and-business-investment/

Marx, Karl, 1981 [1894], *Capital*, volume 3 (Harmondsworth), www.marxists.org/archive/marx/works/1894-c3/index.htm

McLannahan, 2013, "Kuroda Urged to Plan for BoJ Board Games", *Financial Times* (13 March), www.ft.com/cms/s/0/69be2f38-8bc4-11e2-8fcf-00144feabdc0.html

Minsky, Hyman, 2008 [1986] , *Stabilising an Unstable Economy* (McGraw-Hill).

Munchau, Wolfgang, 2013, "Europe's Finance Ministers are Risking a Bank Run", *Financial Times* (17 March), www.ft.com/cms/s/0/b501c302-8cea-11e2-aed2-00144feabdc0.html

Parker, George, and Chris Giles, "Osborne Weighs Monetary Activism Options", *Financial Times* (14 March), www.ft.com/cms/s/0/b5270bbc-8cc2-11e2-aed2-00144feabdc0.html

Pettis, Michael, 2013, *The Great Rebalancing: Trade, Conflict, and the Perilous Road Ahead for the World Economy* (Princeton University Press).

Roberts, Michael, 2011, "Prospects for 2012" (30 December), http://thenextrecession.wordpress.com/2011/12/30/prospects-for-2012Roberts, Michael, 2012, "US: It's Investment not Consumption" (30 November), http://thenextrecession.wordpress.com/2012/11/30/us-its-investment-not-consumption

Roberts, Michael, 2013a, "Japan's Lost Decades—Unpacked and Repacked" (14 February), http://thenextrecession.wordpress.com/2013/02/14/japans-lost-decades-unpacked-and-repacked

Roberts, Michael, 2013b, "Deleveraging and Profitability Again" (25 February), http://thenextrecession.wordpress.com/2013/02/25/deleveraging-and-profitability-again

Roberts, Michael, 2013c, "Goodbye Monti, Hello the Three Bs" (28 February), http://thenextrecession.wordpress.com/2013/02/28/goodbye-monti-hello-the-three-bs/

Roberts, Michael, 2013d, "World Growth Update" (9 March), http://thenextrecession.wordpress.com/2013/03/09/world-growth-update/

Rodrigues, Vivianne, 2013, "Dow Climbs to Record Levels", *Financial Times* (5 March), www.ft.com/cms/s/0/592f4c2a-8542-11e2-891d-00144feabdc0.html

Spiegel, Peter, 2013a, "Cypriot Banks Hit in 10 billion euro Bailout", *Financial Times* (16 March), www.ft.com/cms/s/0/33fb34b4-8df8-11e2-9d6b-00144feabdc0.html

Spiegel, Peter, 2013b, "Cyprus Depositors' Fate Sealed in Berlin', *Financial Times* (17 March), www.ft.com/cms/s/0/f890566a-8f24-11e2-a39b-00144feabdc0.html

Steen, Michael, Alex Barker and Robin Harding, 2013, "US Treasury Comment Triggers Fall in Yen", *Financial Times* (12 February), www.ft.com/cms/s/0/5bef28f4-7471-11e2-b323-00144feabdc0.html

Travis, Alan, 2013, "Labour Outlines Measures to Restrict Benefits for New EU Arrivals in UK", *Guardian* (7 March), www.guardian.co.uk/society/2013/mar/07/labour-measures-restrict-benefits-arrivals

Wagstyl, Stefan, 2013, "China: Investment Still Comes First" (11 March), http://blogs.ft.com/beyond-brics/2013/03/11/china-investment-still-comes-first

Washington Post, 2013, "Transcript of Interview with Japanese Prime Minister Shinzō Abe", www.washingtonpost.com/world/transcript-of-interview-with-japanese-prime-minister-shinzo-abe/2013/02/20/e7518d54-7b1c-11e2-82e8-61a46c2cde3d_story.html

Watkins, Mary, 2013, "Political Instability Tests Draghi Pledge", *Financial Times* (3 March), www.ft.com/cms/s/0/49efb0f0-7459-11e2-80a7-00144feabdc0.html

Watt, Nicholas, 2013, "Tories Tell PM: Lift Poll Ratings or Face Revolt", *Guardian* (31 January), www.guardian.co.uk/politics/2013/jan/31/tories-pm-poll-ratings-revolt

Wheatley, Jonathan, and Peter Garnham, 2010, "Brazil in "Currency War" Alert', *Financial Times* (27 September), www.ft.com/cms/s/0/33ff9624-ca48-11df-a860-00144feab49a.html

Wolf, Martin, 2013, "The Man at Number Ten is not for Turning", *Financial Times* (7 March), www.ft.com/cms/s/0/bf19ad60-8681-11e2-b907-00144feabdc0.html

ALIENATION
An introduction to Marx's theory
Dan Swain, £5, Bookmarks

an introduction to Marx's theory

ALIENATION

Dan Swain

The young German radical Karl Marx began to diagnose the phenomenon of alienation in the early 1840s, and remained pre-occupied with it throughout his life. He sought to explain how capitalist production, with all its dynamism, only took us further away from control over our lives.

This accessible guide to a central aspect of Marx's philosophy takes the reader through the development of the concept from its roots in the Enlightenment through Marx to later debates and controversies.

Dan Swain is a postgraduate researcher in philosophy at the University of Essex. He is on the editorial board of International Socialism.

Bookmarks the socialist bookshop, 1 Bloomsbury Street, London WC1B 3QE 020 7637 1848 | mailorder@bookmarks.uk.com

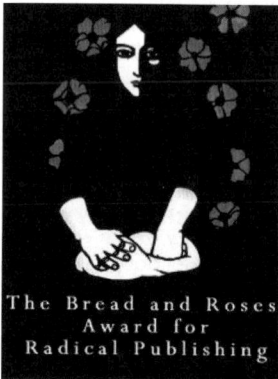
The Bread and Roses Award for Radical Publishing

Alienation has been shortlisted for the Bread and Roses Award for Radical Publishing 2013.

The winner will be announced at the first London Radical Bookfair, Conway Hall, Saturday 11 May 2013.
breadandrosesprize.wordpress.com

Imperialism and instability in East Asia today

Ha-young Kim

During the last two to three years tension and conflict have been increasing in East Asia.[1] In 2012 this tendency was evident in the South China Sea, the East China Sea and the area round the Korean peninsula. Let's look at a few examples:

South China Sea: In early April 2012 there was a confrontation between China and the Philippines over Scarborough Shoal (Chinese: Huangyan Island), one of the Spratly Islands (Chinese: Nansha Islands, Vietnamese: Truong Sa Islands) in the South China Sea. The confrontation between the naval vessels of the two countries continued for almost two months and in the middle of this the United States and the Philippines carried out a Balikatan joint military drill in the vicinity. Japan, Australia and South Korea all sent personnel to participate in this drill. At the time Duane Thiessen, commander of the US Marine Corps Forces Pacific, commented: "If a military conflict were to arise in the Spratly Islands the US military would be able to intervene."

Yellow Sea: In June 2012 South Korea, Japan and the United States held a joint navy drill in the seas to the south of Cheju Island, followed by a joint South Korea and US drill in the Yellow Sea between China and the Korean peninsula. Two things about this were noteworthy: this was the first ever

1:    Thanks to Owen Miller and Kyle Chun for translating this article.

formal joint exercise involving the three countries; this was the first time since the Yonpyong Island incident of 2010[2] that a US aircraft carrier had entered the Yellow Sea. Both of these factors were major provocations for China. In addition to this, in the latter part of April China and Russia held a large-scale joint military exercise in the Yellow Sea. The Chinese defence ministry openly revealed the purpose of this exercise, saying: "This is in response to the recent military exercise carried out by South Korea, the US Pacific fleet and Japan."

East China Sea: The most striking conflict began in the summer of 2012 over the Diaoyu Islands (Japanese: Senkaku Islands). In June there was a confrontation between a Chinese fishery inspection boat and a Japanese coastguard boat and in July Japanese prime minister Yoshihiko Noda aggravated the conflict by playing the nationalisation card.[3] This was followed by a group of Chinese protesters landing on the islands on 15 August. On 10 September the Noda cabinet officially approved the nationalisation of the Diaoyu Islands, immediately ratcheting up the dispute between Japan and China. China responded by declaring that the islands were within its territorial waters and despatched a patrol boat. Over the following few months military tensions increased as patrol boats and warships of the two countries confronted each other in the waters round the islands. They also continued to hold various military exercises. While Japan and the US held joint landing exercises among islands of the East China Sea, China held counter-exercises. The US openly expressed its support for Japan. In July the State Department clarified that the Senkakus "fall within the scope of the US-Japan Security Treaty" and then in December the Defense Authorisation Act approved by the US Congress specifically included a stipulation to the same effect.

The changing structure of world capitalism

In order to understand why tensions and conflicts are on the rise in East Asia at the moment we need to examine the core characteristics of today's global capitalist system. To put it simply, world capitalism is experiencing a long-term crisis of profitability (beginning in the early 1970s), and in the midst of this important changes are occurring in the relative economic power of different states. This has significant geopolitical implications.

2: A major exchange of artillery fire in the Yellow Sea between North and South Korea that took place in November 2010.

3: The Japanese prime minister announced in July 2012 that the Japanese government would buy the islands from their private owner, thus effectively "nationalising" them.

Not only has the current economic crisis made it difficult to cooperate on implementing economic policy, but the changes in relative economic power have been accompanied by changes in political power and this also reduces the possibility of continued cooperation between states. This is giving rise to a situation where those states that want to move up the hierarchy of the international order and those that want to maintain their positions at the top are making a show of strength against one another.

In the early 20th century Lenin stressed the unevenness and contradictions of the world economy, emphasising that the dynamic process of capitalist development itself altered the distribution of this unevenness, thereby constantly changing the balance of power between states. Thus Lenin, in contrast to Kautsky, believed that it was impossible to establish a stable alliance among the ruling powers. In order to understand today's world it is crucially important to understand the political implications of the unevenness and contradictions of the world economy, as well as the changing pattern of this unevenness.

In Lenin's time Britain—then the pre-eminent capitalist state—was faced with the rise of Germany and the US. In the current shifts in the balance of power between states the most striking thing is the relative decline of the US and the "rise of the rest", and in particular, the rise of China. Immediately after the Second World War the US accounted for 50 percent of the world's industrial output, but by the 1980s this had fallen to only 25 percent. Although the US has reigned as the sole superpower since the end of the Cold War in 1991, its economic position has continued to decline. The US has made various attempts to recover its former position, including the Iraq War, but has not been successful. The US National Intelligence Council's report on the outlook for the world system, "Global Trends 2025", argues that looking forward to 2025 the international order is going to become more complicated and while the US will continue to be a superpower, it will be transformed into a less dominant state than it is now.[4]

Meanwhile, China has averaged remarkable economic growth of 8 to 10 percent over the last 30 years and, particularly since the late 1990s, as its economy has grown explosively it has emerged as a potential challenger for US hegemony. Between 1978 and 2009 China's GDP grew by almost 2,000 percent. Table 1 shows how China's share of world GDP (when measured by market exchange rates) was only 1.72 percent in 1980, but by 2010 it had grown to 9.32 percent. When you measure this in purchasing power parity terms that take into account differences in costs the figure rises to 13.37 percent.

4:    US National Intelligence Council, 2008, pp37-39.

On the other hand, during the same period the US's share of world GDP fell from 25.2 percent to 23.13 percent, Japan's from 9.75 to 8.72 and Germany's from 8.37 to 5.25. Figure 1 illustrates how the gap between China's and the US's shares of world GDP has narrowed rapidly.

Table 1: Share of world GDP among six economies, 1980–2010 (%) [5]
Source: World Development Indicators

	1980	1985	1990	1995	2000	2005	2010
US	25.20	33.66	26.26	24.73	30.73	25.57	23.13
	(22.86)	(23.41)	(23.05))	(23.05)	(23.95)	(22.41)	(19.21)
China	1.72	2.47	1.63	2.45	3.72	4.95	9.32
	(2.03)	(2.96)	(3.61)	(5.60)	(7.01)	(9.47)	(13.37)
Japan	9.75	10.97	13.96	17.74	14.49	9.98	8.72
	(8.14)	(8.80)	(9.38)	(8.96)	(7.83)	(6.96)	(5.85)
Germany	8.37	5.70	7.83	8.50	5.90	6.11	5.25
	(6.38)	(5.99)	(5.89)	(5.73)	(5.03)	(4.60)	(4.11)
France	6.28	4.37	5.68	5.30	4.12	4.68	4.06
	(4.37)	(4.09)	(4.02)	(3.78)	(3.70)	(3.30)	(2.95)
UK	4.93	3.73	4.62	3.90	4.59	5.00	3.56
	(3.85)	(3.73)	(3.66)	(3.56)	(3.64)	(3.52)	(3.00)

China became the fifth largest economy in the world in real terms in 2005 and then overtook Germany in 2007 to become the third largest. Only three years later in 2010 China pushed Japan out of the position it had held for 42 years to become the second largest economy in the world.

China's economic status has increased particularly rapidly in East Asia. This region is now the most dynamic in the world capitalist system. China provides a vast export market and plays a pivotal role in regional trade and production that has resulted in a great increase in the mutual interdependence of East Asian economies. Regional trade in East Asia has grown rapidly since

---

5:   Measured according to current currency exchange rates with purchasing power parity in brackets.

the 1990s. Between 1992 and 2007 regional trade increased from 45 percent of East Asia's total trade to 52.23 percent. The principal goods traded within the region are intermediary goods, reflecting the division of labour within the East Asian economy. Core components made in Japan then flow into China, South Korea and the five ASEAN countries (Singapore, Thailand, Malaysia, Indonesia and the Philippines). The components are then reprocessed in South Korea and the ASEAN countries before flowing into China. Thus, Japan, South Korea and the ASEAN countries all have trade surpluses with China. China then assembles these components and exports the finished goods, mainly to the US. China's trade surplus with the US increased by 12.29 times during the period 1995-2008. (The US's ability to import goods relies on money borrowed from China and the rest of Asia.)

Figure 1: Shares of world GDP (purchasing power parity)[6]
Source: IMF World Economic Outlook Database, April 2011

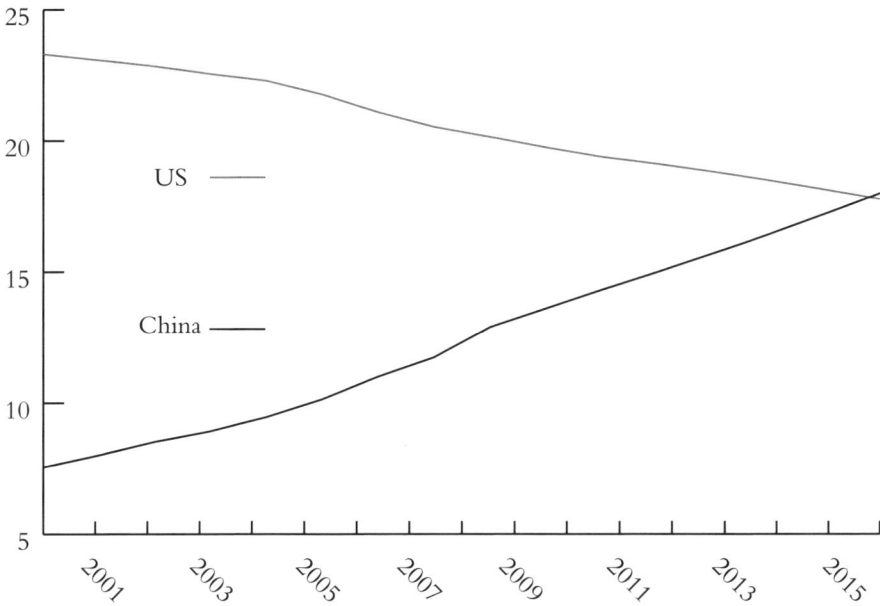

Since 2008 China has been the largest trading partner of both South Korea and Japan. South Korea's degree of reliance on trade with China has

---

6:    Estimates after 2009

increased particularly rapidly, from 9.39 percent in 2000 to 18.43 percent in 2005 and 21.13 percent in 2010. In complete contrast, South Korea's reliance on trade with the US has decreased during the same period from 20.9 percent in 2000 to 10.12 percent in 2010. Figure 2 shows clearly how South Korea's exports to China have soared while exports to the US have rapidly declined. Japan's trade figures have told a similar story. Japan's reliance on trade with China has grown rapidly from 9.95 percent in 2000 to 16.97 percent in 2005 and 21.02 percent in 2010, while during the same period the country's reliance on trade with the US plummeted from 24.99 percent to 12.92 percent. This is a significant shift for South Korea and Japan which have both traditionally achieved economic growth within the context of their close relationships with the US.

Figure 2: South Korean exports to China and the US
Source: Korea International Trade Association

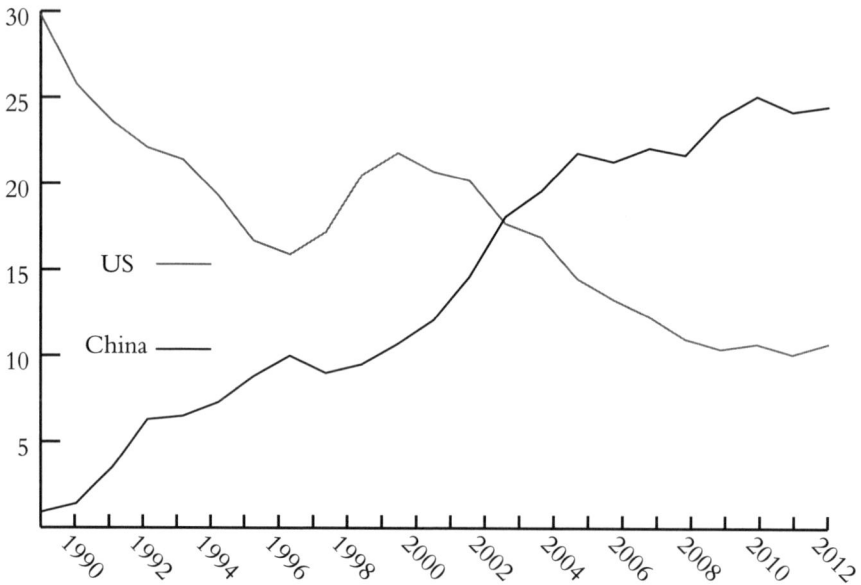

The countries of South East Asia, which have traditionally been the main trading partners for Japan, have also seen a very rapid growth in their trade with China. In fact, China's trade with the South East Asian countries has grown at an average rate of 20 percent a year since the 1990s. As a result, by 2006 their trade with China was about the same as their trade with the US. From 2007 China became the largest trading partner for the ASEAN countries. ASEAN's trade reliance on China grew from 1.4 percent in 1993 to 5.6 percent in 2000, and then to 13 percent in 2006. During the same period the region's trade reliance on Japan fell from 20.6 percent to 15.1 percent.

Geopolitical consequences of the changing world economy

China's economic growth is obviously having a major geopolitical impact. First, as China's political influence grows it is gradually giving rise to changes in the existing world order, dominated by the US. For example, as the "workshop of the world", China's demand for raw materials from Latin American and Africa is huge and as China begins to form close relationships with these countries this is having the effect of peeling them away from the US sphere of influence. At the April 2012 Organisation of American States summit meeting a war of nerves between the Latin American countries and the US broke out over the exclusion of Cuba. The Latin American countries displayed a "completely different attitude to that of the past, when they were America's yes men",[7] and their relations with China have played a role in this change.

China has also been using its huge foreign currency reserves to expand its foreign direct investment and official development aid in Asia, Africa and Latin America and, as this money flows into the whole of the Global South, it is increasing China's influence in these countries. In the past the countries of the Global South had to accept the constraints of neoliberal conditions in order to borrow money from the International Monetary Fund (IMF) or World Bank, but as China expands its support this is changing. In 2007 when China offered to lend money with better conditions Angola broke off its negotiations with the IMF. Since the beginning of the world economic crisis in 2008 China has been pursuing an even more active programme of overseas aid. It has agreed $95 billion worth of currency swaps with six Asian countries, given support to Pakistan, Kazakhstan and others to help them overcome the economic crisis and provided loans to Jamaica, Angola, Mongolia and Ecuador, among others.

The rise of China has also expanded Russia's room for manoeuvre. Russia and China are now cooperating through the Shanghai Cooperation Organisation (SCO) and this institution has had some success in checking the US advance into Central Asia by demanding the withdrawal of US troops from Uzbekistan and Kyrgyzstan. The June 2012 SCO summit

---

7:    *Hankyoreh*, 17 April 2012.

meeting laid out the first comprehensive plan, flaunting the strengthened alliance, and was significantly followed by joint military exercises.

China's increasing political influence is particularly clear among Asian countries. As many Asian countries have seen their trade with China grow rapidly and recorded trade surpluses they have begun to place great importance on their relations with China. For example, at the 2003 Asia-Pacific Economic Forum (APEC) conference the US tried to persuade Asian countries to criticise China's exchange rate policy, but it was not successful and neither was it able to strengthen defence cooperation. In 2006 Alexander Downer, the foreign minister of the US's close ally Australia, cautioned against any US attempt to blockade China, drawing a clear line between the two countries' approaches.[8] This reflected Australia's particular position as it enjoyed an economic boom thanks to its exports of natural resources to China.

The "turning to Asia" policy of Japanese Democratic Party prime minister Yukio Hatoyama, who was elected in 2009, is another typical example of this tendency. He claimed that he would "leave America and enter Asia", in other words that he would look towards China and escape from Japan's reliance on the alliance with the US. However, Hatoyama, who had caused conflict with the US over his plan to move the Futenma US airbase out of Okinawa, then compromised with the US, using North Korea's alleged sinking of the South Korean warship *Cheonan* as an excuse. This led to his resignation as prime minister after only eight months. At the time the US pressured Japan, claiming that "Japanese citizens were also exposed to the threat of attack by North Korea", thus enabling the US to save its key strategic base at Futenma and reinstate the US-Japan alliance.

The move towards stressing the importance of China can also be seen in South Korea. Of the 138 newly elected representatives in the 17th National Assembly elections of 2004, some 55 percent said they regarded China as a more important diplomatic partner than the US. In a survey of representatives elected in the 18th National Assembly elections in 2008, the Democratic Party[9] assembly members took the view that Korea "needs to diversify its diplomatic line". In 2012 the Democratic Party's presidential candidate, Moon Jae-in, criticised right wing President Lee Myung-bak's

8:    Kim Chaech'ol, 2007, p165.
9:    South Korea's Democratic Party (Minjudang) is a liberal bourgeois party, often seen as left of centre or progressive. It lacks much credibility among working class voters because of its association with neoliberal reforms under presidents Kim Dae Jung (1998-2003) and Roh Moo-hyun (2003-2008).

dependence on the US-Korea alliance and pushed the idea of "balancing diplomacy" that stressed Korea-China cooperation. The advocates of "balancing diplomacy" are emphasising the fact that we are now in an age when South Korea's trade with China is worth more than its trade with the US and Japan put together.

These examples illustrate how China's growing influence is making it harder for the US to handle Asian countries in the way it used to. However, the development of East Asian regional cooperation is not without its contradictions. Even while they are expanding their cooperation with China, the countries of East Asia have big concerns about the economic and military rise of China. These countries have historical enmities and territorial disputes with China and these conflicts could grow with the economic crisis. The US has been attempting to use these very concerns and position itself as a "regional balancer" in order to contain China.

Second, China's economic growth has resulted in a military build-up. During the 12 years between 1996 and 2008 China's (officially published) defence budget grew at an average annual rate of 12.9 percent. It is thought that actual military expenditure is higher. According to the estimates of the Stockholm International Peace Research Institute (SIPRI) Chinese defence spending in 2011 was second in the world at $130 billion.

Table 2: China's rapidly increasing military expenditure
Source: SIPRI

2004	$57.5 billion
2005	$64.7 billion
2006	$76 billion
2007	$87.7 billion
2008	$96.6 billion
2009	$116.6 billion
2010	$121 billion
2011	$129.2 billion

China began its full-scale military modernisation and strengthening programme in 2000. It has particularly focused on reinforcing its naval power, which is an extremely rational choice for the Chinese ruling class. For the overseas trade-reliant Chinese economy, which sucks in huge amounts of oil, it is essential that it secures both a stable supply route for oil and stable shipping routes. The energy shipping lane that runs through the Indian Ocean, the Strait of Malacca and the South China Sea to the Chinese mainland is particularly crucial. More than 80 percent of the oil that China consumes comes via this route.

During the 2000s China therefore targeted a large amount of its investment and aid towards countries bordering the Indian Ocean, in its so-called "string of pearls" strategy. This strategy attempts to secure a maritime sphere of influence, using the energy shipping route as its baseline. The key locations for this strategy are the ports of Gwadar in Pakistan, Hambantota in Sri Lanka and Chittagong in Bangladesh, as well as the Coco Islands and Hainggyi Island in Burma, Songkhla in Thailand and Phu Quoc Island in Cambodia. China has been pushing to use these ports and in some cases providing huge amounts of economic support to build new ports at these locations (see figure 3).

Figure 3: China's sea lanes of communication and "string of pearls"

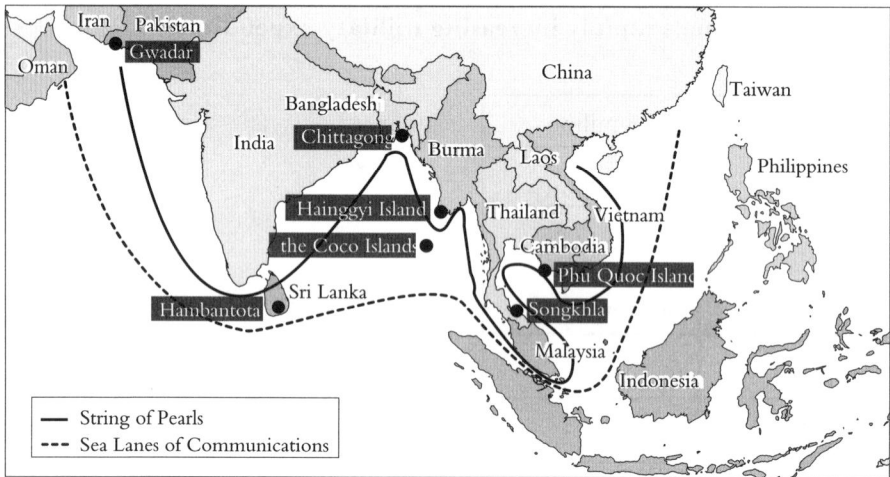

China also regards the fact that the US has dominated the Pacific since the Second World War with dissatisfaction and would like to push the US military out of the seas around China and much further east into the Pacific. China has made the core aim of its naval strategy to develop the capability to deny the US Navy the ability to carry out military operations within the "First Island Chain" (Okinawa-Taiwan-Philippines-Malaysia) and ultimately within the "Second Island Chain" (Ogasawara Islands-Saipan-Guam-Papua New Guinea) too (see figure 4). The intention behind this is to stop the US from intervening in disputes around the Taiwan Strait and the South China Sea region and to protect the shipping lanes in the area. Around 90 percent of China's trade relies on using shipping routes in the South China Sea.

Figure 4: The two East Asian island chains

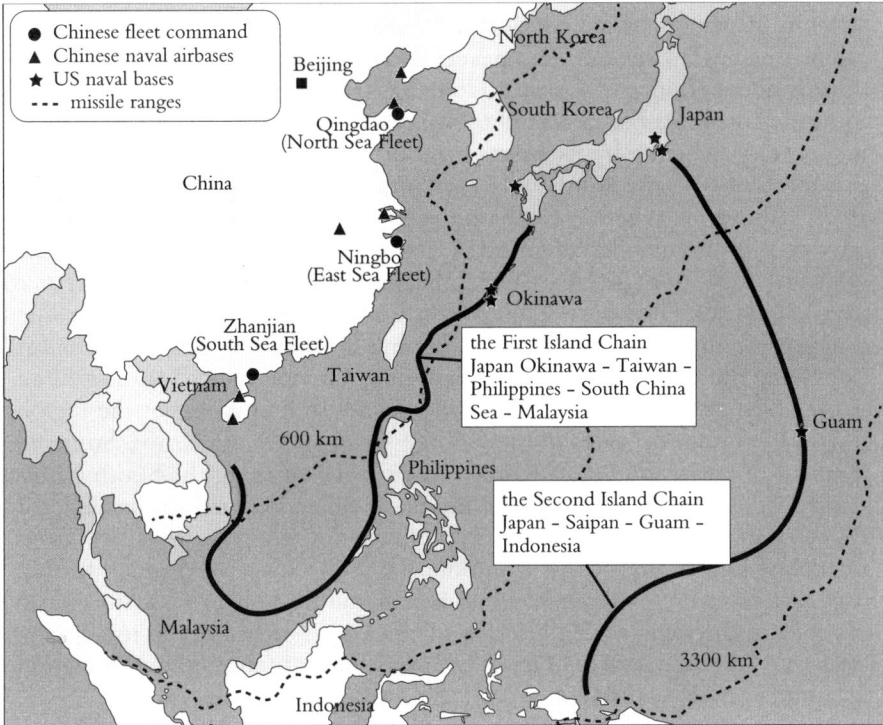

China has been continuously expanding its naval power and in 2012 it successfully commissioned its first aircraft carrier, the *Liaoning*, making it the tenth country in the world to possess an aircraft carrier. It is currently building a further four carriers. It is also known to have procured ten nuclear submarines with ballistic missile capabilities. As for China's air force, it is developing a fourth generation stealth fighter called the Jian-20 and has already carried out a successful test flight. China has also deployed a

3,000 km range anti-ship ballistic missile called the DF 21D, also known as the "aircraft carrier killer". This poses a big threat to the US, which uses aircraft carriers to project its military power around the world. At the recent meeting of the Chinese Communist Party's Central Military Commission new Chinese leader Xi Jinping stressed the defence of territory and sovereignty and emphasised the need for a strong military commensurate with China's international standing.

Of course, it is not the case that China is taking a particularly aggressive stance. Instead for the time being China hopes to construct a peaceful local environment for the sake of continued economic growth. In its 2011 "White Paper on China's Peaceful Development", the Chinese government once again stressed its "peaceful rise doctrine". In contrast to the historical experience of Europe, China says it will not seek hegemony but instead achieve its rise peacefully. Nonetheless China is making its neighbours wary, whether by its moves to secure shipping lanes or its expanding naval activities in the South and East China Seas.

Above all, whether China intends to or not, by expanding its naval power it is directly challenging US dominance in the Indian and Pacific Oceans. The South and East China Seas are both of strategic importance to the US too. The South China Sea is both an important maritime route linking the Indian and Pacific Oceans and at the same time a lifeline for supplying the US bases in the Pacific region. Obviously the South and East China Seas are crucial for the countries of South East Asia, but the region is also important for allies of the US like Japan and South Korea. Some 80 percent of Japan and South Korea's trade relies on using the South China Sea route and 80 to 90 percent of the crude oil and natural gas heading for North East Asia comes this way. The US cannot ignore such a threat to its maritime hegemony. If the US military were to be pushed much further east into the Pacific Ocean it would be difficult for it to provide support to its allies in the region. The US calls China's defence strategy in its adjacent seas an "Anti-Access/Area Denial" strategy and it is currently working out a counter-strategy. (I will deal with this further later in this article.)

The contradictions in US-China relations

China's rise and the US's relative decline have been accelerated recently by two developments. One is the US's failure in the "war on terror" and the other is the economic crisis that began in the US in 2008.

First, the "war on terror" was an attempt by a US in relative decline to recover its former position. The US aimed to consolidate its dominance by using its overwhelming military superiority to seize control of the region supplying oil to the other major powers. The failure of this strategy was a big blow to US hegemony. While the US was bogged down in Iraq other nations and other countries' capitalists were able to use the US's weakness to strengthen their positions. China was presented with an opportunity to expand its influence in East Asia.

Second, the economic crisis that began in 2008 weakened US dominance even further. The US was the epicentre of the crisis and it dragged down the rest of the world economy. Conversely, China escaped from the crisis quickly and was also able to revitalise other countries' economies at the same time. During the course of the economic crisis China became the world's number one exporter and the number one holder of foreign currency reserves. In December 2011 China's foreign currency holdings totalled $3.2 trillion, and of this, 60 percent was held in US dollars, further increasing Chinese influence on both the US and world economies.

However, we must not exaggerate China's rise. Some observers are even of the opinion that China is about to take the US's current position and become a new superpower. Among these observers are those right wingers who adhere to the "China Threat" theory. It has become quite fashionable to predict when China will economically overtake the US. International institutions are all scrambling to predict when that time will come, with Goldman Sachs saying 2027, the World Bank predicting some time between 2023 and 2029, the EU saying 2021, Global Insight 2019 and the IMF 2016. However, the core issue that has to be considered is whether China's current pace of growth can be maintained and this makes the prospects for China's future economic strength quite unclear. The recent global economic crisis did spread to China and the country's growth rate is already falling. It is expected that in the Xi Jinping era China's growth rate will remain below the 7 percent level. If the Chinese property bubble that has grown even bigger under the conditions of economic crisis were to burst it could lead to major political instability. Currently the annual number of demonstrations in China stands at 180,000, meaning that every day, all over China, there on average almost 500 protests and demonstrations of various types.[10] Neither is it an easy matter for China to switch from an economy reliant on exports to one focused on domestic consumption. Currently domestic consumption is thought to make up barely 8 percent of China's GDP and there is a huge gap between rich and poor.

Since the end of the Cold War the US has been able to rule continuously as the world's sole superpower. According to the IMF's statistics

---

10: *Chosun Ilbo*, 16 November 2012.

for 2010, US GDP of $14.657 trillion was almost three times that of China, at $5.878 trillion.[II] In 2012 the gap between US and Chinese GDP was still large (although it had narrowed somewhat), but the gap between the two countries' per capita GDP is far larger. US GDP per capita in 2010 was more than ten times that of China, at $47,240 compared to China's $4,260. With per capita GDP only 46.8 percent of the world average, China is still a poor country. When we examine military strength, the gap between the two countries is even larger. According to SIPRI's statistics for 2011, US military spending is not only the highest in the world, but is equivalent to the defence budgets of the next 5 highest spenders put together (in order: China, Russia, UK, France, Japan). As figure 5 shows, the difference between the defence budgets of the US and China is very great.

Figure 5: US and Chinese defence spending (as proportion of total)

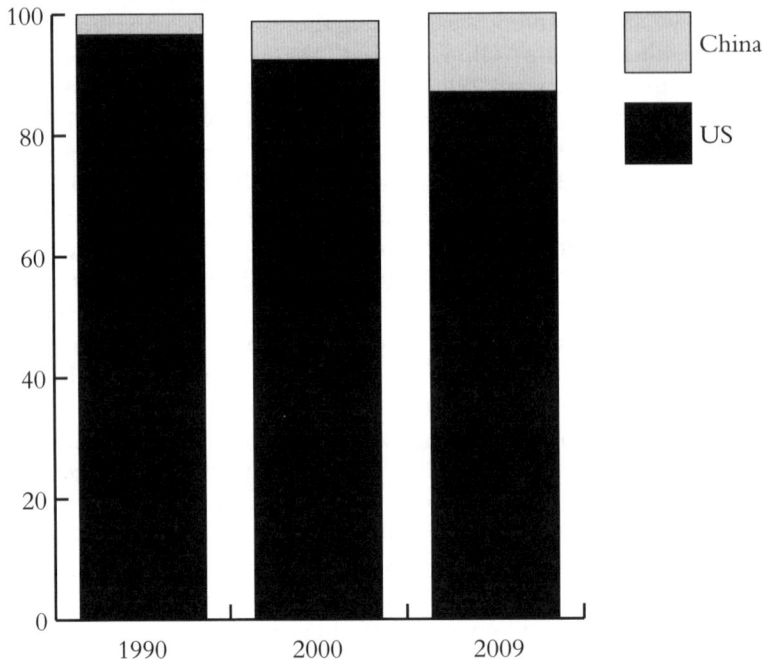

II: These figures are from the IMF World Economic Outlook, 2011.

If we one-sidedly exaggerate the rise of China there is a danger that we make the mistake of overlooking one of the core features of the current world order: the continued existence of an imbalance in strength between the US and the rest of the advanced capitalist states. Having said that, it would also be a mistake to understand today's world as one in which the advanced countries are all actually subordinated to US hegemony. Leo Panitch and Sam Gindin have systematically developed this approach and this has led them to the conclusion that geopolitical competition is now a thing of the past.[12]

We need to recognise that while there is a big imbalance between the US and the other advanced nations, there are also considerable conflicts of interest between them too. We should not ignore the tensions and latent sources of hostility among the major powers. In the context of the recent world economic crisis we are currently seeing the outbreak of severe conflicts over exchange rates and trade between China and the US, whose economies have developed a relationship of mutual dependence. China currently accounts for some 40 percent of the US trade deficit and the US is thus strongly demanding that China allow the renminbi to appreciate. In other words, the US is pressuring China to pay the adjustment costs required for its own economy to recover from the crisis. However, as was the case with West Germany and Japan in the 1970s and 1980s, US pressure on China is not likely to be successful. This sort of economic conflict between the two powers has a geopolitical impact and also combines with moves to occupy a dominant position. Although the effect may not be immediate, in a situation where stagnation continues for a long time conflicts of interest between major powers can give rise to major geopolitical clashes.

The US response and resulting instability in East Asia

Feeling threatened by the rise of China as an economic and military power, the US will actively seek a way to maintain its position at the top of the world rankings. The US already openly stated this in its 2006 Quadrennial Defense Review. This report revealed the superpower's worries, noting that: "Of the major and emerging powers, China has the greatest potential to compete militarily with the US and field disruptive military technologies that could over time offset traditional US military advantages [in the absence of] US counter strategies." It then continued, menacingly, to announce

---

12: On the views of today's Marxists on capitalism and imperialism see Callinicos, 2009, pp16-18. See also Panitch and Gindin, 2012.

that: "It will attempt to dissuade any military competitor from developing disruptive or other capabilities that could enable regional hegemony or hostile action against the United States or other friendly countries, and it will seek to deter aggression or coercion. Should deterrence fail, the United States would deny a hostile power its strategic and operational objectives".[13]

However, after more than ten years mired in Iraq and Afghanistan the US cannot handle the rise of China as an economic and geopolitical competitor so easily and is finding it difficult to maintain its global hegemony. As Alex Callinicos has pointed out, the US establishment seems to be panicked by the idea that while it has been bogged down in the Middle East and Afghanistan the rest of the world has been overtaking it.[14]

This is the background to the emergence of the phrase "Pivot to Asia". Hillary Clinton published an article in *Foreign Policy* in November 2011, entitled "America's Pacific Century". During his nine-day tour of Asian countries in the same year Barack Obama also repeatedly emphasised that "the Asia-Pacific region is my first priority." In his speech to the Australian parliament he stated: "As we end today's wars, I have directed my national security team to make our presence and mission in the Asia Pacific a top priority," adding: "So let there be no doubt: in the Asia Pacific in the 21st century the United States of America is all in."

However, the idea that Asia is important is not exactly a new discovery for the US, which has always regarded itself as an Asia-Pacific power. Its 1990 East Asian Strategic Initiative, which included a plan to reduce the US military presence in East Asia after the collapse of the USSR, did not last long. The US quickly switched back to stating that it would play a core role in the region. This was because of its fears about the rise of potential competitors like China. The 1997 US-Japan Defense Cooperation Guidelines were created in this context. The Pentagon's April 2001 Defense Policy Report also revealed the US's intention to shift its strategic focus from the West to the Asia Pacific region, but during the Bush administration's prosecution of the "war on terror" this inevitably fell by the wayside. However, even the neocon strategy was actually a way of responding to the changes in the world economy: the rise of China and the decline of the US. But, as we all know, this resulted in the Iraq War that ended in defeat for the US.

So Obama's "Pivot to Asia" is not building upon results garnered by the former strategy. It instead takes as its starting point current difficult circumstances, which have been made even worse by recent failures. What's

---

13:   United States Department of Defense, 2006, pp29-30.
14:   Callinicos, 2011, p71.

more, due to its fiscal deficit the US will have to reduce its defence spending over the next ten years by between $400 billion and $1 trillion. It finds itself in a situation where it has to carry out its stated strategy within the constraints of a diminishing defence budget. As it continues to be the world's sole superpower, the US has to show that its capabilities span the whole world and that it intends to maintain its hegemony not just in East Asia but in the Middle East and Europe too. After he was re-elected Obama headed for Burma, but with a military conflict breaking out between Israel and Hamas he could not take his eyes off the Middle East, where US control has been so weakened. In short, with the US bearing the scars of defeat and forced to cut defence spending by the economic crisis, it may feel anxious about the instability in the Middle East but has little option other than turning to Asia.

However, as Chris Harman pointed out in his speech at the Marxism event in Seoul in 2009, a wounded animal is more dangerous. It is clear that the US's strategic adjustment will make the East Asian region even more unstable.

First, it is making efforts to boost its economic and diplomatic influence. It is actively setting out to check China's expanding influence. One example of this is the Trans Pacific Partnership that the US is currently pursuing. The TPP is the main free trade agreement aimed at expanding the US's economic benefits and influence in the increasingly economically important Asian region. At the moment Australia, New Zealand, Singapore, Malaysia, Vietnam and Chile are participating in the TPP. These are all places that have close economic relations with China and have either concluded free trade agreements (FTAs) with China (Vietnam, Malaysia, Singapore, Chile) or are in the process of negotiating one (Australia, New Zealand).

Above all, the US has begun actively to promote the TPP because it wants to recover the influence it has lost in East Asia and the Pacific region and block China's efforts to promote an East Asian Free Trade Agreement (EAFTA) through ASEAN+3 (ASEAN plus China, Japan and South Korea). The US has actually tried to hold back the development of Asian regionalism for some time. During the 1990s the US also used its leadership of APEC to thwart the formation of the East Asian Economic Group and the Asian Monetary Fund. Despite this, with genuine movement towards regionalism in East Asia after the 1997 Asian financial crisis, and against the background of the US's estrangement from Asia during the Iraq War, APEC has become less important. During this time ASEAN+3 has made rapid progress in institutionalisation under the leadership of China. In the case of ASEAN+3, not only the US but all states outside the Asian region are excluded from membership. The US's promotion of the TPP is therefore an attempt to prevent itself from being kept out of East Asian economic integration and even to snatch the leadership of this integration from China.

Of course, there are also economic reasons for the US's promotion of the TPP. Some time ago Obama announced the National Export Initiative that included the target of doubling exports in five years from 2010. In order to achieve this target the US will have to pioneer new markets in East Asia and construct a new economic and trade cooperation system. If an East Asian Free Trade Agreement is concluded with the exclusion of the US it is thought that it might reduce the US's annual exports by at least $25 billion and some 200,000 high income jobs would be lost.[15]

Obama is now making efforts to expand the number of countries involved in the TPP. During his tour of South East Asian countries after his re-election in November 2012 he managed to get a promise from Thailand that it would participate in the TPP negotiations. At the same time the then Japanese prime minister, Noda, also expressed his intention to participate in the TPP and agreed with Obama that preparatory talks should be speeded up. There is also a story that the US officially requested that South Korea participate in the TPP. (The South Korean Ministry of Foreign Affairs and Trade denied these reports when they appeared in the *Bangkok Post.*)

The US is also trying to prevent the leadership of East Asian regional structures drifting over to China and secure its own leading position by actively participating in regional security organisations like the ASEAN Regional Forum and the East Asia Summit (EAS). The US first participated in the EAS in 2011 where, despite opposition from China, it led a multilateral debate on territorial disputes in the South China Sea.

Second, the US is attempting to boost its geopolitical and military influence in the region. It is responding to China's military build-up by making great efforts to maintain its superior position. The US strategic response is well illustrated in its Defense Strategic Guidance (DSG) published in January 2012. Entitled "Sustaining US Global Leadership: Priorities for 21st Century Defense", these guidelines for geopolitical strategy clarify the Obama government's policy focusing on the Asia-Pacific region and aimed at checking the advance of China. This reveals its intention to neutralise China's naval strategy, what the US calls its "Anti-Access/Area Denial Strategy". The guidance document notes in particular: "In order to credibly deter potential adversaries and to prevent them from achieving their objectives, the United

---

15: Bergsten, 2007, p4.

States must maintain its ability to project power in areas in which our access and freedom to operate are challenged".[16]

In summary, the US intends to oppose head-on China's attempts to push the US military out of its neighbouring seas, beyond the First Island Chain and possibly even the Second Island Chain. In other words, the US is sending a message that it will continue to dominate the Asia-Pacific region. This is also revealed in the US attitude towards the territorial disputes in the South and East China Seas. (Both of these seas are within the First Island Chain.) As I pointed out earlier, the US has taken the position that the Senkaku (Diaoyu) Islands fall under the scope of Article 5 of the US-Japan Security Treaty.[17] Thus if there is a confrontation between China and Japan over the Senkakus the US will respond jointly with Japan. The US has also stated openly that it will "take an interest in resolving the territorial disputes in the region", targeting China's disputes with its neighbours over various islands in the South China Sea. In her speech at the ASEAN Regional Forum in July 2010 Secretary of State Clinton noted that "the United States, like every nation, has a national interest in freedom of navigation, open access to Asia's maritime commons, and respect for international law in the South China Sea... The United States supports a collaborative diplomatic process by all claimants for resolving the various territorial disputes without coercion." This puts pressure on China's claims to possession over the South China Sea and offers a protective shield to those countries that are in conflict with China over these issues.

The US Department of Defense has proposed a strategy of "Operational Access", meaning that even in a situation where a country denies access to the US it will have "the ability to project military force into any operational area in the face of armed opposition".[18] In June 2012 US defence secretary Leon Panetta said that the US would station 60 percent of its naval power in the Asia-Pacific region (at the moment

---

16: Department of Defense, 2012, p4.

17: Article 5 of the Treaty of Mutual Cooperation and Security between Japan and the US (1960) states: "Each Party recognises that an armed attack against either Party in the territories under the administration of Japan would be dangerous to its own peace and safety and declares that it would act to meet the common danger in accordance with its constitutional provisions and processes. Any such armed attack and all measures taken as a result thereof shall be immediately reported to the Security Council of the United Nations in accordance with the provisions of Article 51 of the Charter. Such measures shall be terminated when the Security Council has taken the measures necessary to restore and maintain international peace and security."

18: Olsen, 2012, p38.

it is 50 percent) in an effort to raise operational access capabilities.[19] The construction of a Missile Defence (MD) system is one of the most important ways of neutralising China's "Anti-Access/Area Denial" capabilities. The US has been cooperating with Japan on Missile Defence since the late 1990s and trying to get South Korea to participate too. It has also been trying to strengthen Taiwan's military capabilities in order to guard against China's ability to project its military power in the Taiwan Strait. Despite resistance from China, the US decided in January 2010 to sell $6.4 billion worth of the latest weaponry to Taiwan, while in December 2012 the National Defense Authorisation Act passed by the US Congress demanded that the administration sell advanced fighter planes to Taiwan. Aside from this the US has been trying to maintain its maritime dominance in the region by investing in stealth bombers, long distance precision strike capabilities, nuclear attack submarines and cyber-security.

Situated as it is so far from East Asia, the US desperately needs the cooperation of states in the region in order to respond to China's military build-up. Without agreements that guarantee US access, overseas base construction and base improvements as well as joint military exercises with regional states, the US will not be able to pursue its strategy. For this reason, the US is strengthening its existing alliances with Japan, South Korea, Australia and others while reinforcing security cooperation with other states such as Vietnam, Singapore, the Philippines and Indonesia. (To a certain extent this fits well with the interests of the East Asian states, which are concerned about the rise of China and keen to keep it in check.)

US efforts to besiege China by forging alliances in Asia

US strategy in Asia involves seeking "to maintain Japan's strategic subordination, and more generally, developing a coalition of states capable of containing China", as Alex Callinicos points out.[20] Traditionally, Japan has been the most important ally in the region for the US. For a long time, it has pursued a strategy to strengthen its presence by siding with the US. During the late 2000s, especially under the Japanese prime minister Yukio Hatoyama who championed Asia-focused policies, the relationship between the two countries suffered temporary setbacks, but the Obama administration was able to maintain its marine corps base in Futenma and "normalise"

19:   This is from Panetta's speech given at the IISS Shangri-La Dialogue event that took place in Singapore in June 2012—www.iiss.org/conferences/the-shangri-la-dialogue/shangri-la-dialogue-2012/speeches/first-plenary-session/leon-panetta
20:   Callinicos, 2009, p220.

US-Japan relations by exploiting the sinking of the South Korean warship the *Cheonan*. The East Asian Community conceived by Hatoyama eventually came to naught in 2010 when Naoto Kan was sworn into office as the next prime minister.

Japan plays a pivotal role in implementing the US strategy to besiege China with its allies. Accordingly, the US wants Japan to enhance its regional status, which means increasing its contribution to maintaining security in the region. This partly reflects Washington's need to cut its military spending. Recently the US has been asserting such intentions even more openly. At the US-Japan summit held on 30 April 2012 the two countries redefined the nature of their alliance as that of preparing for uncertainties created by the emergence of China in the Asia-Pacific region. At the same time they agreed to facilitate cooperation between the US military and the Japan Self-Defence Forces (JSDF) to contain China and develop the JSDF into a truly "Dynamic Defence Force". The concept of Dynamic Defence is meant to allow the JSDF to operate with greater mobility both at home and abroad, beyond its primary mission of territorial defence. In other words, it is to be freed from a purely defensive mission and expand overseas.

These developments enable Japan, which once imposed brutal colonial rule in Asia, to bolster its military capabilities. Over the last year alone the country relaxed its "three principles" governing weapons exports (deciding to participate in joint weapons development programmes with the US and its allies), revised the Nuclear Energy Basic Law to lay the legal basis for nuclear armament, and issued a report by a committee under the prime minister's office calling for the "amendment of the Constitutional interpretation to allow the country to exercise its collective self-defence rights". In its 2012 defence white paper Tokyo openly warned against a "China threat", and on the basis of this, embarked on a build-up of military forces targeting China. Both the US and Japan deployed Global Hawks, the state of the art unmanned spy drones, off the coasts of Japan including the Senkaku (Diaoyu) Islands to tighten vigilance and surveillance in the area. Japan has already beefed up its military forces in Nansei Shoto (Japan's south western islands) in the wake of the Senkaku flare-up in 2010. It also decided to deploy Osprey aircraft with vertical takeoff and landing capability at Futenma Base, despite fierce opposition from Okinawans. The Osprey is capable of infiltrating deep behind enemy lines or staging surprise attacks with its high cruising speed.

All of this happened under the watch of the Democratic Party of Japan (DPJ). However, Japan's military resurgence is likely to accelerate more rapidly since the Liberal Democratic Party (LDP) secured a majority in the general elections of December 2012. The new prime minister

Shinzo Abe is the grandson of Nobusuke Kishi, a Class A war criminal, and Abe himself is a right wing politician who denies Japan's history of military aggression, colonial rule in Asia and its atrocities. Abe put forth the amendment of the Peace Constitution, recognition of Japan's collective self-defence rights, transformation of the JSDF into a regular military force, and the legislation of its rules of engagement as his campaign pledges. On the day the new cabinet was launched, he announced he would ask a panel of experts for their opinions on the extent to which Japan's collective self-defence rights can be exercised under the existing constitution. He is intent on asserting collective self-defence rights even if it means an amendment of the constitutional interpretation. The right of collective self-defence, in international law means the right of a country to intervene militarily when an ally has been attacked, even if the country itself is not directly attacked. So far Japan has been denied the right of collective self-defence and is allowed a self-defence force capable of engaging an enemy only when attacked first, in accordance with Article 9 of the Peace Constitution, which renounces war and the possession of military forces.

Next to Japan, South Korea is the second most important US ally in East Asia. "The US-ROK Alliance is a linchpin of stability, security and prosperity in the Asia-Pacific region," said Obama in June 2010. The South Korean right wing were overjoyed by the apparently flattering use of the expression "linchpin", but in fact, his comment only reveals how deeply South Korea is tied to the instability in East Asia. The US intends to make South Korea one of the main pillars of its strategy to contain China. The joint statement issued at the conclusion of the 2012 US-ROK Foreign and Defence Ministers' Meeting stipulated South Korea would actively cooperate with the US in implementing its strategy to contain China and implied that the scope of US-ROK cooperation could go beyond North East Asia to the South China Sea—meaning that South Korea can be caught up in regional conflicts in the course of defending US interests in East Asia.

The US wants South Korea to cooperate militarily with Japan. For a long time the US has hoped to strengthen security cooperation between the two countries and form a US-ROK-Japan trilateral alliance, but issues involving Japan's colonial past have been an obstacle. Lately Washington has been hard at work to promote security ties between its allies: thus South Korea and Japan held a joint annual Search and Rescue Exercise (SAREX) and discussed the signing of a military cooperation pact and an acquisitions and cross-servicing agreement.

The Lee Myung-bak government, which secretly attempted to push through a military cooperation pact, postponed the signing when faced with public uproar at home, but the newly inaugurated Park Geun-hye government is very likely to resume the negotiations. The primary focus for the US is to ensure cooperation between South Korea, the US and Japan in building its missile defence system. In other words, the US wants to establish a new command and control structure whereby the three countries share military intelligence and engage in joint operations from the point of missile launch to interception. Although the US uses the "threat" of North Korea as an excuse for building the missile defence system, it is an open secret that its real target is China. As pointed out above, the US missile defence system is crucial in neutralising China's "Anti-Access/Area Denial" strategy.

US exaggeration of the North Korean "threat" has to be briefly mentioned here. The US has used the "threat" posed by North Korea as a pretext for pursuing its strategic interests of maintaining hegemony in East Asia. For example, it accused North Korea of sinking the *Cheonan* warship as a way of strengthening the US-Japan alliance. It even deployed an aircraft carrier for a joint naval exercise conducted right under China's nose off the west coast of Korea. The US also cites the North Korean "threat" as the first and foremost reason for trilateral security cooperation and for the missile defence system. It needs, in other words, to use the poorest and the most vulnerable country in North East Asia as a bogeyman to justify a system that really targets China. In South Korea there is widespread discontent that the US seems to want the tensions on the Korean peninsula to continue. All the same, the US expects South Korea to toe its line in dealing with North Korea.

The South Korean ruling class has posed itself as a loyal ally of the US to promote its own political, economic and military interests and elevate its international status. In the 2000s, the policy of leaning exclusively towards the US became contested by a section of the political elite, but Park Geun-hye from the Saenuri Party, which traditionally placed great emphasis on the US-ROK alliance, won the 2012 presidential election. Park, the daughter of the military dictator who ruled during the 1960s and 1970s, served as an acting first lady after her mother's death; as president, she is certain to lend full support to the US policy of enhancing the US-ROK alliance.

The US is strengthening its security cooperation with other Asian countries too. It is striving to encircle China by promising to provide protection for South East Asian nations which have been alarmed by the rise of China. To this end, the then US secretary of state, Hillary Clinton, defense secretary Leon Panetta and even President Obama have visited Asia several times over the past two or three years.

As a result, the US succeeded in reaching an agreement in 2012 with the Philippines to enhance military cooperation and was given permission to resume its use of the Subic Bay Naval Base and Clark Air Base—once its two biggest foreign bases in the world—by the Philippines government in June the same year. The Subic Base was the most crucial strategic base for the US during the Vietnam War. In April 2012 the Philippines government requested US assistance in the midst of a confrontation with China on Scarborough Island. It is fair to say the Philippines gave the naval and air base to the US in return for the help. With these bases in hand, the US was able to considerably broaden its theatre of operation in Asia and tighten the noose round China.

The US also signed a Memorandum of Understanding with Vietnam to enhance military cooperation between the two countries in September 2011. Having had disputes with China over the Paracel Islands, Vietnam began to allow US naval forces to visit its ports in 2009. In August 2011 it even permitted US naval ships to visit the naval base at Cam Ranh Bay, 36 years after the end of the Vietnam War. On his visit to the base in 2012 defence secretary Leon Panetta stressed that "access for United States naval ships into this facility is a key component of this relationship" with Vietnam, and the Vietnamese government is considering whether to allow US access to Cam Ranh. Cam Ranh Bay, the main base from which the US waged the Vietnam War, is a strategic location for the US, lying within easy reach of the South China Sea.

The US government is also in discussions with the Thai government to enhance its access to the U-Tapao Naval Air Base. The base was used for B-52 takeoffs and landings during the Vietnam War. As illustrated in figure 7, the US is attempting to gain footholds in strategic positions in a number of countries surrounding China.

The US reached an agreement with Singapore in June 2012 to deploy its high-tech littoral combat ships in the country. Furthermore, Obama's visit to Australia in 2011 resulted in an agreement to send 2,500 US marines to Australia's Darwin Naval Base, US fighter jets to the Tyndall Air Force Base, and nuclear-armed vessels and submarines to the Stirling Base. The Darwin Base would serve as a rear base from which to oversee the sea lane that runs from the Indian Ocean through the Strait of Malacca to the South China Sea.

The US is expanding military cooperation not just in the South China Sea but also in the Indian Ocean. In June 2012, Panetta met Indian prime minister Manmohan Singh and talked about a "common security threat". India has been watching with growing alarm China's effort to increase its influence in the Indian Ocean, for instance helping Pakistan and Sri Lanka build ports. As with Japan, the US wants to make India a regional power that will contain China. In 2006 it changed its position against India's nuclear programme and signed a US-India nuclear cooperation agreement as part of this strategy.

Figure 6: Strategic bases in South East Asia that the US is eyeing

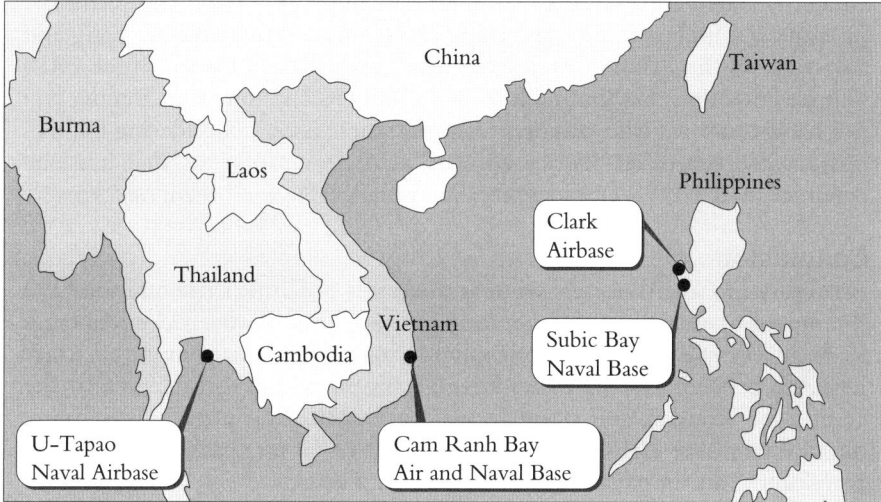

Some of the countries that the US is trying to win over to its side have long histories of opposition to Washington: Burma, Laos and Cambodia—China's traditional allies. Hillary Clinton paid a visit to Burma in 2011 and Laos in 2012, the first time a US secretary of state had visited those countries since 1955. Obama also included Burma and Laos among the first countries to visit after his re-election. Washington wants to pull these countries away from China and make them cooperate with the US. Burma is a case in point. A geopolitically important country for China, Burma has been supported economically and diplomatically by China throughout the last 20 years of economic sanctions imposed by the West. The country serves as a bridgehead for China to make inroads to the Indian Ocean. Currently China is conducting a strategic oil pipeline project with Burma to reduce the amount of oil that passes through the Strait of Malacca and secure more reliable oil supplies. As the *New York Times* noted, the US "embrace" of Burma must have come as a shock to China.

Of course, China does not sit idle, doing nothing about the US encircling it. China has been making continuous efforts to expand its influence not only economically but also geopolitically and to protect its "core interests" from the US and its allies. On his visit to the US in February 2012 China's new leader Xi Jinping argued that China and the US should work out a "new type of relationship between major powers". In other words, they should build mutual trust and respect each other's core interests and concerns. The "core interests" of China include "sovereign and territorial integrity", which means maintaining its rule over Tibet and Xinjiang and adhering to the "One China Principle" regarding Taiwan. Since 2010 China also counts the South China Sea among its core interests. Beijing will not back down easily in disputes regarding these issues, considering China's characterisation of its "core interests" as national interests that must be defended at all costs and under any circumstances, using force if necessary.

Conclusion

Instability in East Asia is growing as the result of China's rise and the US's strategy of maintaining its hegemony in the region. As the US encourages its Asian allies to strengthen their military roles and China responds in kind, East Asia is becoming a powder keg. According to a report released by the Center for Strategic and International Studies (CSIS) in the United States on 15 November 2012, the defence budgets of China, India, Japan, South Korea and Taiwan have doubled over the last decade.

While a war between the US and China is not inevitable, it is nevertheless clear that we are living in a dangerous world. Contrary to the widespread belief that the economic interdependence between China and the US will deter any geopolitical clash between them, increased trade and investment do not bring peace—as the classical Marxist theory of imperialism warns. Germany and Britain had close economic ties before the First World War, and the same was true of the US and Japan before the Second World War. Above all, East Asia is rife with destabilising factors such as territorial disputes and a divided Korean peninsula, any one of which can trigger a rapid escalation of military tension in the region.

Opposing imperialism is a crucial task for socialists. We must oppose the US's imperialist expansion to maintain its world hegemony as well as the Asian governments that ally with the US to increase their own international clout. We must have no illusions or fantasies about Chinese imperialism either. China can never offer a better model for humanity. The answer is not to take sides among competing imperialist countries but to build an anti-imperialist movement from below. Imperialism is not a set of policies thrust upon us by particularly nasty rulers; it is the latest stage of global capitalism driven by capitalist dynamics. Therefore, to oppose imperialism consistently, it is ultimately necessary to oppose capitalism. Socialists have to make every effort to encourage workers' movements to develop into an anti-capitalist movement.

References

Bergsten, C Fred, 2007, "China and Economic Integration in East Asia: Implications for the United States", Policy Briefs PB07-3, Peterson Institute for International Economics.

Callinicos, Alex, 2009, *Imperialism and Global Political Economy* (Polity Press).

Callinicos, Alex, 2011, "Alex Callinicos Korea lecture: Imperialism and international political economy", published in *Marx21*, 11 (autumn).

Kim Chaech'ol, 2007, *Chungguk ui oegyo chollyak kwa kukche chilso* [China's diplomatic strategy and the global order] (Polliteia).

Olsen, Paul A, 2012, *Operation Corporate: Operational Art and Implications for the Joint Operational Access Concept* (School of Advanced Military Studies, United States Army Command and General Staff College), www.dtic.mil/cgi-bin/GetTRDoc?AD=ADA566546

Panitch, Leo, and Sam Gindin, 2012, *The Making of Global Capitalism: The Political Economy of American Empire* (Verso).

United States National Intelligence Council, 2008, *Global Trends 2025: A Transformed World*, www.dni.gov/files/documents/Newsroom/Reports%20and%20Pubs/2025_Global_Trends_Final_Report.pdf

United States Department of Defense, 2006, *Quadrennial Defense Review Report*, www.defense.gov/qdr/report/report20060203.pdf

United States Department of Defense, 2012, *Defense Strategic Guidance—Sustaining US Global Leadership: Priorities for 21st Century Defense*, www.defense.gov/news/Defense_Strategic_Guidance.pdf

CAPITALISM AND SPORT
Politics, Protest, People and Play
Edited by Michael Lavalette
£9.99

The class struggles in Europe

Joseph Choonara

The crisis of global capitalism, now past its half-decade point, remains the key to the political situation across Europe and beyond. It is on this terrain that resistance has begun to develop, one of the most visible expressions of which has been a succession of general strikes in several European countries since 2008.

Greece has witnessed by far the highest number of general strikes—29 since the crisis began. Yet, while exceptional in many ways, Greece is part of a wider pattern. In the Spanish state, unions held a general strike in September 2010, with a second following in March 2012. In Portugal the two main union federations called their first coordinated general strike in 22 years in November 2010, and marked the anniversary in November 2011 with a second on an even larger scale; a third came in March 2012, a week before the action in Spain.

Then, on 14 November 2012, coordinated general strikes across both states took place for the first time since the end of their dictatorships. Some 80 percent of Spanish intercity trains and two thirds of commuter services were cancelled, along with 600 flights; power consumption fell by 20 percent as factories ceased production, with multinational firms such as Danone and Heineken closing; unions reported almost universal support for the strikes in automobile production, shipbuilding and construction; demonstrations and riots took place in Madrid and Barcelona. In Portugal the strike was most solid across the public sector. Postal services and buses were halted; 90 percent of the Lisbon metro was shut down; half of all flights were cancelled; 40 demonstrations took place that evening.

The action across the Iberian Peninsula formed the centrepiece of a European day of action, which also featured a three-hour strike in Greece; a four-hour action by the CGIL union federation in Italy, closing schools, factories, ports and transport networks, accompanied by about 100 protests; protests in 130 cities in France; and demonstrations and strikes by rail workers in Belgium who in some cases physically blocked railway lines. Prior to 14 November 2012 mass one-day strikes also took place in France in spring and autumn 2010, Italy in September 2011, Britain in November 2011 and Belgium in January 2012.

Taken in isolation, these struggles could perhaps be regarded as bureaucratic mass strikes designed to allow rank and file workers to "let off steam"—ineffective and ultimately leading nowhere.[1] Taken together, and viewed with sensitivity to the tensions running through them, we can begin to see them for what they are: part of a developing cycle of struggle with the potential to challenge those presiding over European capitalism.

A new cycle of struggle
Globally, the year 2011 was a turning point. An article by John Molyneux in June that year sought to place the emerging struggles within a Marxist perspective:

> There is now a rising tide of struggle internationally. This kind of generalisation is not easy to make because the struggle is always at different levels and taking different forms in different countries... In 2010 the leading role was played by Greece where there were eight general strikes, plus many major demonstrations and street battles. But there were also general strikes in Spain and in Portugal...and a huge struggle over pensions in France involving mass strikes and huge street mobilisations of up to 3.5 million people. In Iceland the government was forced into a referendum over their IMF bailout and lost it...

> Then...came the "Arab Spring" which lifted the struggle to a whole new level. The Tunisian Revolution, which succeeded in bringing down a dictator, Zine Ben Ali, of 23 years standing, in less than a month led directly to the 25 January [2011] Revolution in Egypt which on 11 February

---

1:    See, for instance, Wall Street Journal, 2012, for a particularly dismissive take on the action.

ended the rule of Hosni Mubarak… It led immediately to uprisings in Libya, Bahrain, Yemen and Syria… Then came…15 May in Spain, and the occupation of Puerta del Sol in Madrid. This spread with enormous speed to other cities, Barcelona, Seville, etc… As I write there is news of 50,000-100,000 on the streets of Milan greeting the defeat of Berlusconi in that city and the revolution continues in Egypt with hundreds of thousands out on 27 May.[2]

For Molyneux the comparisons were with three previous great cycles of workers' struggle. The first, in 1848, saw a series of uprisings in France, Germany, Hungary, Italy, Switzerland and Austria, as well as the mass mobilisations by the Chartist movement in Britain. The second was the revolutionary wave that culminated in the period following the First World War with the 1917 Russian Revolution, the German Revolution of 1918-1923, and revolutionary situations that developed in Italy, Hungary, Austria and Finland. The third was formed by the rebellions of the late 1960s and early 1970s, including the French general strike of 1968, the Italian hot autumn of 1969, the Chilean struggle of 1973 and the Portuguese Revolution of 1974, along with the US civil rights movement and a wave of strike action that brought down a Tory government in Britain.[3]

Whether the current global cycle reaches the heights of its predecessors remains to be seen. Certainly we are not yet witnessing *sustained* workers' struggles; the action in Europe has often been episodic and even in Egypt, where a strike movement helped dislodge Mubarak in 2011, the most consistent factor has been a series of street mobilisations.[4] Nonetheless, there has been a significant shift in the situation. Whether this process continues depends on whether our rulers find a way to stabilise the societies they preside over and decisively defeat enough of those engaged in battle to cow the rest into submission. While there have been setbacks for the movements, in general they have not been crushed, and, in addition, the crisis is currently a factor destabilising societies and restricting our rulers' room for manoeuvre.

The aim of this article is to explore the tensions and complexities in the resistance that has developed in Western Europe. But first it is necessary to consider the lessons of earlier cycles of resistance.

2: Molyneux, 2011.

3: The best account of the third wave of struggle is Harman, 1998.

4: For an excellent account of the tensions that have developed within the Egyptian Revolution see Marfleet, 2013.

From crisis to resistance

Karl Marx's and Frederick Engels's best known comments on the relationship between crisis and resistance were the product of their reflection on the 1848 revolutions. While these struggles ultimately showed that further growth and development of the working class would be needed before it could provide an alternative to capitalism across the continent, they nonetheless gave Marx and Engels their only direct experience of revolution.[5] In his analysis, *The Class Struggles in France*, Marx set out the wider political contradictions that formed the conditions for the explosion, but he added that they were accelerated and ripened by "two world economic events":

> The *potato blight* and the *crop failures* of 1845 and 1846 increased the general ferment among the people. The dearth of 1847 called forth bloody conflicts in France as well as on the rest of the continent. As against the shameless orgies of the finance aristocracy, the struggle of the people for the prime necessities of life... The second great economic event which hastened the outbreak of the revolution was a *general commercial and industrial crisis* in England [which] finally burst in the autumn of 1847... The after-effect of this crisis on the continent had not yet spent itself when the February Revolution broke out.[6]

By 1850, with the revolutions defeated, Marx had concluded: "A new revolution is possible only in consequence of a new crisis. It is, however, just as certain as this crisis".[7] Similarly, looking back in 1895, Engels wrote in his introduction to *Class Struggles*: "The world trade crisis of 1847 had been the true mother of the February and March revolutions, and...the industrial prosperity which had been returning gradually since the middle of 1848 and attained full bloom in 1849 and 1850 was the revitalising force of the newly strengthened European reaction".[8]

The very notion that class struggle could be traced back, in the final analysis, to underlying economic causes was one of the intellectual fruits of the analysis of the first of our three great cycles.[9] It was left to a later generation of Marxists—especially those associated with the early years of the Third International—to develop a more general account of the interaction between crisis and resistance.[10] The second revolutionary cycle would furnish ample

---

5:    See Nimtz, 2000, for a discussion of the two revolutionaries' role in 1848.
6:    Marx, 1950, p132.
7:    Marx, 1950, p210.
8:    Engels, 1950, p111.
9:    See Engels, 1950, pp109-110.
10:   The Third International, Comintern or Communist International was the

raw material. In early 1921 the Third Congress of the Comintern had to deal with the partial restabilisation of Europe under capitalist rule, following the revolutionary wave that accompanied the end of the First World War. While there had been an economic "upswing" in 1919-20, this was followed rapidly by a crisis in late 1920 through to autumn 1921. At the Congress Leon Trotsky sought to assess the prospects for renewed struggle. He cited Marx's and Engels's comments on 1848, but warned against the temptation to derive from these a mechanical relationship between crisis and resistance:

> It would...be very one-sided and utterly false to interpret these judgements in the sense that a crisis invariably engenders revolutionary action while a boom, on the contrary, pacifies the working class. The revolution of 1848 was not born out of the crisis. The latter merely provided the last impetus. Essentially the revolution grew out of the contradiction between the needs of capitalist development and the fetters of the semi-feudal state system. The irresolute and half-way revolution of 1848 did, however, sweep away the remnants of the regime of guilds and serfdom and thereby extended the framework of capitalist development. Under these conditions and these conditions alone, the boom of 1851 marked the beginning of an entire epoch of capitalist prosperity which lasted till 1873.[11]

The first point that Trotsky makes is that the general character of the period is important. "At issue here is not whether an improvement in the conjuncture is possible, but whether the fluctuations are proceeding along an ascending or descending curve".[12] The cycle of boom and bust is an inherent feature of capitalism, but the system also possesses long-term tendencies that, over time, can lead the busts to become more devastating and the booms more ephemeral. Conversely there can be periods of general prosperity in which the bust takes the form of a slight slowdown or contraction in production. The long boom following the Second World War was one such period.

A period of depression would mean "the bourgeoisie will be compelled to exert stronger and stronger pressure upon the working class".[13] The defensive struggles this entailed would allow the revolutionaries to extend themselves into new sections of the class, utilising the policy of the

---

international grouping of revolutionary socialists initiated by the Bolsheviks in 1919. A brief history is provided by Hallas, 1985.

11:    Trotsky, 1973a, p259.
12:    Trotsky, 1973a, pp259-260.
13:    Trotsky, 1973a, p261.

united front that would shortly be adopted by the Comintern.[14] But there would be, within this period, further sharp changes in the economic situation and revolutionaries must grasp the importance of these: "Neither impoverishment nor prosperity as such can lead to revolution. But the alternation of prosperity and impoverishment, the crises, the uncertainty, the absence of stability—these are the motor factors of revolution".[15]

Trotsky's concern throughout the discussion was to defend the proposition: "In general, there is no automatic dependence of the proletarian revolutionary movement upon a crisis. There is only a dialectical interaction".[16] As a counter to the simplistic interpretation of Marx's and Engels's comments on 1848, he provided a Russian example:

> The 1905 Revolution was defeated. The workers bore great sacrifices. In 1906 and 1907 the last revolutionary flare-ups occurred and by the autumn of 1907 a great world crisis broke out. The signal for it was given by Wall Street's Black Friday. Throughout 1907 and 1908 and 1909 the most terrible crisis reigned in Russia too. It killed the movement completely, because the workers had suffered so greatly during the struggle that this depression could act only to dishearten them... In 1910, 1911 and 1912 there was an improvement in our economic situation and a favourable conjuncture which acted to reassemble the demoralised and devitalised workers who had lost their courage. They realised again how important they were in production; and they passed over to an offensive, first in the economic field and later in the political field as well.[17]

The shape of the crisis

If, in the kind of analysis Trotsky was proposing, the overall *shape* of the crisis is important, what does this tell us about the current situation? The crisis that began in 2007-8 is not simply part of the boom–bust cycle or simply the result of a financial or banking disorder. Like the slump of the 1930s, it is the result of a long-term decline in the rate of profit—in this case, one that took place primarily in the decades following the Second World War up to the early 1980s, and one that the years since have failed to reverse. The decline is rooted in the tendency for accumulations of "dead labour" (investment in

14:   This policy involved revolutionaries proposing joint initiatives to reformist leaders and the workers who still remained loyal to them while maintaining their own political independence. See Trotsky, 1989.
15:   Trotsky, 1973b, pp285-286.
16:   Trotsky, 1973a, p261.
17:   Trotsky, 1973a, pp261-262.

machinery, raw material, etc) to run ahead of the amount of "living labour" (wage-workers) employed by the system. If, as Marx argued, living labour is the source of surplus value, out of which profit originates, the progressive build-up of dead labour relative to living will put pressure on profitability in the long run.[18] This tendency does not imply a "final crisis" of capitalism or a theory of its "collapse"; merely that it can reach the point where a new period of sustained growth is premised on the destruction or devaluation of capital on a tremendous scale. This entails a crisis "in which momentary suspension of all labour and annihilation of a great part of the capital violently lead [capitalism] back to the point where it is enabled [to go on] fully employing its productive powers without committing suicide".[19]

However, the sheer scale of the units of capital making up the system, and the way they are bound together with each other, with the financial system and with the state, makes such a clearing out of capitalism today extremely traumatic and risky. The temptation for those presiding over the system is to bail out failing firms and to seek to put a floor under the crisis through forms of state intervention. But this very action can prolong the crisis.[20]

In Europe the crisis is especially acute because it is mediated through the single currency shared by the eurozone countries. The launch of the euro allowed weaker economies, such as Portugal, Spain and Greece, access to flows of cheap credit, often provided by banks of more powerful economies such as Germany and France. An offensive against German workers' wages during these years led to a relative rise in the competitiveness of German exports, and the resulting current account deficits in the weaker economies were financed by their growing indebtedness, much of it taking the form of sovereign debt. When the crisis broke these imbalances grew. The combination of austerity, imposed on these countries in return for bailouts from the IMF, ECB and European Union, which has further undermined growth, along with the action of bond markets, which has pushed interest rates to unsustainable levels, has deepened the debt crisis.[21]

18: Those unfamiliar with Marx's law of the tendency of the rate of profit to fall can consult Harman, 2007.
19: Marx, 1993, p750.
20: This is a summarised version of an account I have advanced in Choonara, 2009, 2011, 2012. For similar accounts, see Callinicos, 2010; Carchedi, 2011; Harman, 2009; Kliman, 2011.
21: Much of the detail is covered well by Lapavitsas and others, 2012, although these authors would disagree with my contextualisation of the problems in a long-term crisis of profitability.

This analysis implies a crisis that is both deep and prolonged, accompanied in the eurozone by profound instability. The duration of the crisis means that many different phases are possible, each accompanied by shifts in the political situation, along with shifts in workers' consciousness—the "absence of stability" discussed by Trotsky.

Conditions for revolt

It is not simply the material conditions of those at the bottom of society that determines whether crisis translates into resistance. Lenin mentions that the conditions for revolution are that the ruled class is no longer willing to be ruled in the old way *and* the ruling class is no longer capable of ruling in the old way.[22] What goes for revolution here applies to struggle more generally. The Marxist who best explored the conditions under which the ruling class can obtain the limited consent required in order to rule without relying solely on repression was Antonio Gramsci:

> The active man-in-the-mass has a practical activity, but no theoretical consciousness of his practical activity, which nonetheless involves understanding the world in so far as it transforms it. His theoretical consciousness can indeed be historically in opposition to his activity. One might almost say that he has two theoretical consciousnesses (or one contradictory consciousness): one which is implicit in his activity and which in reality unites him with all his fellow-workers in the practical transformation of the real world; and one, superficially explicit or verbal, which he has inherited from the past and uncritically absorbed.[23]

The combination of these two contradictory conceptions of the world can lead to a degree of paralysis and passivity on the part of workers, but this is not a static state of affairs. Earlier in the same section of his *Prison Notebooks* Gramsci makes a distinction between "normal times" and abnormal ones.[24] Prolonged periods of crisis can disrupt the coherence of ruling class ideas, and the "common sense" ideas that workers can, for a period, uncritically accept, allowing "good sense", founded on experiences of solidarity and collective activity, to crystallise out.

One of the features of the current period has been the ideological radicalisation of sections of the population, not simply the core of the

---

22: Lenin, 1921, p83.
23: Gramsci, 1998, p333.
24: Gramsci, 1998, p327.

working class but also other groups facing oppression such as students and the unemployed, which often flares up into explosions of protest. The emergence of the Occupy movement in 2011 is an important symptom of this, and such movements can feed into and inspire workers' struggles.[25]

Not only does crisis disrupt the ideological coherence of the ruling idea in society, but, because capitalism is organised as a system of *competitive accumulation*, it can also lead to fissures within the ruling class itself. As Marx put it:

> So long as things go well, competition effects an operating fraternity of the capitalist class... But as soon as it no longer is a question of sharing profits, but of sharing losses, everyone tries to reduce his own share to a minimum and to shove it off upon another... How much the individual capitalist must bear of the loss, ie to what extent he must share in it at all, is decided by strength and cunning, and competition then becomes a fight among hostile brothers.[26]

A crisis can involve schisms between capitalists, or sections of the capitalist class, or the national states that particular capitalists are based in, as rival groupings argue over who will bear the burden of the crisis and over what strategy to follow to escape it. These are not simply economic tensions. As Lenin put it, "Politics are concentrated economics".[27] Political fragmentation is another product of the crisis. The eurozone, where the problems are especially intractable, is a case in point, with clashes between the German and French administrations, the governments of weaker eurozone countries, the ECB and the Bundesbank, and so on, a regular occurrence. But we are likely to see growing tensions too within particular national ruling classes. The emergence of struggles from below can, in turn, widen the splits at the top. In this sense, crisis can form the terrain for the emergence of more or less coherent political and ideological alternatives.[28]

Political polarisation

The political polarisation witnessed in much of Europe is one symptom. As the prescriptions offered by parties of the centre ground no longer fit and the possibilities for reform they offer are progressively closed down, more radical alternatives to the left or right begin to seem more realistic.

25: See Jones, 2012, for a discussion.
26: Marx, 1972, p253.
27: Lenin, 1973, p316.
28: My focus here is on economic crisis, but a deep political crisis, produced, say, by a disastrous military intervention, can have the same effect.

The far right has grown in many European countries. In Greece Chrysi Avgi (Golden Dawn), an openly Nazi organisation, took 7 percent in the June 2012 elections. In France, Marine Le Pen of the Front National (FN) took 6.4 million votes in the presidential elections last year. This electoral expression of the rise of the far right is matched on the ground in some cases by violent street mobilisations and racist attacks.

On the left, the main beneficiaries have in many cases been traditional reformist parties, especially where they have been out of office for a period. The victory of François Hollande in the French presidential election is one example. In Britain too the Labour Party has seen a revival of support during its time in opposition, despite offering a watered down version of the ruling coalition's austerity programme. Although they have generally shifted to the right over recent decades and weakened their ties to workers' organisations, traditional reformist parties have not severed their connection to the working class. They can still win support where they seem to offer a less vicious version of austerity. Nonetheless, in some cases the space to the left of these parties is being filled by more radical forces. In France Jean-Luc Mélenchon, standing on an anti-austerity and anti-racist platform, took 11 percent of the poll in the first round of the presidential elections. In Spain the Communist-led Izquierda Unida was polling at around 13 percent in summer 2012, while in November a coalition between this force and another left wing "eco-socialist" party saw its representation in the Catalan parliament rise from ten to 13 after taking 9.9 percent in regional elections. Greece again shows this pattern at its most spectacular, with the radical left Syriza coalition winning nearly 27 percent in the June 2012 elections; no radical left party has polled higher in Europe since the 1970s.

The left reformist formations have differing roots. Mélenchon's Front de Gauche combines the French Communist Party along with a left breakaway from the Socialist Party and some who have departed from the far-left Nouveau Parti Anticapitaliste (NPA); Syriza draws together most of the Euro-communist elements that emerged from Greece's Communist Party with smaller far-left groups; the Dutch Socialist Party, which retained 15 seats in parliament in September 2012 elections, began life as a Maoist organisation before breaking through in the mid-1990s and drawing in wider layers of supporters opposed to neoliberalism. What they share in common is their capacity to challenge the established left parties by rejecting the pro-austerity consensus. They remain, however, left *reformist*.[29] They reflect struggle from below, or at least an aspiration to it, but seek to transform the

---

29: See Callinicos, 2012b.

capitalist system by reforming it through the existing state institutions and, in some cases, the institutions of the eurozone. As Alexis Tsipras, the leader of Syriza, recently told the Brooking Institution: "Syriza's radical policies have nothing to do with taking Greece out of the eurozone. And if I'm not telling you that it's about reneging on all our agreements with the eurozone, what then does the title 'radical left' refer to? It means that we are ready for radical reforms in the government to create a steady environment of justice, redistribution of wealth and investments".[30]

Nonetheless, the revolutionary left cannot afford to be agnostic about the rise of such currents; their success can raise the confidence and expectations of the working class and mark a shift to the left in the political situation. Any notion that the working class once roused to struggle will *automatically* turn away from its traditional organisations and gravitate towards revolutionary parties, which remain tiny across Europe, is misguided. What Trotsky wrote of the Russian Revolution is true more generally of periods of heightened struggle:

> The fundamental political process of the revolution…consists in the gradual comprehension by a class of the problems arising from the social crisis— *the active orientation of the masses by a method of successive approximations.* The different stages of a revolutionary process, certified by a change of parties in which the more extreme always supersedes the less, express the growing pressure to the left of the masses—so long as the swing of the movement does not run into objective obstacles.[31]

Often it is political factors, evolving in the course of a crisis, that help to precipitate struggle. This was certainly true of struggles that developed during the slump of the 1930s. The great rise in strike action in the US took place in 1933-34, some years after the Wall Street Crash. From a picture of demoralisation and passivity, there suddenly erupted a series of unofficial battles by workers, culminating in the three great strikes of 1934, at Toledo (in the auto industry), Minneapolis (teamsters) and San Francisco (dock workers), that shifted the balance of class struggle in favour of workers. The context was one in which there was a widespread belief that the Great Depression had bottomed out. But workers also gained confidence when the New Deal inaugurated by the Roosevelt administration

---

30: Tsipras, 2013, pp13-14.
31: Trotsky, 1985, p18.

helped to trigger a wave of unionisation.[32] Similarly in France, mired in deep economic crisis from 1931, the great explosion of struggle took place five years on, following a period of sharp political polarisation in which workers, enthusiastic for unity against the threat of fascism, greeted the 1936 election of a Popular Front government supported by Socialists and Communists with a wave of strikes and factory occupations.[33] In both cases the radicalisation of sections of the working class ran far beyond the politics that helped to spark the mobilisation.

The condition of the class

A shift in the consciousness of the mass of workers does not simply involve ruling class ideas breaking down or a political crisis for the establishment; it also involves new forms of consciousness and organisation crystallising out of the real activity of workers. The conditions of the class when it enters a crisis, which might make it more or less confident to fight, are therefore important. As Trotsky put it, "the effects of a crisis…are determined by the entire existing political situation and by those events which precede and accompany the crisis, especially the battles, successes or failures of the working class itself prior to the crisis".[34]

However, it is not simply the case of a fixed working class becoming more or less confident or organised. The periodic restructuring of capitalism eradicates some of the old bases of class strength, while drawing workers into new areas. It often takes time and an experience of struggle for such groups of workers to develop the self-confidence and organisation required to fight collectively and for the older groups that remain to regain their confidence.

So the third of our cycles of struggle, which began in the late 1960s, followed a long period of growth which, in many advanced capitalist states, allowed new class forces to form and develop, often through localised and sectional struggles for better wages or conditions—which capitalists and governments were sometimes prepared to concede. In Britain in the period running up to 1972 as many as 95 percent of strikes were unofficial, powerful examples of what Tony Cliff referred to as "do it yourself reformism". In France the run-up to the general strike of 1968 was marked by two years in which there were "outbreaks of violent industrial disputes" and "demonstrative strikes including one-day general strikes" organised by the

---

32: Newsinger, 2009, pp69-71.
33: Danos and Gibelin, 1986.
34: Trotsky, 1974, p76.

CGT union federation. The number of strike days rose from just under 1 million in 1965 to over 4 million by 1967.[35]

Despite these signs, commentators of the period often mistook the absence of the kind of revolutionary upsurges that had characterised the inter-war years for an absence of workers as a force capable of transforming society. For instance, the new "affluent workers" of the car plants and other similar industries were supposedly more interested in obtaining consumer goods than they were in striking. Famously, the left wing French theorist André Gorz declared in early 1968 that "in the foreseeable future there will be no crisis of European capitalism so dramatic as to drive the mass of workers to revolutionary general strikes".[36] But as the developing class forces clashed with a system no longer capable of meeting their rising expectations from the late 1960s, the potential for revolutionary explosions nurtured within capitalism's long boom came to the fore. It was only in the late 1970s that the partial restabilisation of bourgeois institutions, combined with the reorientation of social democratic and Stalinist organisations to absorb and channel the militancy in safer directions, contained this upsurge.[37]

The run-up to the current crisis was quite different, certainly not characterised by a boom or a "golden age" for reformism. But, again, new class forces developed over the preceding period—forces which will confound the pessimists who have sought to confine workers' struggle to the dustbin of history. One noteworthy example is the exceptional prominence of public sector workers in the current wave of strikes in Europe. Modern capitalist societies rely not simply on the direct exploitation of productive workers to generate profits, but also on wider sections of the working class to ensure that the right kind of labour power is available. The healthcare and education systems are vital to capitalists who want to compete within the global division of labour by exploiting skilled, relatively healthy and reliable workers. The infrastructure and security that governments help to provide are necessary for capitalists, just as the civil servants who collect taxes allow the whole system to function.

The expansion of the public sector, and of work in services more generally, does not mean that we have to accept myths of sweeping "deindustrialisation". The bulk of manufacturing output remains concentrated in the rich OECD countries, even if it now takes place with fewer

---

35: See Cliff, 1985.
36: Cited in Harman, 1998, p4.
37: Harman, 1979. As Harman points out, there was also a subjective factor at work: the failure of the revolutionary lefts across Europe to provide a coherent political alternative for workers' movements.

workers. In fact, the rise in productivity over recent decades means that relatively small groups of workers, perhaps tied into multinational networks of production, can impact disproportionately on capitalist profits. There has also been an expansion of service sector jobs that involve the same kinds of drudgery and exploitation as in the manufacturing sector—and with it the potential to organise.

But in many countries the continued growth and relative stability of the public sector has allowed it to develop and retain levels of unionisation not currently seen in the private sector. These are areas in which many increasingly feel subject to the same pressures and attacks as the wider working class and look to unions to defend themselves. To be a newly qualified teacher or lecturer today is no longer seen as entering a privileged or venerated profession.

The objection that such groups do not have power in society because they do not directly generate profits is misplaced for two reasons. First, they are indirectly indispensable for capitalists, both in the long term but also in the day to day functioning of the system. For instance, strikes by teachers leading to school closures, in particular, entail considerable disruption to the economy. The British government was certainly keen to claim that the 30 November 2011 one-day strike by 2.5 million public sector workers would cost the economy £500 million—£200 per worker per day![38] Second, given that they are the largest organised groups of workers in many countries, a victory by public sector workers can encourage other groups to follow their lead, to organise and to fight.

The movements' tensions

There are real tensions within the strike movements. In a general sense, working class consciousness is always uneven. Gramsci's description of contradictory consciousness, cited above, implies that the quite different experiences of different sections of the class will lead to different degrees of confidence and combativity even within particular countries.

The predominantly reformist consciousness of most workers most of the time is also reflected in and reinforced by reformist *organisations*. For instance, the tradition of Labourism in the British working class has been the rock on which waves of struggle in 20th century frequently crashed. Labour, ably assisted by union leaders, and often appealing to the British "national interest", sought while in power in 1964–1970 and 1974–79 to blunt workers' militancy by driving through productivity deals to undermine union stewards'

38: BBC, 2011.

power to negotiate bonuses, and by creating a layer of full-time union convenors and senior stewards who were more distant from the shopfloor.[39]

There is a division of labour between reformist organisations. If social democratic parties offer the promise of piecemeal political reform within the capitalist state, on the economic terrain the key role in negotiating the terms of exploitation of workers is played by the trade union bureaucracy. In countries with established unions and the space to develop stable reformist organisation, unions tend to produce a layer of full-time officials detached from the workplace.[40] The social role of this bureaucracy—negotiating within capitalist economic relations—is reinforced by its privileged position. If the workers they represent lose their jobs, the officials do not. If the wages of union members fall, it does not automatically lead to changes in the pay or conditions of the officials. Tony Cliff and Donny Gluckstein argue:

> The bureaucracy balances between the two main classes in capitalist society—the employers and the workers. The trade union officials are neither employers nor workers. Union offices may employ large numbers of people, but, unlike a capitalist employer, it is not this that gives the union official his or her economic and social status… The union official does not suffer like the mass of workers from low wages, being pushed around by the employers, job insecurity and so on. The trade union bureaucracy is a distinct, basically conservative, social formation… It holds back and controls workers' struggle, but it has a vital interest not to push the collaboration with employers and state to the point where it makes the unions completely impotent… If the union fails entirely to articulate members' grievances, this will lead eventually either to effective internal challenges to the leadership, or to membership apathy and organisational disintegration… If the union bureaucracy strays too far into the bourgeois camp it will lose its base.[41]

This analysis does not mean revolutionaries are indifferent to the question of who leads unions. There can be significant divisions between left wing and right wing officials. Splits in the bureaucracy can weaken its conservative influence, and the election of a left union leader can, under the right conditions, raise the confidence of workers. But in the final analysis, the role of the union bureaucracy as a conservative social layer takes

---

39: Cliff and Gluckstein, 1996, pp328-331.
40: Cliff and Gluckstein, 1986, pp13-20.
41: Cliff and Gluckstein, 1986, pp27-28.

precedence over the division of this layer into left and right, especially at times of deep crisis.[42]

How can these conservative tendencies be overcome? In periods of heightened struggle workers themselves can develop rank and file movements consisting of workers mobilised at the base of unions. Rank and file organisation of this kind can perform two functions: it can act as a pressure on the union bureaucracy, making action more likely and seeking to prevent sell-outs, and it can, if necessary, allow workers to fight independently of the bureaucracy by taking unofficial action.

The best brief statement of this role was provided by the Clyde Workers' Committee, one of the unofficial bodies that developed during the upsurge in workers' struggle in Britain from 1910 onwards: "We will support the officials just so long as they rightly represent the workers, but we will act independently immediately they misrepresent them. Being composed of delegates from every shop and untrammelled by obsolete rule or law, we claim to represent the true feeling of the workers. We can act immediately according to the merits of the case and the desire of the rank and file".[43]

Such a movement can only be built through struggle. If the bureaucracy simply exerted itself to shut down strikes, building a rank and file movement would rely on the gradual accumulation of forces through limited unofficial action. Fortunately the bureaucracy is also subject to pressure to initiate action. This can come from below, from the anger of ordinary union members and their politicisation through wider changes in society, but it can also be driven from above. For instance, if the scale of attacks is such that the union leaders fear they will lose their ability to negotiate on behalf of workers—through significant reductions in the number of union members in employment or a dismantling of union rights—they can feel it necessary to act.

Indeed, this has been the pattern in recent years. The level of economic strikes in the private sector has fallen across much of Western Europe since the 1970s, from an average of 419 working days per 1,000 employees each year in that decade, down to 51 days in 2000-2004. But the number of general strikes called by unions has risen; there were 19 from 1980 to 1989, but 39 in the 1990s and 40 in the period from 2000 to 2008.[44] General strikes were disproportionately directed at governments that sought to introduce sweeping changes to employment rights, welfare or pensions, without

---

42: Cliff and Gluckstein, 1986, p28.
43: Cited in Callinicos, 1995, p33.
44: Kelly and Hamann, 2009, p1.

meaningful consultations with the unions.[45] Under these conditions, even a conservative union bureaucracy can feel forced to act to maintain its position. There is a key question facing the far left in many countries today. Can they take advantage of brief, large-scale, official strikes taking place to lay the basis for independent workers' organisation to develop? Or will these actions simply remain tightly controlled bureaucratic mass strikes?[46]

The experience so far

Rather than attempting the near impossible task of a comprehensive survey of European struggles, it is more helpful to point to some of the key experiences in four countries that illustrate general points.[47]

Greece

Greece experienced only a partial downturn in militancy after the struggles of the 1970s. For a time, from the early 1980s to the late 1990s, the union bureaucracy maintained a tighter grip on workers. But even this period saw action against attempts by successive governments, whether led by the right or the social democratic Pasok, to impose neoliberal measures—for instance the wave of strikes and protests that greeted the election of the conservative New Democracy party in April 1990,[48] including the extremely militant and weeks long action that came as the government sought to privatise the Athens Bus Company in 1992. These struggles were strengthened by the presence of significant forces to the left of Pasok—including the anti-capitalist left generally, the Eurocommunist Synaspismos (which later formed the core of Syriza) and the Communist Party. By 1998 a new phase of escalating struggle was beginning, marked by an all-out strike against privatisation by Ioniki bank workers and a teachers' strike over changes to the education system, and followed in 2001 by a powerful general strike that defeated attacks on pensions.

At the time the crisis hit, about a third of workers were unionised, concentrated in the substantial state-run sector. Unionisation is lower in the private sector, though union density figures are often misleading; some

45: Kelly and Hamann, 2009, pp10-12.
46: Cliff, 1985, is a brilliant study of the different kinds of mass strike.
47: Writing this section would have been impossible without the assistance of Miguel Sanz Alcántara and Jesús M Castillo of En Lucha in the Spanish state, Denis Godard of *Que Faire?* and the NPA in France, and Nikos Loudos of the Greek Socialist Workers Party, who allowed me to quiz them on the workers' struggle in their respective countries. Any errors are, of course, my own.
48: Styllou and Garganas, 1991.

workplaces with extremely low levels of membership can organise effective strikes that include non-unionised workers. Greek unions take a range of different forms, organising on a general, industrial or geographical basis, with two national confederations—GSEE for private industry and large companies owned or formerly owned by the state, ADEDY for the public sector. Although not formally affiliated to political parties, union representatives are elected through party lists, with Pasok generally commanding the highest level of support; the Communists also control a number of unions that are grouped together within the broader confederations.

Initially union leaders were extremely reluctant to call action, especially under the Pasok government in power from 2009 to 2011. A push from groups of rank and file workers where the far left had significant influence was essential in forcing the bureaucracy to act, and each time strikes were sanctioned ordinary workers rushed to participate, raising the pressure for further action. For instance, action by teachers, a sector where the left is particularly strong, provided an example of militancy and self-confidence early in the crisis. Subsequently the presence of a strong left in this sector proved double-edged—the sectarian traditions of sections of the left and the years in which teachers often fought alone allowed ideas such as the notion that "nothing will change until the political balance of forces changes" to flourish. Recently teachers have had a presence in general strikes, but a lower level of struggle outside these mobilisations. Nonetheless, their early action helped give others the confidence to fight.

The most dramatic sign of the new militancy in Greece has been the succession of general strikes against austerity measures. These began under the Pasok government and continued after it collapsed in 2011 and was eventually replaced by a coalition led by the right wing New Democracy. The strikes helped crystallise a network of workplace militants, encouraging their political generalisation and allowing them to mingle with workers from different sectors. While early strikes were characterised by workers obeying the strike call and staying at home, increasingly they have involved high levels of rank and file activity, with mass meetings, large mobilisations for demonstrations and picketing of workplaces. The power of these networks was revealed in February 2012 when a 48-hour general strike was called at a day's notice, in the same week as another one-day general strike, and workplace militants were able to ensure its success.

Each recent general strike has been the culmination of sectional action, and the general strikes, usually after a short lull, help to generate new waves of sectional action. A central debate in the movement today is over sustained action—workers want to know how they can go beyond one-day or two-day strikes. This explains why the government has cracked down hard on groups of workers who took such action, including sailors and Metro workers in Athens, who were subjected to "civilian conscription" in an attempt to break their strikes.

The degree of contention between workers and the union bureaucracy is now such that leaders of the union confederations have avoided rallies called during general strikes over the past year. Mass workplace meetings now also show a willingness to challenge union officials. For instance, during a recent bus strike workers overturned their leadership's opposition to more action, forcing them to resign. In hospitals too, left militants have collected signatures to demand mass meetings to challenge bureaucratic inertia, and organised occupations and blockades to force unions to call coordinated action between hospitals across an area. In local government occupations of town halls and offices have laid the basis for the formation of groups of workers who organise picketing and mobilise for the general strikes. The revolt of rank and file workers extends into areas where there is little recent tradition. In August 2012 Agrotiki bank workers were called into a mass meeting to accept the calling off of a strike—the workers refused and began organising picket lines and further mass meetings. There have also been occupations of small workplaces with no union.

The meltdown of Pasok (currently below 10 percent in polls) has further undermined union leaders allied to it. So far the rise of the left reformist Syriza has not led to major organisational shifts; the Communists have a far larger presence in the unions, and even the far-left Antarsya coalition is more visible in many sectors. But the ideological impact of the rise of left alternatives to Pasok has helped to further fuel the revolt.

In this context the far left, which includes the Greek Socialist Workers Party (SEK), has sought to develop the pressure from below within the unions—for example, by publishing rank and file papers for media workers, teachers and hospital workers. It seeks to raise the confidence of workers to act independently, as well as taking advantage of official calls, such as a recent one from a leader of the electricity workers' union for escalating action. In addition, SEK is involved in beginning to coordinate action by initiating and participating in forums that draw together workers from different sectors. The far left has also been able to intervene effectively over political and ideological questions—seeking to construct a united front against the fascist Golden Dawn, for example.

The struggle has reached heights that many on the left across Europe would be envious of, but this does not for a moment reduce the challenges and complexities faced by the forces of the revolutionary left.

The Spanish state

When the crisis began union density was about 17 percent across the Spanish state. Workplaces are organised on a "one-union" basis, rather than on sectional or industrial lines, with workers mostly belonging to the UGT, linked to the Socialist Party, or the CCOO, which was historically closer to the Communist Party but is now close to the Socialists in practice.[49] Traditional industrial sectors such as mining and metal working are well unionised, along with much of the public sector. Many large workplaces are 15 or 20 percent unionised, but all workers in the workplace benefit from collective bargaining, can go on strike and participate in the election of workplace delegates.[50]

From 1996 to 2006 the number of strikes recorded, excluding general strikes, lay between 618 and 807 a year. Strikes in this period were often relatively long in duration and typically involved large numbers of workers. The most important single action was in 2002—a successful one-day general strike against the right wing Aznar government. This was highly infused with the wider anti-capitalist mood of the time and, like many of the large strikes of the period, challenged a government policy affecting society at large, in this case reductions in unemployment benefit.

After the crisis broke, Spain witnessed a rise in strikes centred on private industry as employers stopped conceding wage rises through collective bargaining and the CCOO and UGT began to initiate action. According to Ministry of Labour figures, this peaked in 2009 at 1,001 strikes, falling back slightly in 2010 and 2011.[51] Many of the strikes were now relatively short-lived and the numbers involved were not especially high, but the offensive produced breakthroughs in some sectors, such as metal working, threatening to generalise into a wider upturn in struggle. However, despite the successes, the union leaders agreed to concede "flexibility" measures and signed a deal with the employers' organisation that undermined the growing movement.

This concession was followed by a major attack on the public sector by the Socialist Party government, which in May 2010 imposed a series of austerity measures including a 5 percent cut to public sector wages, triggering a strike across the whole public sector that June. This failed to force the government

---

49: Though this pattern varies regionally. For instance, in the Basque Country the main unions are nationalist.

50: Most union financing is from the state, based on the number of delegates elected, adding to the bureaucratic nature of the two main unions, which together control over 85 percent of delegates and which do not directly depend on the dues of their members—see Durgan and Sans, 2011.

51: Again, the figures exclude general strikes to show the pattern more clearly.

to retreat and a further attack followed—an attempt to reverse many of the workplace rights won over the preceding 35 years—leading to the September 2010 general strike. The government remained intransigent and the unions, facing "their own", Socialist, government, capitulated. The combination of the attacks on workers' rights, a sharp rise in unemployment as the crisis deepened and the defeat of the general strike (the first time such action had proved entirely unsuccessful since the transition from dictatorship in the 1970s) led to a significant decline of action in private industry. What strikes did now take place were increasingly of a defensive character, concerning job losses or unpaid wages.[52] Now the momentum shifted to the public sector, where, by the end of 2011, there was again a rise in industrial action.

Up until this point the strike movement had been driven by calls for action from above with little organised pressure from below. But from mid-2011 dissatisfaction with the union leaders' collaboration with employers and the government over austerity came together with the wider radicalisation taking place across the Spanish state. The Indignados movement (also known as 15M, named for the date, 15 May 2011, on which the movement first mobilised) launched a series of occupations of public spaces and protests, mainly attended by students, the unemployed and underemployed youth, and inspired in part by the Egyptian Revolution.[53] Initially this movement was quite distant from, even hostile to, traditional workers' organisations. Its cry of "Nobody represents us" was directed as much at Socialist politicians and the unions as it was against the elite, even if many individual union members, especially younger workers and those from the public sector, participated within it and brought its influence back into the workplace. Despite its distance from the unions, the scale of street mobilisations, which increasingly included demands for a general strike "without unions" in its slogans, did impose a pressure on the official movement.

The movement on the streets has not translated into a generalised upturn in struggle—it has not been able to overcome the hold of the bureaucracy or the impact of unemployment (now running at about a quarter of the workforce), labour law reform, which makes it far easier and cheaper to fire workers, and demoralisation due to the defeat of the Socialist Party government in the December 2011 elections. But there has been an expansion of smaller, more politically radical unions, and Madrid teachers have

---

52: In 2006 and 2007 about half of strikes had been offensive, demanding improvements to wages and conditions. By 2011 only about a fifth were offensive.

53: See Durgan and Sans, 2011, for a discussion of the roots and development of the movement.

held organising assemblies modelled in some ways on the Indignados movement. Struggle has also grown in parts of the public sector, such as health and education. In these areas unofficial networks, known as *mareas* (tides), now help organise regular protests. And there was one especially important exception to the decline of the strike movement in industry: the two-month miners' strike in Asturia in summer 2012. Here the social movements and the unions did come together—with mass demonstrations, hundreds of thousands strong, greeting the miners' march on Madrid in summer last year. But the mood on the streets was not matched by the solidarity it needed from the leaderships of UGT and CCOO and the struggle was contained and defeated.

Large-scale set-piece action has also continued, with general strikes called in March and November 2012, the latter involving over 8 million workers, as the main unions were forced to respond to both the pressure from the streets and workplaces, and the sheer scale of the austerity being imposed by the government. Again these actions had wide support from the social movements and in some cases saw more combative picket lines as groups of workers sought to organise from below. If these strikes are included in the figures, they show a significant rise in industrial action. But there were limits to the action in 2012: the seven months between general strikes, in which there was little or no direction given by union leaders, saw a wave of job cuts. The social movements were left to lead mass protests against these attacks.

New opportunities arose in early 2013 as the right wing government's popularity plummeted, its leading members engulfed in a corruption scandal. At the same time the Indignados movement has shown signs of revival; large, coordinated protests of the *mareas* movement were set for February; and a series of local strikes are now taking place in the public sector, especially in health. The time is ripe for a challenge to the government. The question is whether there can be a sustained, general rise in struggle and in the confidence of workers to fight in the coming months, despite the concessions made by the major unions and the climate of unemployment and austerity. While there is discontent at the base of the unions, and tensions between activists and the highly bureaucratised leaderships, this discontent is not effectively organised. There are particular areas in which the main unions are considered especially combative, and there are a number of smaller left wing unions with a better record of taking action, even if these often see their role as recruiting from the larger unions, rather than influencing or developing links with their grassroots members. There are also some examples of workers in UGT and CCOO organising in their workplace to strike or occupy, sometimes outside of the official structures. One challenge for the small forces of the revolutionary left will be to try to draw together, organise and coordinate such efforts.

France

If Spain shows how mass strikes can ebb, but rise again under pressure from social and political factors, France shows how the struggle can be contained, at least temporarily.

As in Spain, unions are concentrated both in traditional bastions of the working class, such as car plants, steel and chemicals, and in the public sector. A range of different union federations vie for support, including the two largest—the CGT traditionally associated with the Communist Party (and today the Front de Gauche of which the Communists are a component part) and the CFDT connected, though less organically, with the Socialists—and a range of smaller ones including the radical SUD union federation.

Entering the crisis, France already had a recent history of militancy that belied its low union density (below 9 percent). November 1995 saw an explosion of union activity over attacks on pensions. While the strike movement was official, it soon spilled over into unofficial action, being driven from below by mass meetings of strikers and near daily protests mobilising millions. By the end of the year the right wing administration was forced to withdraw many of its attacks. Further large strikes concentrated in the public sector followed in 2003, and again in 2006 over changes to the education system. In addition, in 1999-2000 there was a wave of localised strikes over the implementation of a new law setting a 35-hour working week, this time in the private sector.

In the years preceding the crisis France consistently had the highest number of days of strike action per worker in Western Europe.[54] Against this backdrop, unions called a series of seven national strikes in autumn 2010 against a new assault on pensions, amid large street protests and student mobilisations. The strikes were the result of pressure from low-level union officials (typically representatives based in workplaces but employed full-time on union duties) along with the scale of the attack mounted by Nicolas Sarkozy's right wing government and its intransigence in the face of opposition. A number of "Days of Action" were called by the *Intersyndicale*—a body coordinating between the various national union confederations—which, while the movement was rising, gave the call a particularly strong resonance. The resulting action was focused on the public sector but included sporadic struggles in the

---

54: Eurofound, 2010, table four. The figure in 2007 was 128 working days lost per 1,000 employees. The next highest were Spain (58.1 days) and Italy (47.6 days). Of course, these crude figures can give a distorted picture, especially when one or two large strikes occur against a low background level of action. In 2008 Denmark registered one of the highest numbers of days lost anywhere in Europe over the past decade—because of a two-month strike by nurses, carers and educators which alone accounted for 98 percent of the strike figure that year!

private sector. It involved some of the biggest strikes in French history and consistently won the support of about two thirds of the public.

The revolutionary left was able to influence the strike movement in this phase, taking up the widespread call for indefinite stoppages, which briefly seemed like it might become a reality. But where there was such action, it was isolated. One example was the stoppage and blockade of oil refineries, which closed a third of petrol stations across France. This might have been the signal for an all-out general strike, but ultimately the union leaderships, both at a national level and more locally, were able to contain the pressure from below. Police were deployed to attack pickets and clear the oil blockade.

The unions had succeeded in maintaining a succession of one-day actions that expressed the anger among workers but ultimately allowed the momentum to dissipate and Nicolas Sarkozy to pass his law raising the pension age. By the end of October the momentum of the protests and strikes was waning and less radical components of the *Intersyndicale* began to distance themselves from the action. An aid to the leader of the CFDT told one newspaper: "Secretly, several leaders of the confederation wouldn't look unfavourably on a petering-out of the movement. They know [Sarkozy's government] is never going to give in. The longer the movement lasts, the more the frustrations of the protesters are difficult to manage internally".[55] The CFDT opened the door to negotiations and the CGT followed shortly after. The far left was not able to take advantage of the situation to coordinate the militancy from below and overcome the vacillations of the union leaderships.

The bitterness has found a political expression in the wake of the setback, with the election of a Socialist Party government and the strong showing of the Front de Gauche.[56] But strike action declined from 2011. Recent action has largely consisted of defensive battles over pay and plant closures. These are, however, often militant struggles, as with recent strikes in the car industry. Hundreds of workers occupied PSA Peugeot-Citroen's Aulnay-sous-Bois plant in January and February, led by a committee composed primarily of members of the CGT and SUD unions, joined by non-unionised workers and some members of the CFDT.[57] Strikers have sought to link up their fight with similar disputes at Renault's plants.[58] It remains to be seen whether such action can overcome the inertia of many of the other unions in

---

55: Erlanger, 2010.
56: The NPA, by contrast, has fallen into a crisis, dramatically undermining its capacity to influence events. See Callinicos, 2012a; Godard, 2013.
57: Auto Critique, 2013.
58: CGT PSA Aulnay, 2013.

the industry and whether the fight can be spread to wider groups of workers. Certainly such sparks show that the movement in France has not been broken—but the fact that one of the most powerful workers' movements in Europe could be contained, even if temporarily, is a warning for the left.

Britain

Britain witnessed appallingly low levels of strike action in the years leading up to the crisis. From an average of 12.9 million days per year of strike action in the 1970s and 7.2 million per year in the 1980s, the figure for the 1990s had fallen to 660,000—and has not recovered since. The peaks in recorded strike activity from the 1990s onwards generally reflect one-day strikes by large numbers of public sector workers, for instance in 2002 and 2007.[59] Union membership has fallen since the early 1980s, with union density now standing at about a quarter of the total workforce, though it remains at 56.5 percent in the public sector.[60] The decline is a result of the scale of the defeat inflicted upon the British working class under the Thatcher government in the 1980s.

Three big unions account for over half of the membership of the TUC, Britain's union federation. Unite and the GMB are general unions based primarily in the private sector, but with substantial public sector memberships. Unison organises in the public sector, for example in hospitals and councils, though privatisation means that it now also contains members who are in the private sector. Smaller unions organise particular industries or occupations—for instance, teachers (NUT and NASUWT), communication workers in the postal service and telecoms (CWU), lecturers (UCU), civil servants (PCS), or construction workers (UCATT). The TUC has historically been closely tied to the Labour Party and most unions pay substantial amounts to fund the party.

The immediate impact of the crisis, which began under a Labour government, was to encourage union leaders to end a campaign over public sector pay that had seen 400,000 civil service workers, teachers and lecturers strike in spring 2008, followed by two days of action by 650,000 local government workers in summer. As the impact of the recession began to feed through to the private sector there were by 2009 a scattering of unusually militant strikes, including a small number of occupations of threatened plants, and action at oil refineries and construction sites. But these sparks failed to generalise and the overall level of strike action remained miserable—the

---

59: Hale, 2010.
60: Brownlie, 2011.

12 months in the run-up to March 2011 saw the lowest number of days of industrial action in Britain since records began in 1931.

Yet by the end of 2011 the annual figure was the highest for two decades. This is almost entirely accounted for by a series of one-day public sector strikes. The political context was the election in May 2010 of a governing coalition of Conservatives and Liberal Democrats that was both weak, with a limited mandate, and determined to drive through austerity, including an attack on pension rights that unified the public sector in opposition.

In this context, action by smaller unions where socialists had a stronger presence helped pressure the larger unions to fight over pensions. The UCU lecturers' union held a national strike in March 2011. The same month saw a TUC-backed protest of over half a million in London; one slogan with particular resonance on the day was "We've marched together, now let's strike together". In June the UCU, PCS and NUT organised a coordinated one-day strike by 750,000 workers. Now the big battalions of the union movement began to act—and on 30 November 2011 a one-day strike by 2.5 million in 23 unions took place, drawing in the Unison, Unite and GMB unions across much of the public sector. It was the largest strike in Britain since 1926 and featured vibrant demonstrations across the country.[61]

But the other side of the union bureaucracy was shown over the coming weeks. By Christmas the larger unions had signed an outline agreement with the government to end the struggle. This time the big unions were able to exert pressure on the smaller ones to contain the action. All the left could do by spring 2012 was to try to stop the rout, organising a strike by the lecturers, joined by some civil service and health workers, in May. Despite this, one by one the leaders of the smaller unions called off and contained strike action, and members of the larger unions, faced with a situation in which there was little prospect of a fight, in most cases grudgingly voted the pension deal through. By autumn 2012 the NUT teaching union that had been widely expected to strike also pulled back from action. Now the call for coordinated action, a factor that had raised the confidence of workers in 2011, became an excuse for passivity, with the NUT leadership citing unwillingness of the other large teaching union, NASUWT, to strike.

A second TUC-backed national demonstration, in October 2012, was 200,000-strong, and reflected a continued desire for action alongside the bitterness felt by many activists. In the aftermath of the sell-out leaders of the major unions have combined talk of a possible general strike with calls

---

61:   A survey of 60 of the biggest of the hundred or so demonstrations on the day showed 300,000 marching in support of the strikes. See Kimber, 2012.

to support Labour in forthcoming elections. As Len McCluskey, leader of Unite, the largest union in Britain, put it: "As the working class reasserts itself, Labour is the natural, historic, vehicle for their voice… And that is the alliance [between unions and Labour] I see delivering a victory for Labour in 2015".[62]

The left has focused on attempts to reignite official action over the rapidly accelerating attacks being driven through by the coalition government. One improvisation in the recent period has been the launch of Unite the Resistance, an attempt by the Socialist Workers Party (SWP) to form an alliance with those left officials prepared to support strike action. The initiative has held a number of successful rallies and conferences, in which the SWP has been able to draw wider forces from the working class into a debate on the way forward for the movement and to initiate solidarity with groups of workers who take action.

Unite the Resistance is partly inspired by the minority movements of the 1920s, initiated by the Communist Party, which then had a few thousand militants in Britain. That movement similarly aimed to draw together workers and left union officials to stop the decline and demoralisation that followed a major defeat for workers in 1921. Beginning in mining and metal working, and ultimately leading to a national minority movement, it gave greater confidence to those workers who wanted to see a fight. It helped restore union membership and militancy in a range of industries and allowed the recently formed Communist Party to expand its working class base. However, by the mid-1920s pressure from Moscow and the confusion and disorientation among the party's leaders led the movement to accommodate to the left wing bureaucracy. By the time of the General Strike of 1926 it simply called for "the concentration of all power in the general council of the TUC", supporting the bureaucracy as they led the movement to a catastrophic defeat.[63]

Avoiding such a trajectory means that Unite the Resistance cannot simply draw the left officials together with ordinary workers; it must also encourage workers to put pressure on and raise criticisms of the officials. And it must have as a clear goal assembling the workers who can be the basis of genuine rank and file movements. But, however well-conceived this approach is, the possibility of building a rank and file movement depends on something that a small revolutionary left can influence but certainly not guarantee—a sufficiently powerful revival of working class struggle.

62: McCluskey, 2013.
63: Cliff and Gluckstein, 1986, p117; see pp103-140 for a more general account of the minority movements.

Conclusion

The complex relationship between crisis and resistance makes it impossible to generalise about the tactics the left should employ. The different tempo and depth of crisis, the different political factors and trade union structures, and the different scales on which the revolutionary left exists in different countries necessitate quite different approaches.

But one observation that can be made is the centrality of politics to the emerging struggle, all the more so as in general there has not been a gradual accumulation of struggle in the preceding period on a sufficient scale to give workers the confidence to act independently from below. This makes it necessary to take advantage of political upheavals to raise the possibility of action in the workplace and to use official strikes to strengthen rank and file organisation. A second observation is that the embryonic cycle of struggle that became apparent in 2011 continues, but it does so with complications and tensions. We should expect setbacks as well as advances. Yet the period remains one characterised by ideological turmoil, political instability and intense pressure on workers. In some cases this has translated into a rise in workers' struggle since the beginning of the crisis. In others there is little sign of a sustained rise in self-activity, merely the potential for it to happen in the coming months or years.

Gramsci once described himself as a "pessimist because of intelligence, but an optimist because of will".[64] Given the combination of the possibilities that may open up in the coming period and the enormous challenges for the small forces on the revolutionary left if we are to take advantage of them, his words seem especially apt.

References

Auto Critique, 2013, "Renault et PSA: La Convergence des Luttes à l'Ordre de Jour!" (29 January), www.npa-auto-critique.org

BBC, 2011, "War of Words Over Claim Strikes 'Could Cost Jobs'", BBC News online (25 November), www.bbc.co.uk

Brownlie, Nikki, 2011, "Trade Union Membership 2011", BIS.

Callinicos, Alex, 1995, *Socialists and the Trade Unions* (Bookmarks).

Callinicos, Alex, 2010, *Bonfire of Illusions: The Twin Crises of the Liberal World* (Polity).

Callinicos, Alex, 2012a, "France: Anti-Capitalist Politics in Crisis", *International Socialism* 134 (spring), www.isj.org.uk/?id=794

Callinicos, Alex, 2012b, "The Second Coming of the Radical Left", *International Socialism* 135 (summer), www.isj.org.uk/?id=819

Carchedi, Guglielmo, 2011, "Behind and Beyond the Crisis", *International Socialism* 132 (autumn), www.isj.org.uk/?id=761

64: Gramsci, 2011, p299.

CGT PSA Aulnay, 2013, "PSA—Renault, Même Combat!", *Journal de Grève* 3, http://cgt-psa-aulnay.fr

Choonara, Joseph, 2009, "Marxist Accounts of the Current Crisis", *International Socialism 123* (summer), www.isj.org.uk/?id=557

Choonara, Joseph, 2011, "Once More (with Feeling) on Marxist Accounts of the Crisis", *International Socialism 132* (autumn), www.isj.org.uk/?id=762

Choonara, Joseph, 2012, "A Reply to David McNally", *International Socialism 135* (summer), www.isj.org.uk/?id=829

Cliff, Tony, 1985, "Patterns of Mass Strike", *International Socialism 29* (summer), www.marxists.org/archive/cliff/works/1985/patterns/index.htm

Cliff, Tony, and Donny Gluckstein, 1986, *Marxism and Trade Union Struggle: The General Strike of 1926* (Bookmarks).

Cliff, Tony, and Donny Gluckstein, 1996 [1988], *The Labour Party: A Marxist History* (Bookmarks).

Danos, Jacques, and Marcel Gibelin, 1986, *June '36: Class Struggle and the Popular Front in France* (Bookmarks).

Durgan, Andy, and Joel Sans, 2011, "'No One Represents Us': the 15 May Movement in the Spanish State", *International Socialism 132* (autumn), www.isj.org.uk/?id=757

Engels, Frederick, 1950 [1895], "Introduction to *The Class Struggles in France 1848-1850*", in Karl Marx and Frederick Engels, *Selected Works* (Lawrence and Wishart), www.marxists.org/archive/marx/works/1895/03/06.htm

Erlanger, Steven, 2010, "French Unions at Critical Point as Strikes Continue", *New York Times* (25 October), http://www.nytimes.com/2010/10/26/world/europe/26unions.html

Eurofound, 2010, "Developments in Industrial Action 2005-2009", European Foundation for the Improvement of Living and Working Conditions, www.eurofound.europa.eu

Godard, Denis, 2013, "The NPA in Crisis: We have to Explain because we have to Start Again", *International Socialism 137* (winter), www.isj.org.uk/?id=874

Gramsci, Antonio, 1998 [1929-1935], *Selections from Prison Notebooks* (Lawrence and Wishart).

Gramsci, Antonio, 2011 [1926-1930], *Letters from Prison, volume 1* (Columbia University Press).

Hale, Dominic, 2010, "Labour Disputes in 2009", *Economic and Labour Market Review*, volume 4, number 6 (June).

Hallas, Duncan, 1985, *The Comintern* (Bookmarks), www.marxists.org/archive/hallas/works/1985/comintern/index.htm

Harman, 1979, "The Crisis of the European Revolutionary Left", *International Socialism 4* (spring), www.marxists.org/archive/harman/1979/xx/eurevleft.html

Harman, Chris, 1998, *The Fire Last Time* (Bookmarks).

Harman, Chris, 2007, "The Rate of Profit and the World Today", *International Socialism 115* (summer), www.isj.org.uk/?id=340

Harman, Chris, 2009, *Zombie Capitalism: Global Crisis and the Relevance of Marx* (Bookmarks).

Jones, Jonny, 2012, "The Shock of the New: Anti-capitalism and the Crisis", *International Socialism 134* (spring), www.isj.org.uk/?id=796

Kelly, John, and Kerstin Hamann, 2009, "General Strikes in Western Europe 1980-2008", paper for Political Studies Association annual conference, April 2009.

Kimber, Charlie, 2012, "The Rebirth of our Power? After the 30 November Mass Strike", *International Socialism 133* (winter), www.isj.org.uk/?id=774

Kliman, Andrew, 2011, *The Failure of Capitalist Production: Underlying Causes of the Great Recession* (Pluto).

Lapavitsas, Costas, and others, 2012, *Crisis in the Eurozone* (Verso).

Lenin, Vladimir Ilyich, 1921, *"Left Wing" Communism: An Infantile Disorder* (The Marxian Educational Society), www.marxists.org/archive/lenin/works/1920/lwc/index.htm

Lenin, Vladimir Ilyich, 1973 [1922], "Closing Speech on the Political Report of the Central Committee of the RCP (B)", in *Collected Works*, volume 33 (Progress), www.marxists.org/archive/lenin/works/1922/mar/27.htm

Marfleet, Philip, 2013, "'Never Going Back': Egypt's Continuing Revolution", *International Socialism 137* (winter).

Marx, Karl, 1950 [1850], *The Class Struggles in France 1848-1850*, in Karl Marx and Frederick Engels, *Selected Works* (Lawrence and Wishart), www.marxists.org/archive/marx/works/1850/class-struggles-france/index.htm

Marx, Karl, 1972 [1894], *Capital*, volume 3 (Lawrence & Wishart), www.marxists.org/archive/marx/works/1894-c3/index.htm

Marx, Karl, 1993 [1857], *Grundrisse* (Penguin), www.marxists.org/archive/marx/works/1857/grundrisse/

McCluskey, Len, 2013, Ralph Miliband lecture, London School of Economics (15 January), http://bit.ly/milibandlecture

Molyneux, John, 2011, "The Rising Tide of Revolution" (1 June), http://johnmolyneux.blogspot.co.uk/2011/06/rising-tide-of-revolution.html

Newsinger, John, 2009, "1934: Year of the Fightback", *International Socialism 122* (spring), www.isj.org.uk/?id=530

Nimtz, August, 2000, *Marx and Engels: Their Contribution to the Democratic Breakthrough* (State University of New York).

Styllou, Maria, and Panos Garganas, 1991, "The Political Crisis in Greece: an Interview with Maria Styllou and Panos Garganas", *International Socialism 52* (autumn).

Trotsky, Leon, 1973a [1921], "Report on the World Economic Crisis and the New Tasks of the Communist International", in *The First Five Years of the Communist International*, volume one (New Park), www.marxists.org/archive/trotsky/1924/ffyci-1/ch19.htm

Trotsky, Leon, 1973b [1921], "Summary Speech from the Third Session of the Third Congress", in *The First Five Years of the Communist International*, volume one (New Park), www.marxists.org/archive/trotsky/1924/ffyci-1/ch20.htm

Trotsky, Leon, 1974 [1921], "Flood-Tide: The Economic Conjuncture and the World Labour Movement", in *The First Five Years of the Communist International*, volume two (New Park).

Trotsky, Leon, 1985 [1930], *The History of the Russian Revolution* (Pluto), www.marxists.org/archive/trotsky/1924/ffyci-2/06.htm

Trotsky, Leon, 1989 [1931], "What Next? Vital Questions for the German Proletariat", in *Fascism, Stalinism and the United Front* (Bookmarks), www.marxists.org/archive/trotsky/germany/1932-ger/index.htm

Tsipras, Alexis, 2013, "Greece and the Economic Challenges Ahead: A Conversation with Greek Opposition Leader Alexis Tsipras", The Brookings Institution (22 January), www.brookings.edu/events/2013/01/22-greece-economy#ref-id=20130122_Tsipras

Wall Street Journal, 2012, "Big Europe Strikes Have Little Effect", (14 November), http://online.wsj.com/article/SB10001424127887324556304578118263611154772.html

From mobilisation to resistance: Portugal's struggle against austerity

Catarina Príncipe

Portugal, as one of the countries in the European Union taken hostage by the Troika (the International Monetary Fund, the European Central Bank and the European Commission), has been subjected to increasingly harsh austerity policies that have led the country into a recession of historic proportions, the result being mass impoverishment. The mandate from the Troika is being compounded by additional cuts being made by the current government in what amounts to the fastest and most brutal neoliberal programme ever introduced in Portugal. The right wing Portuguese administration is using the crisis and the memorandum with the Troika as a pretext to attack labour rights and dismantle the Portuguese welfare state; the demands for further austerity presented by the Portuguese and European ruling classes seem endless.

However, these extreme attacks have not translated into a rising tide of resistance. Moments of mass mobilisation have happened during the last two years—above all in the monster demonstrations against austerity on 15 September 2012 and 2 March 2013. But these were unable to transform themselves into generalised resistance capable of shifting the balance of class forces in Portugal. This article seeks to understand this disconnect by proposing that the mass mobilisations happen almost "apart" from the structures in the country that would be capable of organising a rooted long-term resistance. This gap between the mobilisations and the social structures has occurred because of the decision by the social movements over the last five or six years not to organise in the workplace or local communities. Although this choice was the correct one at the time it was made, its limitations are now being revealed. This article aims to summarise and analyse the story of the resistance in Portugal during the last few years, highlighting both our successes and limitations and contributing to the strategic debate in a spirit of solidarity.

"They want us precarious—We will be rebellious!"

In 2007 a group of activists coming out of the student movement decided to bring the "Euro May Day" concept to Portugal.[1] The trade unions with their bureaucratised and closed structures were slow to respond to the growing number of precarious workers. Precarity was seen as a generational problem—older workers were (supposedly) not affected by it and some saw precarity as the fault of young workers unwilling or uninterested in fighting for their own rights. Within the unions this scapegoating of younger workers could also be found. Moreover, precarity was an unknown term for most Portuguese workers, who lacked a collective definition of their working conditions. Many people viewed the issue through a strictly individual lens, saying: "I have a fixed-term contract. I'm not precarious", or: "I have an individual contract through a temporary work agency, but that's particular to my profession; it's not a generalised problem."

In this political context the decision to import the Euro May Day as a fresh, young and new way of protesting was the appropriate political choice for several reasons:

1) We understood that it was necessary to see precarity as something affecting all spheres of life. The idea of "precarity in life" as a common point of departure allowed us to discuss precarity not only as a labour condition but also to discuss how it related to questions of independence, self-determination and life planning, as well as discrimination and racism.

2) Because of the broad framing of the conflict and the novelty of a new, creative movement led by young people, we were able to change the public narrative on precarity. It was no longer seen as an individual choice, but rather as the result of political and economic processes. This means that today in Portugal there is a collective understanding of what precarity is and how it concerns everyone, no matter what age.

1:    "They want us precarious—We will be rebellious!" is one of the most important and well known slogans of the anti-precarity movement.

3) Because we knew that precarity was a coming reality for the entire Portuguese working class, we rejected the notion that it was a generational issue. Thus we did not organise Euro May Day in competition with the traditional trade union demonstrations (as was the case in several other countries), but sought to "add struggles to the struggle" by pursuing connections and joining and mobilising for the trade unions' protests (so, for example, the Euro May Day participants always join the trade unions' May Day demonstration). This choice helped to form a new connection between the trade unions and the social movements that, however fragile, is very important for the protests against the Troika today.

In Portugal more workers are unemployed than are unionised, and most precarious workers are not unionised. Portugal's largest trade union confederation, the CGTP, was not addressing this issue adequately and thus left a large political vacuum to be filled. Given the low level of struggle and our lack of connections to the trade unions, we chose at that moment to organise outside of the workplace. This was a correct political choice—at the time.

The CGTP is a fairly militant trade union confederation and is politically very close to the Portuguese Communist Party (PCP), but it has a very closed apparatus and a bureaucratised structure and is very suspicious of any activity that does not come from inside its own organisation. Moreover, many of the young activists who started the anti-precarity movement in Portugal are from or close to Bloco de Esquerda (Left Bloc, the party of the radical left) or from more autonomist organisations, and thus have little or no influence inside the unions. In this difficult situation real collaboration between the union leadership and the movement was more or less impossible. Excluded from the traditional structures of organised labour, the movement was forced to adapt by organising precarious workers *away* from the point of production. It was a necessary and correct decision to make, but a decision prompted by weakness, not strength. It is the conversion of this necessity into a virtue that holds the movement back today.

The Euro May Day parade has been held in Lisbon since 2007 and in Porto since 2009. Two very important organisations emerged out of these demonstrations: the *Precários Inflexíveis* ("Inflexible Precarious") in Lisbon and *Ferve—Fartos d'Estes Recibos Verdes* ("We Are Tired of these Green Receipts") in Porto. These two groups managed to keep the question of precarity on the political agenda all year round (the Euro May Day networks are only active in the months leading up to 1 May) and served as important public platforms to criticise precarity, becoming well known in the media and developing their own campaigns. However, the fact that we continually tried to organise outside the workplace left us in a fragile position of being unable to directly address the workers and their daily problems; having no strength, capacity or resources to organise local struggles, let alone a strike. The core of these organisations is composed of some of the most active and dedicated activists, but lacking a social field in which to intervene, the growth of the organisation is either slow or non-existent. We have no influence in the workplaces and therefore lack the necessary response that a workers' organisation needs to have. Nevertheless, the core of these organisations was always present in the organisation and mobilisations of the most important protests in Portugal over the last two years.

The "Desperate Generation"

Since 12 March 2011 there were several moments of protest that deserve to be mentioned: the "Desperate Generation" demonstration (12 March 2011), the "Real Democracy Now" demo (15 October 2011) and the two "Screw the Troika" demos (15 September 2012 and 2 March 2013).

In January 2011 a Portuguese folk music group released a song entitled "How Silly I Am" denouncing widespread precarity and lack of perspective among the youth. The song went viral online and inspired a group of four friends to call for a demonstration on 12 March through Facebook. Almost half a million people took to the streets in many cities across Portugal, joining in one of the biggest demonstration since the Portuguese Revolution of 1974-5.

The focus of the demonstration was the unbearable situation of a generation without a future. But because the manifesto was very broad, neoliberal voices tried to appropriate it. Confronted with this problem, the main organisers decided to request help from anti-precarity, LGBT and other movements, who provided them with advice and support while respecting their political autonomy. The result was that the movement was able to overcome appropriation by the right and attempts to frame the issue as one of a conflict between generations, fostering displays of genuine intergenerational solidarity. Ultimately the demonstration consisted of young precarious workers accompanied by their parents and grandparents, who attended out of solidarity but also to express their own opposition to the ruling Socialist Party's (PS) proposed cuts.

Part of the success of this demonstration can be ascribed to the media attention it received—occurring in the wake of the Arab Spring and the debates about the role of the new media in organising protests. Something similar happening in Portugal caught the attention of the media and cast a lot of attention on the mobilisation. Moreover, the PS government of José Sócrates already found itself in a severe crisis of public opinion following the passage of several rounds of austerity. The media opportunistically aided the mobilisation to harm the government, but quickly lost interest after the demonstration

It would be a mistake, however, to credit the demonstration's success to media attention alone: 12 March also represented a new form of popular mobilisation. Because of its indeterminate character, it attracted a wide variety of people and extended into layers of the population far beyond the normal reach of the unions and left parties, so much so that the unions and the Communist Party initially treated the mobilisation with suspicion, distrustful of a mass movement beyond their control.

It is worth noting that the mood of popular discontent and the popular criticisms of democratic institutions was not reflected in the general election results of 5 June 2011. The content of the Troika memorandum (which was signed by the PS, PSD and CDS[2] before the elections) was not made public for a long time, so most voters did not understand what its implications would be at the time of the election. A feeling of inevitability and to some extent a popular belief that the austerity measures were necessary to "save" the Portuguese economy clearly worked to the detriment of the anti-memorandum left: the Bloco's share of the vote fell from almost 10 percent in 2009 to 5.2 percent, with an abstention rate of around 40 percent. The PCP was able to maintain its result as it has a very established base of support, but was also not able to win new votes. Why the Bloco faced such a drastic defeat at the polls will be addressed later. Nevertheless, the positive experience of the 12 March mobilisation gave the social movements a needed breath of fresh air for the coming year.

15 October 2011—"Real Democracy Now!"

The "movement of the squares" also took root in Portugal in 2011. It started as an attempt to imitate the enormous occupations of squares in Spain and Greece but on a much smaller scale. Beginning in mid-May in the heat of the electoral campaign some one hundred activists occupied a central square of Lisbon for two weeks. There were also occupations of squares in Porto, Coimbra and Ponta Delgada. Emulating the politics of the Indignados, the demands went from a singular focus on precarity towards a systemic critique. The occupations of the squares linked up with activists from the 12 March

2:    Social Democratic Party (PSD): the right wing party now in power; Christian Democratic Party (CDS): the conservative party now in power in coalition with the PSD.

mobilisations and established a network to join the international call for a demonstration against austerity on 15 October 2011.

On 13 October the government presented the plan for the 2012 state budget. It called for, among other things, deep wage cuts and the elimination of holiday bonuses for public sector workers. Over 100,000 demonstrators protested against the budget in Lisbon and 15,000 in Porto. In Lisbon the demonstrators surrounded the parliament and conducted an assembly that lasted through the night. Amazingly the assembly decided to call for a general strike, despite many of the participants being completely new to political activism.

Building upon this momentum, Portugal's two trade union confederations called for a general strike on 24 November. It should be noted that the Portuguese trade unions had also called a general strike against austerity in November 2010. Different this time was the initiative from the movements for the strike, as opposed to the ritualised one-day actions the unions seem to call every year.

The 15 October protests marked several important political developments in Portugal. The clearest was the qualitative change in the political demands since 12 March. The demonstration of 12 March had been politically indeterminate and mixed—the anti-capitalist left was present, and the social movements (feminist, LGBT, anti-precarity, anti-racist), sections of the political right and even some elements of the far-right tried to insert themselves in the demonstration. By October the focus had become clearer: it was not limited to a critique of precarity and an uncertain future, but was a more focused critique of the government and the austerity policies as whole. Quantitatively the October demonstration was smaller, but qualitatively it was much better.

The October demonstrations also witnessed the introduction of other political elements of the Occupy movement. These included: the questioning of parliamentary democracy and democratic institutions; opposition to the rule of the "1 percent"; and a general distrust of established political parties and organisations—a feeling that already existed in Portugal, but not as clear or as loud as now. The terrible electoral results for the left, the 40 percent abstention rate and an ongoing process of institutionalisation of the radical left created a mood and political space for the distrust of political organisations and the trade unions. This is an important fact to understand as it remains one of the major problems continuing to face the radical left today.

The last important aspect is the relation to the CGTP. The process of dialogue between the movements and the unions that began in 2007 has strong limitations. On the one hand, the cooperation between social movements and the union bureaucracy, however limited, is a welcome sign. It shows that movement activists do not oppose traditional workers' organisations. At the same time, however, the reach of the movement remains very limited. The movements lack any sort of rank and file organisations that could serve as conduits into the wider working class and remain utterly dependent on the bureaucratic leaderships.

"Screw the Troika—we want our lives"

Following the October demonstrations there were no mass protests for almost a year. Portugal saw a general strike on 22 March and some sectional struggles, but in mainstream news media and politics Portugal was portrayed as the well behaved student of the European south. The people of Portugal understood the need for austerity; they agreed they had lived beyond their means and therefore had to make the appropriate sacrifices. The Portuguese people and government were portrayed as embracing the Troika as a good friend.

This portrayal is not completely untrue: the notion that austerity was inevitable was very powerful in the minds of the people. Many thought there was no other way out and initially hoped to weather the coming period through individual solutions. It was also difficult to respond politically, as some of the government's proposed measures were delayed until 2013, thus mitigating the effects on the population. Portugal seemed to be acquiescing to the demands of the Troika and was held up as a good example in contrast to Greece, whose left was already beginning to transform that country's politics at the time.

Faced with this lull in activity, organisers from the anti-precarity movement together with others—some of them public figures—called for a demonstration on 15 September 2012. The timing corresponded to the "restart" of the political year when the state budget for 2013 would start to be discussed. Simultaneously, these activists knew the beginning of the school year would bring with it discontent, since thousands of teachers were not going to have a job due to government cuts in education. The demonstration was mainly called through Facebook and once again the media gave it significant coverage.

On 7 September prime minister Pedro Passos Coelho and finance minister Vitor Gaspar announced the austerity measures contained in the 2013 state budget. Alongside further cuts to wages and pensions and the elimination of holiday bonuses, the budget also foresaw a dramatic increase in social security taxes. In practical terms it would mean the transfer of one month's salary a year from the workers to the bosses, a further drop in internal consumption and the penalisation of the poorest members of society.

These measures prompted a wave of resistance in society. After the announcement of the new measures the call for a demonstration grew massively on Facebook and in the media. The informal network of people that called for the demonstration also established contact with the trade unions, from whom they got no answer. It is important to say that although the trade union bureaucracy decided not to actively be part of the organisation of the demo (though the general secretary stated on 14 September that he would individually join the demonstration), the rank and file activists and members joined the demonstration in a massive way.

"Screw the Troika—We want our lives" was the motto for the demonstration that took place on 15 September in Portugal. Roughly 1 million people took the streets of 40 cities around Portugal (in addition to solidarity demonstrations across Brazil and Europe). At the end of the demonstration the organisers called for a popular general strike and decided to establish contact with the trade unions in order to make this demand possible.

The reactions to the announcements regarding the social security tax were deeply negative. No one publicly supported this measure, not even members of the Troika committee. At the same time the Portuguese constitutional court declared the measure unconstitutional in the public sector. The government decided to retreat on both proposals and said that they would announce new measures soon.

Meanwhile, the CGTP decided to call for a demonstration on 29 September. This demonstration mobilised more than 200,000 people in Lisbon. The leader of the CGTP, Arménio Carlos, announced during his speech that the unions would meet the widespread demand for a general strike, though without setting a specific date.

On 3 October the finance minister announced new measures while speaking on television. Having been forced to retreat on the two main measures—the changes to the social security tax and the elimination of holiday bonuses—the government instead presented the biggest single income tax hike in Portuguese history, amounting to an increase of 35 percent. Essentially the government sought to compensate for the cuts they could not enact with tax increases.

After this brutal attack the CGTP called for a general strike for 14 November and its Spanish counterparts announced their intention to participate and suggested an Iberian general strike. The European Confederation of Trade Unions met on 16 October to discuss the possibility of widening the wave of general strikes throughout Europe. These discussions resulted in the first multi-state general strike in European history.

The general strike of 14 November had a strong impact in Portugal, not only because participation was extremely high, but also because it gave an international perspective to the struggle and was the first step to developing protests against austerity on a European scale. One of the most interesting things in this process is that the impetus for a strike emerged from the mobilisations that preceded it and were organised by groups outside of the trade unions. At the same time, it clearly shows the weakness of these movements—although there were one million people on the streets, the organisers have no influence in the decisions of the trade unions and had to wait for the leadership of the CGTP to support the strike to make it possible.

The weaknesses of the resistance

These three moments of mass mobilisation in Portugal have clear similarities: the three of them came from "rootless" organisations, they showed that the potential level of participation is much bigger then the number of people who are already organised, they happened as a momentary reaction to a concrete political proposal from the government and they all received above-average media coverage. The incredibly positive response to the movement's critique of austerity underlines what possibilities lie on the horizon for Portugal's radical left. So what is the problem? Why are we not seeing any big mobilisations now? Why has the working class not been able to exert pressure on the government through sectional struggles or sympathy strikes? Why has the impact of austerity not generated a mood of resistance? These are the most important questions for the Portuguese resistance right now.

As previously stated, when we started the anti-precarity mobilisations in 2007 we made a correct political choice that allowed the creation of a collective identity and an important pole of political attraction in Portuguese society. However, the choice to organise outside of the workplace was made out of weakness: we had no capacity politically to influence the trade unions and no networks inside the union structures. Besides, the trade union bureaucracy has little interest in creating grassroots networks of rank and file activists that could potentially slip out of their control and challenge the stability of the system. The Portuguese CP views the fight against the Troika as a struggle of "national liberation" and proposes a "patriotic left government". It sees the political and economic struggles as occurring in different, separate spheres. In such a context this rootless social movement—*of* workers but not rooted *in* the workplace—is at the mercy of the leadership of the CGTP. The potential pitfalls of this situation were demonstrated both on the 15 October 2011 and on 15 September 2012 when, although they were the biggest demonstrations in Portugal since 1974, their organisers had to wait for the leadership of the CGTP to put the general strike in motion and had very little power to actually influence this process. This is part of the reason why the general strikes in Portugal have been organised "following the calendar" and never as a confrontational struggle in a specific political moment to challenge the government's agenda.

It is also helpful that the anti-precarity networks have been able to create a vibrant political space in Portugal—unfortunately this space is more virtual than concrete. These groups work very efficiently with new media: they have established a series of blogs and websites used by precarious workers to share experiences and discuss politics and have also built up good relations to the traditional media, allowing them to highlight demands and campaigns in the mainstream news. But the core group of organisers is small and has grown very little through the years, precisely because of their rootlessness.

The political situation in Portugal is unstable and liable to change rapidly. Rootless networks such as our own are not always capable of giving fast answers—this was clearly the case when Angela Merkel visited Portugal on 12 November: one month after a demonstration of over 1 million people and two days before a European general strike only around 100 people showed up to the demonstration.

Since 2007 the anti-precarity activists have been at the heart of the resistance. The group of activists from Precários Inflexíveis has not dissolved into the broader movement but persists as an independent organisation and initiates its own projects, one being a national petition in support of a law against austerity. This demanded a lot of the movement's resources, as such a petition requires the signatures of 35,000 people to be valid and cannot be conducted over the internet—this is only the second time in Portuguese history that such a signature drive has been undertaken. The group also became a legal association, allowing membership and offering an organisational response to the isolation and atomisation of precarious employment. However, the core of the organisation is still very small and has not grown. The movement has punched above its own weight on multiple occasions, giving many of us the illusion that we are stronger than we actually are. This is a problem as it means we neglect building rooted sustainable networks of resistance in the workplaces and communities, but rather focus on large one-off demonstrations that are not followed up with further struggle.

Precarity and traditional forms of workers' organisation

Precarity pushes workers into a life of constant instability and to an uncertain future. The precarious condition, starting in the degradation of the labour relations, affects all dimensions of life. It is also important to explain what we in Portugal understand as precarity. Precarity is not only temporary work: it is the so-called "false green receipt"[3] used massively by the Portuguese state that denies a labour contract to hundreds of thousands of people; it is the subcontracting companies which retain around half of the worker's wage; it is the reality of informal work. Half of the Portuguese active population fluctuates between different forms of precarity, underemployment and unemployment.[4] Above all, precarity makes collective organisation more difficult through the individualisation of the work relation and the blackmail of unemployment. Precarity is growing in all professional sectors and it is intergenerational; it's a labour and social recomposition of huge dimensions based on super-exploitation and the permanent blackmail of unemployment.

For these reasons, we don't understand precarity as an emerging class in opposition to the working class, but as the rapid destruction of the labour relations gained by the workers' mobilisations of the 20th century: the eight-hour workday, the right to leisure, the freedom of association and expression, the right to protection in sickness and unemployment, the right to paid holidays, the right to contracts with rights and guarantees, the right to collective bargaining and contracting, the construction of the welfare state that grants access to health and education to us all. In this sense, precarity is about all of us and the working class is, in fact, the class most affected by precarious conditions.

This political understanding—that it is important to unify those affected by precarity in articulation with the traditional forms of the organisation of the working class to strengthen and amplify class struggle—was what made our articulation with the trade unions possible.

The trade unions are still today the most representative associations of workers. However, there is an urgent need for a change inside the trade unions and their structures. The fact that in Portugal workers can only become unionised by their work sector (in the sectoral trade unions) leads to the difficulty of organising those who live in precarious conditions changing sectors frequently. Also it is not possible for someone who is unemployed to become unionised. Informal work relations also do not allow workers to organise, and this is also the experience of many migrants. Moreover, closed and bureaucratised structures add many limitations to the struggling possibilities of rank and file members. But to force an antagonism between those

3:   The false green receipts are a form of independent contract used illegally by many employers and the state to avoid permanent employment and paying for social security, illness, holiday and unemployment funds.

4:   Numbers given by the association Precários Inflexíveis with data from the National Institute of Statistics. It can be found at: www.precariosinflexiveis.org/?p=4241

who are detached from the experience of organisation and the workers'
organisations is a path that will lead nowhere and that weakens the whole of
the working class. Therefore precarity challenges the trade unions to transform their structures and their activity into a more combative, more open to
dialogue and more articulated struggle which has to include the strength of
the precarious, the underemployed and the unemployed workers

The Bloco and the movements

It is also relevant to discuss the role of the Bloco. It was formed in 1999 by
three small radical parties and a wide layer of independent activists. It aimed
to be an oppositional party and to occupy the political space to the left of
both the Stalinist CP and the social liberal Socialist Party. The Bloco sought
to bridge the gap between the emerging anti-capitalist milieux and the social
base of the Socialist Party (people who have been in the Socialist Party for
many years but are unhappy with its neoliberal turn). The Bloco's relation
to the social movements was to be one of mutual respect and collaboration.
The activists from the Bloco would participate in and build social movements in a comradely fashion, respecting and debating with other political
currents and building the movement for the movement's sake.

From 1999 to 2009 the party's electoral fortunes went up and up,
peaking in 2009 with a result of around 10 percent. However, in the snap
elections of June 2011 the result dropped to 5 percent. This prompted an
intense strategic debate within the party, where it was clear to most militants that Bloco was sending contradictory messages to its supporters. On
the one hand, there was an attempt to be a "respectable" party and try to
win over the disaffected supporters of the Socialist Party, which was in
power until 2011. On the other hand, it was important to maintain Bloco's
image as a different kind of party and try to still be seen as an alternative to
the existing political system. This led to the party being seen as *too* radical
by some and not radical *enough* by others, throwing the party back to the
results of 2005. Out of this debate emerged the party's current line: a call
for a government of the left based on four points of unity:

1) Annulment of the abusive debt: reduction of the debt to 60 percent of
GDP, renegotiation of deadlines and interest with all the lender institutions,
public and private, national and international.
2) Reversal of all wage cuts and guarantee of essential social goods: public
education, public health system, public social security system.
3) Nationalisation of all the banks receiving bailout money from the
state, redirecting of investment for the public good and reversal of the

nationalisations of formerly public economic sectors (energy, telecommunications, etc).

4) Strengthening of financial regulations, fighting of fiscal fraud and a shift of the burden of taxation from labour to capital.

These four points are to serve as the basis for a possible left government, which is to be formed by any and all political forces who agree to the four points. Given that the Bloco received only 5 percent of the votes in 2011, the call for a left government (which can include the CP and the Socialist Party if the latter is willing to renegotiate the memorandum of the Troika) cannot be seen as the result of any electoral calculus but is rather an attempt to open new political avenues in Portugal entirely. However, this proposal has short-term (let alone middle and long-term) limitations. The CP is extremely sectarian and unwilling to support a project it cannot control (and has always approached the Bloco with suspicion at best); the PS is not in power (as opposed to Pasok when Syriza called for a left government in Greece) and would not accept the four proposed points anyway, since it also signed the memorandum and is itself in the middle of a small rhetorical shift to the left. The PS leadership is talking left in an attempt to marginalise the Bloco—why should it join a government of the left?

These political calculations aside, the greatest limitation lies in the lack of sustained grassroots resistance in Portugal. If the call for a left government rests upon the assumption that there has to be a seismic shift on the Portuguese political map spurred on by growing mobilisation and resistance, that resistance has to come before any potential government could even have a social base. The Portuguese left has had extremely important moments of mobilisation but they have not yet turned into organised resistance. To fight against this weakness by proposing an institutional/parliamentary solution is to put the cart in front of the horse—before we can talk about a political sea change, we need to be laying the groundwork.

In 2012 a survey was published about the quality of democracy in Portugal.[5] The results are very interesting and provide some clues to how we can formulate our strategy: 78 percent of the respondents agreed that politicians are only concerned with their own interests, and 77 percent said that major political decisions favour large corporations. There is also a clear distrust of political parties, and social movements are considered to be more able to voice the people's concerns. Public trust in democratic institutions is

---

5:    Pinto, Magalhães, Sousa and Gorbunova, 2012.

continually decreasing, aided by the perception that the Portuguese government is essentially held captive by international institutions. In this situation, a purely or even primarily institutional answer is an even more problematic and limited one. Elections and parliamentary manoeuvring do not fundamentally transform society—what changes people's relationship to politics is activism, collective experience and organisation.

The Bloco needs to use the immense capacity of its activists to build local branches capable of organising broad campaigns to defend local institutions and public goods. Especially as local elections approach, this could prove phenomenally successful. At the same time the Bloco needs to be more present in the movements and strengthen solidarity networks to, for example, prevent evictions or organise collective kitchens. This would not be with the aim of replacing the obligations of the state but to be able to in practice communicate that collective problems (like unemployment, poverty, hunger, the lack of housing) cannot be dealt with individually. It is also important that the activists from the Bloco are able to contribute to addressing the political challenges of the movement by broadening the understanding that this is not a temporary problem but a systemic crisis. The party must articulate the possibility and necessity of alternatives to capitalism and help people believe that they are possible if we build them together.

From mobilisation to resistance—a few conclusions
The biggest challenge for the Portuguese left is to turn the spontaneous and uneven moments of mobilisation into organised resistance. It is necessary to rethink our relationship to the traditional workers' organisations, how to negotiate the new reality of precarious employment and how to challenge the political line of the trade unions to see past the artificial division of political and economic struggle. We need to grow roots and bring new experiences to the workers' and the social movements: re-energising the rank and file, organising the unemployed and building networks of solidarity with sectional struggles. Ultimately it comes down to growing roots and being able to turn a feeling of generalised discontent into organised action and collective experiences.

The group of activists that organised the demonstration on 15 September broadened the organisation and prepared a new demonstration for 2 March 2013. According to the organisers, there were 1.5 million people on the streets of Portugal, making it one of the biggest demonstrations in Portuguese history. There are two differences in the success of this demonstration: the media attention wasn't as great as during the lead up to 15 September, and the government hadn't presented any new austerity measures in the preceding days—2 March 2013 therefore marked a clear qualitative growth in the capacity of mobilisation of the social movement in Portugal. It is also important to note that the leader of the CGTP publicly supported and called for the demonstrations, a change in Portuguese political dynamics. Moreover, the anthem of the revolution of 1974-75, "Grândola, Vila Morena", was the demonstration's main slogan: the memory of the revolution is becoming more and more tangible, allowing the recovery of a more radical political standpoint as well as the opening up of a wider field of possible alternatives. This demonstration is a new lease of life for the resistance in Portugal. However, from this experience new forms of organisation and mobilisation have to come forward in order to transform periodic mobilisation into new forms of active resistance.

Reference

Pinto, António Costa, Pedro Magalhães, Luís de Sousa and Ekaterina Gorbunova, 2012, *A Qualidade da Democracia em Portugal: A perspectiva dos Cidadãos* (ICS-UL), www.bqd.ics.ul.pt

New from Redwords
Poems of Protest
by William Morris
with an introduction by
Michael Rosen
£6.99

Though most know him for his design work, William Morris was also an accomplished writer whose poetry was used as songs and chants for the socialist movement.

This volume includes work that has not been published since first appearing as propaganda in *The Commonweal*, the paper of Morris's Socialist League. Michael Rosen argues that his socialist poetry was part of a long tradition of protest writing and a signpost for future struggles.

Also included are "How I Became a Socialist" by William Morris and an afterword, "The Communist Poet-Laureate" by the Morris scholar Nicholas Salmon.

www.redwords.org.uk

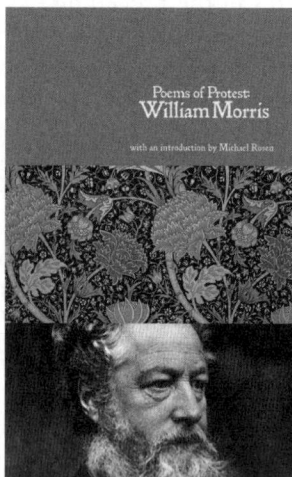

Marxism and women's oppression today

Sheila McGregor

We live in contradictory times: they reflect how much in society in relation to women has changed, but also how much appears to have stayed the same. Women make up almost half the workforce and just over half of trade union members.[1] The level of unemployment among women has risen by 19.1 percent since 2009 and by only 0.32 percent among men, although more men are unemployed than women.[2] Some £11.1 billion of George Osborne's £14.9 billion savings since 2010 have come from women although women earn less than men.[3] Small wonder that we saw the biggest strike of women workers in British history in response to the government's attack on pensions on 30 November 2011, and that hundreds of women turned out to lobby parliament on 24 October 2012 in protest at the impact of austerity on women, chanting slogans such as "Hey, ho, patriarchy has to go."

David Cameron has introduced a law to allow "gay" marriage but simultaneously wants to introduce tax changes to support marriage while being personally in favour of the tightening up of time limits for

---

1: www.homeoffice.gov.uk/equalities/women/women-work/
2: Gold, 2012.
3: Quoted in Martinson, 2012.

abortion.[4] Cameron wants to appear "modern" but blame the poorest in society for being poor and make women and the family subsitute for the cuts in the welfare state. Meanwhile the Church of England can't even countenance women bishops. Raunch culture has become ever more pervasive, but there are also protest movements against overt sexism such as the SlutWalks in 2011 and 2012.[5] The revelations about Jimmy Savile's paedophile behaviour led to an outpouring of anger while exposing the continued disgraceful sexist culture of the BBC and other institutions. And mass popular demonstrations erupted across India in protest at the appalling gang rape of a 23 year old woman on a bus on 16 December 2012.

Revolutionary socialists take part in all struggles against exploitation and oppression, whether they are against austerity measures, sexual violence, the impact of war, police racism or the growth of fascist organisations, attempting to unite the maximum number of forces in any given struggle. At the same time, revolutionary socialists are concerned not only with combatting the particular effects of exploitation and oppression, but also with taking the struggle forward so as to break the very chains of exploitation, which give rise to all forms of oppression.

Thus involvement in struggle is both a practical question of how best to build a protest or strike and an ideological question of how to win those you are struggling alongside to an understanding that it is not enough to win over the particular struggle, but that what is required is a revolutionary transformation of society. When people embark on a struggle over an issue, they usually come with a mixture of ideas about the society they live in, what they are fighting for and how best to achieve their goal. Inherent in any struggle is a debate about how to take it forward. Struggles against sexism are no exception to this.

In 1975, in the first battle to defend the 1967 Abortion Act against the James White Bill, there was a debate in the National Abortion Campaign over whether to take the fight to defend abortion rights into the trade unions as a class issue that obviously affected working class women but also affected men. The success of socialist women in both winning and implementing this strategy led to the Trades Union Congress

---

4: www.guardian.co.uk/politics/2012/oct/24/suffragette-great-granddaughter-march-parliament. The recent death of a woman in the Republic of Ireland, as a result of being refused an abortion, is a reminder of the importance of the right to free, legal abortions.

5: The SlutWalk protest marches began on 3 April 2011, in Toronto, Canada, after Constable Michael Sanguinetti, a police officer, suggested that to remain safe, "women should avoid dressing like sluts." Participants expressed their rage at trying to explain or excuse rape by referring to any aspect of a woman's appearance. Similar marches were held across the world.

(TUC) leading the successful demonstration against John Corrie's 1979 bill to restrict abortion rights.

Women not only raised the issue in mixed unions, but also in union branches with only male members such as among miners and boilermakers. Male trade unionists were faced with the argument that the right of women to control their own bodies was a trade union issue. The slogan "No return to backstreet abortion" encapsulated the fact that it was working class women who suffered most from the lack of free and legal abortions.[6]

Today, as women and men protest against sexism on SlutWalks, in defence of abortion rights, and against austerity measures with their specific impact on women, the "common sense" of many, if not most, is that "patriarchy" is to blame for what is happening to women. The concept of patriarchy is sufficiently elastic and imprecise as to appear to explain the behaviour of individual men, sexism, discrimination, the unions as well as the state. There is also a resurgence of interest in ideas about women's oppression such as Wages for Housework, dating from the 1970s, as well as using Marx's *Capital* to explain women's oppression. However, Frederick Engels's contribution to understanding women's oppression is often rejected.[7]

The purpose of this article is to look at three things: first, the importance of Engels in understanding the roots of women's oppression; second, the way in which the drive to accumulate at the heart of capitalism transforms the position of working class women inside society and the nature of the working class family; and third, the importance of being part of the waged workforce and working class struggle for women's liberation.

Engels and the origins of women's oppression

The relation between man and woman is the most fundamental, or as Marx puts it, "the immediate, natural and necessary relation of human being to human being is also the 'relation of man to woman'".[8] Thus relations between men and women are a measure of the "humanness" and extent of equality of society. In addition, women's oppression is the oldest oppression and will be the most difficult to overcome as the roots are located in an institution that shapes the most intimate sphere of human life, in relationships between men, women and children in the family.[9] This leads

---

6:   www.socialistworker.co.uk/art.php?id=3143. If my memory serves me correctly, it was the then national secretary of the International Socialists who suggested the slogan when I was women's organiser and editor of *Women's Voice*.

7:   See Federici, 2012, and Vogel, 1983 (but about to be reprinted).

8:   Quoted by Brown, 2012, p28.

9:   This point will be further developed in later sections of the article.

many people to assume that all human societies have been based on unequal relationships between women and men and that it is inherent in "human nature" or if not in "human nature", then in all forms of society. The commonsense view today, as in the time of Engels and Marx, is still that women's oppression has always existed.

Marx and Engels, however, both insisted on tackling our evolution historically. Human beings emerged historically as social beings. And, as Heather Brown argues, "men and women always exist and interact within concrete circumstances mediated by definite social relations".[10] Both Marx and Engels were profoundly influenced by Charles Darwin's theory of evolution, and in 1876 Engels wrote his short pamphlet *The Part Played by Labour in the Transition from Ape to Man,* in which he presented the arguments for us emerging as "gregarious" beings with the use of tools driving our evolution.[11] He then wrote a later text, *The Origin of the Family, Private Property and the State,* to establish that the oppression of women arose historically and had not always existed.

Some writers are willing to look to Marx but not to Engels. For example, Heather Brown, in her excellent book *Marx on Gender and the Family,* rejects Engels's contribution to understanding the family because she believes he suffers from economic determinism, linking women's oppression to private property and failing to "challenge the distinction between the public and private spheres".[12] She argues that since women's oppression existed in Greek and Roman times where private property was not fully developed and in societies such as the Soviet Union based on state property, Engels's analysis must be fundamentally flawed.

On the first point, the development of the analysis of the Soviet Union as state capitalist by Tony Cliff involved rejecting the view that capitalism could only exist based on private ownership by individual capitalists. Furthermore, when the state owned and controlled the means of production, as in the case of the Soviet Union and similar societies, the state could function as a single capitalist in competition with other capitals on a global basis and the separation of workers from any control over the means of production meant they were exploited as a class in a similar way to workers in the West. That being the case, the reproduction of labour power in the Soviet Union could be analysed in a similar way to other capitalist societies.[13]

10: Brown, 2012, p28.
11: Quoted in Harman, 1994, p85-86.
12: Brown, 2012, pp54-55.
13: Cliff, 1974.

On the second point, where she objects to Engels's argument that a communist society would "make the relations between the sexes a purely private affair, which concerns only the two people involved", Brown concludes that this could lead to women remaining in the home, "or if the society was run more communally, a few women would remain to do the housework".[14] Elsewhere in the same text Engels talks about society being based on an association of all individuals who take decisions about the direction that society would go in and women and children no longer being economically dependent on men.[15] It is true he does not spell out how the task of reproduction would be organised, but then he doesn't give a blueprint for how production would be organised. In that light, it is surely better to interpret his comments about relations becoming a "private affair" as an indication that personal relationships would be based on personal choice.

Unfortunately, Lise Vogel in *Marxism and Feminism* dismisses Engels's analysis of women's oppression as "a defective formulation".[16] Some of her criticisms may be accurate, but she dismisses an important text for explaining women's oppression historically. Engels's arguments need to be taken more seriously.

The road to the emergence of *homo sapiens sapiens* is a long one going back three to seven million years.[17] In 1994, Chris Harman undertook a review of Engels's *The Part Played by Labour in the Transition from Ape to Man* and *The Origin of the Family, Private Property and the State*. Harman surveyed the existing knowledge of the behaviour of pygmy chimps and gorillas, our nearest relatives, pointing to a series of features, two of which are particularly salient to any discussion about the relations between males and females in our evolution: 1) the degree of social cooperation; and, 2) the role of the female in initiating sexual contacts. He also noted that "their cooperation is essential if males are to have special relationships with them".[18] Philippe Brenot and Pascal Picq, in a book which looks at the development of sexual relations

14: Brown, 2012, p55.

15: "Above all, it [the new social order] will have to take the control of industry and of all branches of production out of the hands of mutually competing individuals, and instead institute a system in which all these branches of production are operated by society as a whole—that is, for the common account, according to a common plan, and with the participation of all members of society... It will, in other words, abolish competition and replace it with association"—Engels, 1847.

16: Vogel, 1983, chapter 6.

17: This depends on dating skeletons from the human line, Brenot and Picq, 2012, p85.

18: Harman, 1994, p89. In its narrowest sense, sexual reproduction does not change, how individuals make sexual approaches to one another, and what sexual practices are considered acceptable or otherwise are shaped socially and historically.

in human evolution, observe that the sexual practices of orangutans, which are more distant from us in evolutionary terms than pygmy chimps, are quite remarkable in that they are about satisfying desire, not just reproduction: "Orangutans practise face to face copulation, and what may surprise us, amuse themselves with a variety of preliminaries: caresses, touching, reciprocal masturbation, oral sex, kissing of the genital areas and all that at tens of metres above the ground".[19] They argue, reasonably in my view, that practices that involve both seeking and giving pleasure presuppose a capacity to conceive of the needs and desires of the other.[20]

The task of trying to establish the transition of ape to man is complex and hampered by the scattered record of skeletons which can be used as a basis for analysing how our ancestors lived their lives. Nevertheless, there are certain features about human beings which have a bearing on understanding the evolution of human society and relations between human beings:

1) Walking upright and the attendant vulnerability.
2) Regular meat consumption.
3) Sophisticated tool making and use.
4) The separation of the sex act from ovulation and the oestrus cycle.[21]
5) The whole human body as an "erogenous" zone.
6) The length of gestation for a human baby.
7) The vulnerability of the human baby and the length of time and socialisation required to attain adulthood.

These features are strong indicators of human beings having evolved both as social beings and with a tendency towards forming couples. The fact that sexuality is not tied to reproduction is a clear indicator of the potential for same sex sexual practices. The emergence of desire and response to the needs of the other in other primates should also be a caution against automatic assumptions about male predatory sexual practices that have to be tamed.

In *The Origin of the Family, Private Property and the State* Engels presents evidence from his day of the existence of egalitarian hunter-gatherer societies with non-hierarchical, non-oppressive relations between men and women. Contemporary evidence that groups of human beings have lived in this way until relatively recently has been thoroughly presented

---

19: Brenot and Picq, 2012, p42.
20: Brenot and Picq, 2012, p43.
21: You can't see whether a woman is ovulating by looking at her body, so a "desire" for sex has to be signalled in other ways.

in the pages of this journal.[22] There are several important points that we can draw from our knowledge about such societies. First, what underpins egalitarian relationships is the autonomous but essential contributions men and women make to the survival and well-being of the group regardless of the existence and extent of any sexual division of labour[23] beyond the obvious one inherent in women's childbearing capacity.[24] Second, women's childbearing role is not an impediment to their autonomy. Third, childcare is a shared responsibility of the band, not uniquely of the biological parents. Fourth, at least some hunter-gatherer societies have accepted a choice of "gender" role.[25] Fifth, the public nature of such groups meant that interactions between people would be within sight or earshot of others, not hidden behind four walls as in today's world of the nuclear family.

Equally important for Marxists is to be able to account for the rise of women's oppression. Engels focused on the emergence of agriculture and on changes in ways of producing food, which over time led to societies creating a surplus sufficient to sustain a group or class not directly involved in food production. But why the change if many hunter-gatherer societies experienced a luxury of time as well as reasonable conditions for survival?[26] And why should such changes lead to the emergence of male dominated ruling classes, with subordination of women in the family in every class?

Harman gives an extended account of the impact of accumulated changes in food production, use of metals, diversity of tasks, trade, rising population and warfare to illustrate the rise of class society in Mesopotamia around 3000 BC.[27] He also depicts how changes in agricultural techniques linked to the male role in agriculture, such as harnessing oxen to the plough, improved productivity and shifted control away from women to men. Such changes, alongside the increasing importance of childbirth for a settled agricultural society, the emergence of systematic warfare to defend stored surpluses and trade, would lead to the loss of women's autonomy.

22: See Harman, 1994. Harman draws heavily on the writings of anthropologists like Eleanor Leacock, Richard Lee and Colin Turnbull among many.

23: A survey of the accounts of hunter-gatherer societies shows a huge range of tasks undertaken by women. See Harman, 1994, and McGregor, 1989.

24: Marx sees this as essential for the reproduction of the species, a position with which I would hope most people would concur.

25: See Blackwood, 1985, pp27-42.

26: In fact, Marshall Sahlins coined the term "the original affluent society": quoted in Harman, 1994, p118.

27: Harman draws heavily on the Marxist archaeologist V Gordon Childe and C K Maisels for this account—Harman, 1994.

The rise of the family with women subordinate to men then secured control over the means of producing the surplus and the surplus itself.[28]

Once the transition to class society occurs, in which the surplus generated is sufficient to sustain a ruling class and a range of occupations such as warriors, priests, traders and the like, there is no way back to some "golden age" hunter-gatherer society. From that point the majority of men and women are subjected to exploitation and all women are oppressed, hence Engels's linking of the rise of the family to the rise of class society and the state. But this too has to be grasped historically. In the chapter on the family Engels discusses the changing nature of love and desire in the Middle Ages compared with Antiquity while projecting forward to the potential for different ways of living inherent in the overthrow of capitalist society:

> Thus what we can now conjecture about the way in which sexual relations will be ordered after the impending overthrow of capitalist production is mainly of a negative character, limited for the most part to what will disappear. But what will there be new? That will be answered when a new generation of men who never in their lives have known what it is to buy a woman's surrender with money or any other social instrument of power; a generation of women who have never known what it is to give themselves to a man from any other considerations than real love, or to refuse to give themselves to their lover from fear of the economic consequences. When these people are in the world, they will care precious little what anybody today thinks they ought to do; they will make their own practice and their corresponding public opinion about the practice of each individual—and that will be the end of it.[29]

The family is not a static institution that transcends the mode of production, but a form of reproduction which is moulded by society and by class. Engels ends the chapter with a quotation from the great American anthropologist Lewis Morgan:

> When the fact is accepted that the family has passed through four successive forms, and is now in a fifth, the question at once arises whether this form can be permanent in the future. The only answer that can be given is that it must

---

28: Harman, 1994, pp134-139.
29: Engels, 1978.

advance as society advances, and change as society changes. It is the creature of the social system and will reflect its nature.[30]

Capitalism and the family

Capitalism is a highly dynamic system "constantly revolutionising" the way we live our lives. Marx and Engels's writings are necessarily located in analyses based on early capitalism. Their observations of the impact this had on workers' lives led them to conclude that the basis for the family in the working class had disappeared: "First, they said, private property and its associated property rights are irrelevant to the working class of the towns and the cities—who have no property. Second, the mass employment of women and children in the factories would abolish the dependence of women on men".[31]

Moreover, Marx left a rather unhelpful formulation for future generations of Marxists: "The maintenance and reproduction of the working class remains a necessary condition for the reproduction of the working class. But the capitalist may safely leave this to the workers' drives for self-propagation".[32] Although this is a somewhat terse statement, and some would argue, a trifle reductionist, there are three points which should be made about this: first, men, women and children do seek to eat, drink and find shelter in the most horrendous of circumstances such as war and famine. Men and women have sexual relationships leading to women continuing to give birth. Second, Marx and Engels were both personally horrified by and amply documented the devastating impact on the living and working conditions of the working class even if they failed to appreciate the impact industrialisation would have on the ability of the working class to reproduce itself.[33] But neither of them looked at the way in which the capitalist class began to intervene in society, taking certain elements of the old patriarchal household and "recombining them into the new working class family".[34] Third, any reference to nature in Marx, such as "workers' drives", needs to be historicised and grasped in its social and historical context. Human beings do need to eat, drink, sleep and develop relationships with others, but how we do so is always shaped by society at particular times and in particular places.[35]

30: Quoted in Engels, 1978, p97.
31: Cliff, 1984, p196. See also German, 1981, p37, and Harman, 1984, p5.
32: Marx, 1976, p718.
33: Marx, 1976, Engels, 1993.
34: Harman, 1984, p7.
35: See Brown, 2012, pp72-76.

So Marx and Engels were wrong in the mid-19th century about the possibilities for the construction of a working class family. But they were right that the mass employment of women has had a crucial impact on relations between men and women since the latter part of the 20th century until today, and has significantly undermined the model of the working class family which finally emerged by the end of the 19th century.

The failure of Marx and Engels to provide an analysis of the working class family is one reason cited by socialist feminists and academic Marxists for criticising them. There are many others. Juliet Mitchell argued that "the problem of women becomes submerged in the analysis of the family".[36] Lise Vogel herself talks about both Marx and Engels being "imprisoned within the limited and sexist horizons of their period", adding that Marx was a "Victorian husband and father with traditional attitudes in his own family life".[37] Indeed, Engels is often accused of an over emphasis on heterosexuality and homophobia because of his derogatory remark about homosexuality in *The Origin of the Family, Private Property and the State*.[38] Vogel also blames Engels for formulations that led socialist feminists to develop "dual systems" theories. The conclusion is very often that Marx and Engels could—or can—explain class and exploitation, but they couldn't—or can't—explain women's oppression that requires other tools such as patriarchy theory. This is a pity, as the reasons that socialist feminists and Marxist feminists seized on a formulation in Engels,[39] to justify a dual approach, lie in how those writers perceived the issue of women's oppression, rather than in Engels's formulation. Vogel herself does not go down this route although her own analysis is, in part, about establishing the potential for cross-class alliances among women.[40]

However, Marx and Engels provide a historical method and a theoretical understanding of capitalism that allows us to overcome the limitations in their analysis of the family. In *Capital*, volume one, Marx

---

36: Quoted in Vogel, 1983, p35.

37: Vogel, 1983, p34.

38: "They fell into the abominable practice of sodomy and degraded alike their gods and themselves with the myth of Ganymede", in a discussion about the low status of women in Greek society—Engels, 1978, p74. There is a debate about the translation of the German, as the expression is *"die Wiederwärtigkeit der Knabenliebe"* , which could perhaps be better translated as "the unpleasant nature of sodomy". Regardless of that, this is a case of condemning Engels for not rising above the prejudices of his day. He didn't in this case, but his overall approach to understanding how society shapes men and women provides a sympathetic reader with necessary tools of analysis.

39: "According to the materialistic conception, the determining factor in history is, in the final instance, the production and reproduction of immediate life"—Engels, 1978, p4.

40: Vogel, 1983, p168.

points to the central importance of the reproduction of labour power (the working class) for capital:

> The capital given in return for labour power is converted into means of subsistence which have to be consumed to reproduce the muscles, nerves, bones and brains of existing workers, and to bring new workers into existence... It is the production and reproduction of the capitalist's most indispensable means of production: the worker. The individual consumption of the worker, whether it occurs inside or outside the labour process, remains an aspect of the production and the reproduction of capital, just as the cleaning of machinery does, whether it is done during the labour process, or when intervals in the process permit.[41]

So the reproduction of workers is essential for capital accumulation. However, the form this takes is not predetermined by the drive to accumulate. Writers in the tradition of *International Socialism* have long argued that, for historical reasons in Britain and many other capitalist societies, this has been done by the working class family, defining the family as the privatised reproduction of labour power. However, this is not always the case. In West Germany (pre-1989 Germany was divided between West and East Germany) after the Second World War, Turkish and Italian *Gastarbeiter* (guest workers) were housed in hostels while any family they might have were forced to remain outside Germany. The apartheid system in South Africa also had similar arrangements. In addition, certain aspects of the process of the reproduction of labour power can be and have been undertaken by the state to varying degrees.

Kath Ennis, Irene Breugel, Chris Harman and Lindsey German all argued convincingly that while the reproduction of labour power is essential, this does not necessarily have to take the privatised form of the family.[42] Ennis points out:

> Housework could be eliminated if a small fraction of the technology which can send men to the moon was to be applied to the household. Cooking could be socialised instead of everyone doing their own. And new forms of social care for the young, the old and the sick, could leave women free to lead their own lives.[43]

41: Marx, 1976, pp717-718.
42: Breugel, 1976, German, 1981, Harman, 1984.
43: Ennis, 1974, p27.

However, Ennis also argues, rightly: "In theory, capitalism could do without the family", but: "In practice, however, this would require such fundamental changes in society, it is hard to imagine them ever being carried out".[44] Not only would the level of investment be enormous, but it would also mean fundamentally attacking and challenging the ideas that underpin the family. This is unlikely outside of all-out war, where as many people as possible have to be drafted into fighting on the front line or on the production line. Equally, no individual employer in constant competition with other employers is going to go down that road. It is also fairly obvious that in current economic conditions the capitalist class is unlikely to see any need to socialise or take over the tasks of the family.[45] A further point is that the family, all appearances to the contrary, serves the interests of capital in maintaining the reproduction of labour power.[46]

Domestic labour and women's oppression

There was an attempt to argue that women's work in the home should be seen as a direct contribution to surplus value and therefore be equated with the sale of labour power in work. In 1976 Irene Breugel, followed by Judith Hamilton and Elana Dallas, wrote a convincing critique of the demand for wages for housework, pointing out that housework is not unpaid wage labour: more importantly, a wage would trap women in the home whereas the focus should be on the power of women workers in social production and the fight for the tasks of the household to be socialised.[47] To put it in Marxist terms, work in the home has a use value but no exchange value and therefore is not part of the process of the production of surplus value.

Perhaps inevitably, the focus on domestic labour leads to seeing husbands and male partners as the beneficiaries and thence to the conclusion that men are the enemy. In some cases it leads to the demand for wages for housework. Silvia Federici, a long-time proponent of wages for housework, argues in the preface to *Ground Zero*:

> capitalism requires unwaged reproductive labour in order to contain the cost of labour power, and we believe that a successful campaign draining the source of this unpaid labour would break the process of capital accumulation, and confront capital and the state on a terrain common to most women.[48]

44: Ennis, 1974, p27.
45: Ennis, 1974, p27.
46: Ennis, 1974, p26, German, 1981.
47: Breugel, 1976, p22, and Dallas Hamilton, 1976, p22.
48: Federici, 2012, p8.

Federici argues that waged work is not a path to liberation.[49] In a different variation, Pamela Odih, for example, argues that the exclusion by Marx of domestic labour as a category of capitalist accumulation "is part of the more general economic dominance and hegemony of men over women".[50] She fails to see that the oppression of women is nonetheless real for all that domestic labour does not generate surplus value, and that women workers are "equally" as exploited as male workers. The fact that domestic labour is mainly done by women does not place male workers in an alliance with capital.

Arguments around domestic labour as the cause of women's oppression also suffer from being incoherent and ahistorical, failing to take account of the changes that have occurred over the last 50 years. Single men and single women have to do all their own housework.[51] Does this mean that single women are not oppressed and that single men are not the enemy, but only male partners of women?

Housework and childcare are shared by couples. Overall men today are contributing more in terms of housework and childcare, even if women still do more. Where both work fulltime, housework and childcare are shared more equally, but men work longer hours and travel further to work than women. And men still do most of the DIY.[52] Many fathers would like to spend more time with their children. This is not to say that men and women should not share equally both housework and childcare, but that the argument about who does what misses the obvious solution: as far as possible to socialise domestic labour. It also misses the devastating impact on everyone of the stressful long-hours culture in modern Britain.

Moreover, the logic of the arguments around domestic labour is to argue for two struggles: one against exploitation, the class struggle, and another against patriarchy, women against men. This is quite different from locating women's oppression in the family as the privatised reproduction of labour power for capital, which traps men, women and children in hierarchical gender relations. The solution in the latter case is the socialisation of reproduction, with men and women workers combining together for social and economic change.

The rise of the working class family

The re-emergence of the working class family, despite Marx and Engels's

---

49: Federici, 2012, p9.
50: Odih, 2007, p11.
51: Women spend on average ten hours a week and men seven—German, 2007, p112.
52: German, 2007, p111.

predictions that it would disappear, led to a key debate between Marxists and patriarchy theorists. Did male workers collaborate with the ruling class to exclude women from jobs and impose a family wage?

Heidi Hartmann, a leading patriarchy theorist, argues that: "the material base upon which patriarchy rests lies most fundamentally in men's control over women's labour power".[53] According to Hartmann, male workers, in alliance with capital, ensured women were excluded from economically productive resources and also controlled their sexuality. Male workers feared economic competition from women workers as well as the threat to their authority. She goes on to argue: "In the absence of patriarchy a unified working class might have confronted capitalism, but patriarchal social relations divided the working class, allowing one part (men) to be bought off at the expense of the other (women)".[54]

Jane Humphries undertook a forensic examination of these arguments in "Protective Legislation, the Capitalist State, and Working Class Men: The Case of the 1842 Mines Regulation Act". This was the first piece of protective legislation that specifically mentioned women. Essentially, Humphries analyses one type of mining where women were employed underground. She shows that the male miners preferred to recruit their own wives and children to work alongside them as this was both safer and also ensured the wage paid to them did not have to be shared with anyone outside the family. The male hewer's or miner's wage acted as a "family" wage. Members of the family tended to look out for one another more, were more dependable, honest about the amount of coal dug out, and parents were less harsh towards their own children. Male miners preferred employing their own daughters rather than other people's sons.[55]

Humphries also shows that male miners did not appear to object to the independent attitudes of their wives and daughters, nor necessarily consider them "inferior homemakers" compared with other working class women.[56] The degree of comfort of the family home appeared to relate more to income than to whether women worked or not.[57] The organisation of the work as a "family" effort had an impact on personal relations between men and women in another way: it led to earlier marriage as men wanted wives to work with them rather than to have "to pay wages to their assistants which were a substantial drain on their wages". It also led to large families. Humphries continues:

53: Quoted in German, 1981, p36.
54: Quoted in Humphries, 1981, p3.
55: Humphries, 1981, pp13-14.
56: Humphries, 1981, p17.
57: Humphries, 1981, p15.

"Not only did women's employment promote early marriage, it also allegedly affected the choice of a partner. Strength was the usual criterion, rather than 'aptitude for domestic duties' or 'liking'."[58] Young women stood up for themselves with one witness to the commissioners who compiled the report for the 1842 legislation recounting: "If a man was to offer any insult to a girl in a pit she would take her fist and give him a blow in his face".[59]

Life was extremely tough down the mines and took its toll on everyone, but particularly on nursing mothers and pregnant women, who often gave birth in the pit and returned to work within days of childbirth. Miscarriages and stillbirths were frequent.[60] In contrast, the subcommissioners who compiled the report were less concerned about the level and nature of accidents, the impact on all miners' health, never mind the impact on pregnant women and nursing mothers, than with the sexual mores of the women miners.[61] This reflected their own bourgeois attitudes shaped by their experience of the bourgeois family, morals and sexuality. They were mortified by seeing half naked men and women together: "The youths of both sexes work often in a half naked state and their persons are excited before they arrive at puberty. Sexual intercourse frequently occurs in consequence...women brought up in this way lay aside all modesty, and scarcely know what it is by name".[62]

In a more practical vein, the mine owners themselves believed that if women were no longer allowed to work underground it would discipline the men to turn up more regularly and be prepared to work for longer hours to compensate for the loss of their wives' wages.[63] In other words, protective legislation which banned women from working would help discipline male workers.

Humphries's analysis points to the importance of careful historical research which investigates concretely the situation of male and female workers as well as the different class interests at play in the 1840s, both from the point of view of individual mine owners, the capitalist class and men and women workers themselves. Of all the forces which contributed to the introduction of the 1842 Act, it is clear that Hartmann's theory of patriarchal structures uniting male miners, mine owners and the bourgoisie is a myth, which does not stand up to examination.

58: Humphries, 1981, p14.
59: Humphries, 1981, p26.
60: Humphries, 1981, p22.
61: Humphries, 1981, p23.
62: Humphries, 1981, p25.
63: Humphries, 1981, p23. Too many miners celebrated Saint Monday!

The same can also be said about other versions of patriarchy theory, whether they are based on ideology, arguments about a patriarchal state, biology and the like, which collapse very quickly when subject to serious historical class analysis. Historically, part of the purpose of patriarchy theory in all its forms has been precisely to replace a class analysis with one based on sex in order to further an argument for cross-class alliances of women to fight men.[64]

Other extensive accounts of how and why a working class family was created have been given by Tony Cliff and Lindsey German in particular.[65] They both draw extensively on research done by historians of the working class and the family in the 19th century. They both show that although the driving force to constitute a working class family came from above, there was not huge resistance from either women or men:

> So there was a coincidence of interests between the capitalist class and the working class. But this did not flow from a patriarchal convergence, as some feminists argue... For working class men and women it came from the wholehearted desire for a better life.[66]

Both Cliff and German assume, in my view rightly, that men and women do seek relationships with one another and very often do want to have children and bring them up in decent conditions. The conditions wrought by early capitalism were literally wrecking the lives of men, women and children and as German argues: "It was out of these conditions that the demand for protective legislation and the family wage came".[67]

The consequences for women.

German asserts that the development of the family wage in mid-19th century Britain, with women supposedly becoming homemakers while men continued to go out to work, came at a price:

> However, as a solution to the problems of the working class family it was an extremely narrow and backward looking approach. It implied that women

---

64: See German, 1981, for a review of Juliet Mitchell and Heidi Hartmann in particular, Harman, 1984, for a review of the debate in *International Socialism*, and Molyneux, 1979, for a review of Christine Delphy.

65: Cliff, 1984, and German 1989, 2007.

66: German, 1989, p34.

67: German, 1981, p37.

had to be dependent on men for their livelihood, and that men had a greater right to work than women.[68]

More than that, it led to a development of gender roles allocated to women and men on the basis of a sexual division of labour: the male bread-winner going out to work and the female homemaker responsible for child rearing and work in the household, all because women can bear children. The nuclear family, man, woman and children, came to ossify gender roles and hierarchical relationships with children at the bottom of the hierarchy. It became a prison as well as a haven, a source of conflict as well as solidarity.

However, possibilities of forcing the ruling class to socialise the reproduction of labour power by providing 24-hour nurseries, cafes and restaurants and the like were totally unrealistic in the aftermath of the defeat of the Chartist movement in 1848.[69] Instead:

> the ruling class was concerned to secure the family as a means of reproducing labour power. The same period also saw serious attempts by the state to regulate sexuality. This was a ruling class offensive designed to impose bourgeois norms of family life on the working class. The Poor Law Amendment Act in 1834, by outlawing outdoor relief for unmarried mothers, helped break earlier patterns of premarital sex. Other laws in the 1880s raised the age of consent for girls, regulated obscenity, prostitution and homosexuality and were part of a drive to establish the marriage bed as the sole legitimate place for sexual relations, at least for women.[70]

Despite all this, the reality did not live up to the ideology about the working class family. Many working class women found they still had to work as their husbands did not get a family wage. Hilary Land argues:

> Married women were not expected to make an economic contribution to the household and if they did it was often not perceived to be "productive work". Men were assumed to earn a family wage. In practice not every man did earn a wage high enough to support a wife and children. Charles Booth's and Seebohm Rowntree's poverty surveys carried out at the turn of the century showed that irregular or inadequate wages accounted for a substantial proportion of poverty. Indeed, low wages were the largest single cause of

---

68: German, 1989, p35.
69: Cliff, 1984, p202.
70: McGregor, 1989, p10.

poverty among working class families. Booth, for example, estimated that in London's East End 30 percent of the population was unable to rely solely on the man's wage. The economist Arthur Bowley estimated on the basis of the census of 1911 that only 41 percent of working class families were dependent on a man's wage alone. On average the man's wage comprised 70 percent of the family income.[71]

Unsurprisingly, in such circumstances: "Married women had to find some way of contributing to the family income and, not finding it in factory employment, they were forced to earn a little by taking in washing, going out charring, taking in lodgers and childminding—all extensions of women's normal domestic work".[72]

From the post-war boom to today

Marx and Engels write in the *Communist Manifesto*:

> The bourgeoisie cannot exist without constantly revolutionising the instruments of production, and thereby the relations of production, and with them the whole relations of society. Conservation of the old modes of production in unaltered form was, on the contrary, the first condition of existence for all earlier industrial classes. Constant revolutionising of production, uninterrupted disturbance of all social conditions, everlasting uncertainty and agitation distinguish the bourgeois epoch from all earlier ones. All fixed, fast-frozen relations, with their train of ancient and venerable prejudices and opinions, are swept away, all new-formed ones become antiquated before they can ossify. All that is solid melts into air, all that is holy is profaned.[73]

The long period of capitalist expansion that started in the 1930s and continued into the early 1970s brought about enormous changes which have continued until now. In many ways, by 2000, the way of life for women, children and men was unrecognisable compared with a century earlier.

It is worth looking at the changes brought about, by looking first at the changing role of women going out to work, before looking at other important changes and the impact of working class struggle and social movements such as second wave feminism and the LGBT movement. It

---

71: Land, 1980, pp55-77.
72: Land, 1980, pp55-77.
73: Marx and Engels, 1848.

is also worth stressing that the impact of the long boom on women and the family has to be firmly embedded in the understanding that women bear the brunt of childcare and housework in the family. Women going out to work means women being both oppressed and exploited, with their working lives shaped by the fact of being women and the nature of the oppression being shaped by the question of exploitation.

The key change for women has been their entry into the labour market as wage workers. This started in the 1930s, accelerated with the impact of the Second World War (an aspect of the war made famous by the film *Rosie the Riveter*) and then slowed for a short time in the aftermath of the war. This trend then accelerated once more, continuing through the period of the long post-war boom and through the various economic crises from 1973 until now. Crises are "sex blind" in the way they work, in the sense that the choice of workplace to close is not decided primarily by whether women or men work there but by the sector undergoing the crisis. The closure of the mines, steel plants and docks in the 1980s, in the main, threw men onto the dole. The differential impact on women today is because of the high percentage of women working in the public sector and the decision by government to cut back the welfare state.

Women today are no longer part of the industrial reserve army of labour but a permanent part of the modern waged workforce. From 1971 to 2011 the economic activity rate among women rose from 59 percent to 74 percent while the female employment rate rose from 56 to 69 percent. In the same period the economic activity rate among men fell from 95 percent in 1971 to 83 percent in 2010 and the employment rate fell from 92 to 75 percent. The employment rate plateaued through the 1990s until today and is lower than in other OECD countries.[74]

At the same time, the fact that women still do the majority of housework and childcare means that their working lives are still shaped by their role as mothers and homemakers. Women do not leave their oppression inside the door when they go off to work. When they get to work they find they have taken it with them. This shapes women's lives, regardless of whether they are single, married, cohabiting, divorced or lesbian. Women's oppression is structured into the world in which we live. Women still do not get equal pay with men. The hourly rate for full-time women workers is still 14.9 percent less than that of men.[75] This is a

---

74: From "The Missing Million" report—www.resolutionfoundation.org/media/media/downloads/The_Missing_Million.pdf
75: www.fawcettsociety.org.uk/index.asp?PageID=23

decline of 1.28 percent since 2011. Gaps in pay between men and women vary according to sector, rising to 55 percent in the finance sector and 33 percent in the banking sector.[76]

The gap between part-time women's pay and men's pay is much greater as part-time women's rate of pay is lower than full-time women's rate of pay. In 2005-6 it was 26 percent lower than full-time women's pay. In 1975 the gap was only 10 percent. One of the reasons for this is the greater "part-time pay penalty" in the UK than in other parts of Europe. More women move jobs when they move from full-time to part-time work after having a child.[77] This often leads them to taking less skilled and therefore less well-paid work than when they worked full-time. Part-time work is in any case more prevalent in less-skilled and less well-paid sectors:

> Compared with women who work full-time, part-time women are more likely to have low levels of education, to be in a couple, to have dependent children that are both young and numerous, to work in small establishments in distribution, hotels and restaurants and to be in low-level occupations. Almost 25 percent of part-time women are shop assistants, care assistants or cleaners. 15 percent of full-time women are managers but only 4.4 percent of part-time women.[78]

The reason the majority of women work part-time is connected to their role in childcare in the family.

> Existing research reveals in broad terms why women work part-time. These reasons include: domestic circumstances; the lack of affordable childcare, access to qualifications; and labour market conditions and opportunities. These circumstances and conditions operate as constraints on women in the labour market. Part-time working is also associated with specific stages in the life cycle. In particular, many women with young children find that only by taking part-time employment can they balance the responsibilities and demands of family life and work.[79]

In 2010, 29 percent of overall jobs were part-time, of which

76: www.fawcettsociety.org.uk/index.asp?PageID=321
77: In my school the head will not contemplate a head of faculty going part-time, so any woman who needs to go part-time has to give up her responsibilities and therefore take a substantial pay cut.
78: http://cep.lse.ac.uk/pubs/download/CP194.pdf
79: Grant, Yeandle, and Buckner, 2005.

75 percent were women's, with an increase in 10 percent of male part-timers compared with 3 percent of women part-timers.[80] However, women's attitudes also seem to be changing, possibly as a result of the impact of some of the government's austerity measures.[81] For example, an analysis by the TUC shows "that while the number of women who are working part-time but would like to be full-time is on the rise, the number of women working part-time who don't want a full-time job, often because of family and caring responsibilities, has been falling".[82]

One thing is certain, that men and women in the UK have higher childcare costs compared with other parts of Europe: 66 percent of mothers in the UK are in work, compared with 72 percent in France and 86 percent in Denmark.[83] Some of the recent changes in childcare support implemented by the government since April 2011 are perverse. Single parents working over 16 hours a week and second earners are worse off. The overwhelming majority, of course, in those two categories are women.[84] "By cutting the maximum level of support available through the child care element of Working Tax Credit from 80 percent of costs to 70 percent of costs, the average claim has fallen over £10 per week".[85] At the same time low to middle two-parent households are becoming more than ever dependent on the contribution of women's pay. In 1968 women's pay made up 11 percent of the household total, whereas by 2008-9 it had risen to 24 percent.[86] If that were not enough, the government is intent on damaging childcare provision by permitting an increase in the ratio of child to carer in nurseries from 1:5 to 1:8.

The changing rate of employment of women has been driven by the needs of capital, even if the hours they work are determined by childcare. But the vast expansion of women's role as wage-labourers has had enormous social consequences, extending their expectations and powering the rise of the women's movement.

The working class came out of the Second World War expecting

80: www.flexibility.co.uk/flexwork/time/part-time-2010.htm
81: The interaction of the changes in the tax and benefit system for adults with young children needing childcare are complex. Each individual/couple has to look carefully at their income to see where and how the changes will impact on them. Very often a second earner will find she is working for nothing, such are the costs of childcare. See Alakeson and Hurrell, 2012.
82: Harris, 2012.
83: McVeigh, 2012.
84: Alakeson and Hurrell, 2012.
85: Daycare Trust, 2013.
86: www.resolutionfoundation.org/media/media/downloads/The_Missing_Million.pdf

changes and sections of the ruling class fearing revolution. The net result was the development of the welfare state, a system comprising a National Health Service, universal benefits, the building of decent council housing, benefits paid for through national insurance, a safety net for the temporarily unemployed, pensions and maternity services. Thus some of the tasks of the reproduction of labour power were socialised.

Longer schooling and mass university education for young women and men transformed the lives of children and adolescents,[87] providing not only some kind of education and training, but arenas for socialisation and experience away from the family. Increasingly, household tasks were mechanised. Washing, which previously took all day and involved heavy work, was transformed with the use of washing machines that washed, then spun clothes, sheets and babies' nappies. The latter, in turn, have often been replaced by a disposable version. Cleaning was lightened through electrical appliances and different materials used for kitchens and bathrooms. Gradually coal fires came to be replaced by central heating. All these changes have led to a decline in the time spent on household chores, although women still do more than men.[88]

The same period also brought changes which facilitated a transformation in women's ability to control their own lives, including their sexuality: the development of reliable forms of contraception, access to legal abortion, easier access to divorce, the right to take out loans, to name but a few: "The conservative mood of the 1950s, reinforced by the Cold War, gave way to a liberalisation of social attitudes".[89] British society continued to become more equal overall,[90] with increasing levels of trust, better social relations and increased status of women.[91] Working class adults formed couples on the basis of mutual desire or love rather than on the basis of supporting one another in work.

In the 1960s, as these changes were taking place, the level of working class confidence was rising in the key industries of car making, engineering and the mines. In the universities students were starting to agitate over issues such as Ban the Bomb, the Vietnam War and student grievances. The civil rights movement in the United States spilled over into the student

---

87: "Between 1960 and 1965 there was a 57 percent increase in women gaining degrees (the equivalent rise for men was 25 percent)"—Orr, 2010, p 31.
88: German, 2007, p111.
89: McGregor, 1989, p12.
90: Danny Dorling dates the start of the process of becoming more equal in the UK and France to the 1930s lasting through until the 1970s—Dorling, 2012, p102.
91: Wilkinson and Pickett, 2010, p58.

movement. A mass student movement developed in Germany and then France culminating in the French general strike of May-June 1968.

All these struggles were mutually reinforcing, raising the confidence of all involved and opening vast numbers of people to new ideas. The ideas of the Women's Liberation Movement or second wave feminism chimed with the experiences of women workers coming up against problems of unequal pay, job discrimination, problems of childcare and the like. The Ford women sewing machinists' strike of 1968 forced Barbara Castle, Labour Minister of Employment, to introduce the Equal Pay Act. The ideas about gay and lesbian liberation, arising out of Stonewall, touched a chord with all those who felt unable to openly articulate their same sexual desire.[92] Women demanded access to the pill outside of marriage and attitudes to women's sexuality began to change with the demands of women for sexual satisfaction. Arguments about the appropriateness of wearing short skirts and the picketing of the Miss World competition in 1968 made the point forcibly that women were not sex objects. At the same time, women's refuges and rape crisis centres were opened in the 1970s to address the very real problems of domestic and sexual violence that the development of the movement made more visible.[93]

The impact on the form of the family

Entry into work and the changes outlined brought about significant changes to women's traditional role as mother and housewife. The *Social Trends* report in 2009 described what has occurred since 1971: a 20 percent decline in births to women under 25; a 51 percent drop in marriage of women by the age of 30. Adults living alone had increased from 6 percent to 12 percent. Single parent households had increased from 4 percent to 11 percent between 1971 and 2008.

The number of married couples in 2009 was the lowest since 1895. In the Second World War there were 471,000 marriages in England and Wales and by 2006 this had dropped to 237,000 marriages. The number of children living with an unmarried couple has risen from 1 million in 1999 to 1.66 million in 2009, while the numbers of children with married couples has dropped from 9.57 million to 8.32 million in the same decade.

Even though the majority of children appear to be born to couples David Wallop reports that 1.12 million children with married couples face a

---

92: For a comprehensive analysis of the period, see Harman, 1988.

93: The first one opened in London in 1976—Cochrane, 2012.

family break up by the age of five compared with 1.2 with cohabitees who face a family break up by the age of five.[94]

According to Gingerbread, 23 percent of households with dependent children are headed by single parents, 90 percent of whom are women. These households care for 3 million children. 57.2 percent of single parents are in work—an increase of 13 percent since 1997. The rate of employment of single parents varies according to the age of the youngest child but at 71 percent is similar to that of women in couples once the youngest child is 12 years old.

However, a report commissioned by the Department of Work and Pensions (DWP) concluded: "It does not appear that becoming a lone parent is a 'decision' taken easily, lightly or wantonly. The single and non-cohabiting lone mothers appear to have the least choice".[95] This lack of choice reflects the extent of damage caused by inequality in the UK. International comparisons of data on single parent families show: "There is no connection between the proportion of single parents and national standards of child well-being." In Sweden only 6 percent of children with a single parent in work and 18 percent of those without were in relative poverty. In the UK the figures are 7 percent for single parents with jobs and 39 percent for those without.[96] Equally, there is a strong connection between inequality in society and child well-being. They stand in inverse relationship to one another.[97]

Teenage mothers are often denounced as being "feckless",[98] even though they only make up 2 percent of single parents. Richard Wilkinson and Kate Pickett point out that "there is a strong tendency for more unequal countries and more unequal states to have higher teenage birth rates—much too strong to be attributable to chance".[99] They also argue there is a strong link between poverty and deprivation and teenage births.[100]

Women's status as workers continues to underpin many of the advances that have been made, bearing out Marx's prediction about the undermining of the traditional family and a tendency towards the equalising

---

94: Wallop, 2009.

95: http://statistics.dwp.gov.uk/asd/asd5/rrep006.pdf

96: Wilkinson and Pickett, 2010, p187.

97: Wilkinson and Pickett, 2010, p23.

98: Wilkinson and Pickett, 2010, p119.

99: Wilkinson and Pickett, 2010, p125.

100:Wilkinson and Pickett, 2010, pp125 and 142. They present a case for teenagers becoming mothers in response to low self-esteem. The conception rate is similar across teenagers, but abortion is a way out.

of relationships.[101] Today men and women who enter relationships with one another can get married, cohabit, separate, remarry, cohabit with someone different in either heterosexual or same sex relationships or stay single. Those with children can do the same.

Marriage, cohabitation and single parenthood do not change the fact that couples or single women (and sometimes men) bear the burden of reproduction. Underneath the surface there are possibly class differences between those who marry and those who cohabit that are likely to be reinforced by the £20,000 now spent on the average wedding. What is certain is that single parenthood certainly goes hand in hand with poverty and poverty has the biggest bearing on educational and health outcomes for children.

Changes in sexual behaviour

A great deal is written, rightly, about the commodification of sexuality, but there are also indications that changed attitudes to sexuality have influenced people's sexual behaviour. German writes:

> When the pioneering gynaecologist Helena Wright asked her working class patients in the 1930s what they got out of making love, most of them blinked uncomprehendingly. Sex was much more likely to be something which men wanted, and women suffered... The difference from modern women was total. As Helena Wright says, today "the contrast is extraordinary. The girl's face shines brilliantly and she says, 'Oh Doctor, it's glorious'."[102]

There have been other particular changes: "Only 3 percent of women who started having sex in the 1950s had ten or more partners during their lifetime, while 10 percent of women starting intercourse in the 1970s claimed this figure." "Being in love" is given less frequently as the reason for first intercourse. Based on a study from the 1990s, German continues: "In the age group 16-24, of those who had ever experienced vaginal intercourse, 85 percent had also experienced oral sex".[103]

But the invisible hand of the market that pulls women into work intrudes everywhere, even into the most intimate sphere of people's

---

101: "However terrible and disgusting the dissolution of the old family ties within the capitalist system may appear, large-scale industry, by assigning an important part in socially organised processes of production, outside the sphere of the domestic economy, to women, young persons and children of both sexes, does nevertheless create a new economic foundation for a higher form of the family and of relations between the sexes"—Marx, 1976, pp620-621.
102: German, 2007, p20.
103: All quotes from German, 2007, p43.

lives. Women's bodies became central to advertising and women were encouraged to buy all sorts of products to make themselves look like the advertising images of their own bodies. Since the impact of the Women's Liberation Movement ebbed away, there has been a resurgence of a new sexism. Sex itself has become yet another commodity to be bought and sold; women reshape their bodies into objects for male pleasure, including putting them under the surgeon's knife. All this with the added twist that the more sexually alluring a women appears to be, supposedly, the more she is empowered. Judith Orr writes about these developments:

> This is what marks the new sexism from the old. It reflects and has absorbed the history and language of women's struggles to assert their sexual needs and desires, to be more than mere objects for the enjoyment of others, all the better to continue that very process. Raunch culture is sold to us as a liberated way to express our sexuality and so, paradoxically, it has persuaded us to accept being objectified in ever more crude and shocking ways.[104]

So entry into work has partially transformed women's and men's and children's lives with important gains for both women's autonomy and a degree of sexual freedom unheard of since the establishment of the working class family in the middle of the 19th century. Homophobia continues, but same sex relationships are acceptable. And transexuality is becoming more familiar to a wider number of people in society.

However, the family, regardless of the form it takes, still embodies the privatised reproduction of labour power. And whatever kind of relationship men and women happen to be in, none of us can escape the socialising force of the nuclear family. It is still based on the assumption that a woman should play a particular role as partner and mother because she is able to bear children while men cannot. Thus the gender roles for women and men and the normative view of heterosexuality continue. Commodified sexuality coexists with a prurience about teaching children and adolescents about sexuality. Since our species does not teach sexuality through observation of the sex act, unlike other species, everyone has to learn the best way he or she can, through trial and error, and pornography in a society where women are supposed to be eternally young and sexually alluring for men and patterns of long hours of work and stress make the real prospects of satisfying personal relationships more and more difficult.

104: Orr, 2010, p36.

Domestic and sexual violence

"No one walks down the aisle in a white dress thinking they are doing this for the benefit of capital or to reproduce the next generation of workers".[105] The family is the place women and men expect to be loved and cherished, perhaps to bring up children, whether their own or those of their partner. However, the stresses and strains of daily life can make that a nearly impossible task. The family creates expectations about hierarchy and gender roles for all men and women and children, which can be unbearable for individual family members. Often relationships creak under the strains they are expected to bear; sometimes the family is an unbearable place to be and at times it explodes.

The facts about domestic and sexual violence make this all too clear.[106] Some 54 percent of UK rapes are committed by a woman's current or former partner. On average, two women a week are killed by a male partner or a former partner. Serious sexual assault is most likely to be committed by someone known to both female and male victims. "Abused women are more likely to suffer from depression, anxiety, psychosomatic symptoms, eating problems and sexual dysfunction." Children also suffer: "They are at increased risk of behavioural problems and emotional trauma, and mental health difficulties in adult life... In 75 percent to 90 percent of incidents of domestic violence, *children* are in the same or the next room."

The almost constant stream of revelations about sexual harassment and worse in the public domain are a reminder, if one were needed, that women are not necessarily safe at work. The Jimmy Savile scandal is appalling, showing that a serial child abuser close to Margaret Thatcher and the political establishment was allowed to prey on young people for decades. This is appalling not just because it revealed the extent of the sexist culture within the BBC in Savile's time, but what emerged about the BBC today. An article about the BBC in the *Observer*, written by an anonymous TV producer, recounts one incident after another of women having to listen to sexual innuendos (so-called "banter"), or being groped by "sleazy" men. She concluded: "In an industry with virtually no job security, with even the channels themselves turning a blind eye to sexual harassment, it's little wonder that women are resigned to putting up and shutting up. It's why you won't find my name on this piece—and perhaps why the likes of Jimmy Savile got away with it for so long".[107]

105: German, 2007, p58.
106: Statistics from www.womensaid.org.uk/core/core_picker/download.asp?id=1602
107: Anonymous, 2012.

As explained at the beginning of this article, feminists and socialists combined in the 1970s to campaign successfully in defence of abortion rights. Today there is no reason why a similar campaign in unions and workplaces could not be equally successful in establishing that sexual harassment of any kind is unacceptable. The acceptance of sexist language in society should be challenged.[108] Far from empowering women, it reflects the view that women are subordinate to men and reducible to their sexuality. The problem of sexual harassment is very often linked to the power of the employer and fears women have of losing their job or chance of career progression. Women, gay, lesbian and trans people need to be encouraged to join the relevant union and get the unions to take up their complaints.[109] Indeed, in the Russian Reolution of 1917, women workers settled accounts with sexist foremen and employers. Equally, employers should be forced to combat sexual harassment in workplaces and to keep their hands and comments to themselves.[110]

The centrality of wage labour

Marx and Engels, Rosa Luxemburg and Clara Zetkin, Lenin and Trotsky were all insistent on the importance of women workers. The reason is, in part, what Rosa Luxemburg said so succinctly: "Where the chains are forged there they must be broken".[111] The only power that can contest the power of the ruling class and the state lies in the ability of the working class to take control over the whole of production and the functioning of society. Collectively, workers are powerful.

But there are also other reasons that are intrinsic to Marx's theory of revolution. Being in work changes the individual from being a private citizen into a social citizen. Whatever the task, paid work makes an individual part of a collective with independent means—a wage or salary that belongs to him or her. It inserts the individual into a collective with contact with other workers, people you can talk to and socialise with.[112]

108: The words "bitch" and "cunt" are often used by women and some people, like Laurie Penny, argue it is empowering.

109: Schools already have to provide "Child Protection Officers" so children and adults know who to report suspected child abuse to.

110: This is an adaption of a formula used in schools where children are in the habit of fighting and making nasty comments to themselves.

111: Luxemburg, 1918.

112: Over the last five months I have been struck by the way in which work has provided a form of community for a group of women who were all pregnant about the same time. Not only could they discuss among themselves how best to tackle everything, but other women, mothers, were on hand to pass on their advice. It also served to educate others, including

It also has an impact on gender roles. Engels wrote up his own observations of the impact of industrialisation on men and women in *The Condition of the Working Class in England*. He draws attention to the way in which older and younger women break out of their normal roles as wives and children, going to the pub straight after work, drinking away their wages and defying the authority of their husbands and fathers.[113] Engels continues:

> We must admit that so total a reversal of the position of the sexes can have come to pass only because the sexes have been placed in a false position from the beginning. If the reign of the wife over the husband brought about by the factory system, is inhuman, the pristine rule of the husband over the wife must have been inhuman too.[114]

These kinds of insights are borne out by the way in which modern women's behaviour is becoming more like that of men in such matters as drinking, smoking and socialising. Similar effects have been identified in relation to women's response to rape inside marriage: "A woman's ability to leave marriages after being raped is also heavily conditioned by economic factors. Most women, some 87 percent in fact, tried to leave and 77 percent succeeded".[115]

Being at work is also potentially a great leveller. When the employer attacks pay and conditions, brings disciplinary charges or wants to make changes, the only means of effective resistance is a collective one. And developing a collective response requires meetings, discussion and decisions. Frequently it is the younger workers who are most daring.[116] A meeting in

fathers to be, about the different phases of pregnancy and what it entailed. There is also a tradition of informally introducing babies to the staff. So new fathers and mothers bring in their babies who get passed around the staff to hold, with a great many men showing their expertise when taking their turn.

113: Engels quotes Lord Ashley in the House of Commons on this: "A man berated his two daughters for going to the public house, and they answered that they were tired of being ordered about, saying 'Damn you, we have to keep you!' Determined to keep the proceeds of their work for themselves, they left the family dwelling, and abandoned their parents to their fate"—Engels, 1993, p15. Marx is also often ambiguous in his comments about the impact of the new factory conditions on women. See Brown, 2012, pp84-92, for a sympathetic analysis of Marx and morality.

114: Engels, 1993, p156.

115: McGregor, 1989, p18.

116: Where I work it is often, but not always, the young women who are most vociferous about fighting back.

January of London National Union Teachers school representatives was dominated by women speakers articulating the anger of their members at government attacks and demanding the union lead a fight.

When votes are taken at workplace meetings, everyone, whether man or woman, gay, lesbian or straight, black or white, Christian, Muslim or atheist has only one vote and therefore finds themselves in a position of equal status with the other. Thus the process of class struggle itself sets up a dynamic which is both democratic and gives a voice to everyone. That is why Marx could talk about the potential transformation of relationships between men and women as a result of the creation of the modern working class.

The impact of austerity

In the UK today work is not a route out of poverty and single parent households are twice as likely to be poor as households with couples. The UK is already one of the most unequal societies. The wave after wave of austerity measures being implemented by the government can only make that inequality worse as support systems for the most vulnerable are whittled down and kicked away. But cuts to the public sector hit women doubly hard as they make up 65 percent of the public sector workforce. So women public sector workers find their pay is frozen and that they have to work longer for a reduced pension. The cuts in services are hitting women hardest, followed by pensioners.

The cuts are reaching to every corner of people's lives from transport costs through education to housing. The cap in housing benefit due to come into force in April 2013 will set in train a form of class cleansing as "poor" families are forced out of areas where they can no longer pay the rent. The uprating of benefits by the Consumer Price Index rather than the Retail Price Index hits women more than men as 30 percent of women rely on state support compared with 15 percent of men. Some 50,000 jobs in health are set to go to achieve the £15 to 20 billion savings demanded by the government. Cuts in mental health provision will hit women who are twice as likely to suffer from anxiety and depression and from domestic and sexual violence. Social care budgets for the elderly are being cut on average by 8 percent. The majority of users of such services are women as the carers. The Sure Start budget, which provides services for 68 percent of parents with children under one year, is no longer being ring fenced; 3,000 posts for youth workers are being cut. Support provided by councils for rape crisis centres is disappearing.[117] On every single measure, those who are already vulnerable will be hit hardest.

There is no way that women and existing family structures will be able to substitute for state provision as it disappears. Life at the bottom of society is going to get meaner and tougher as a direct result of government policy, with single women and single parents with their children among the worst affected.

We have seen how the aftermath of the Second World War led to a transformation in women's lives with women being drawn into work and elements of the reproduction of labour power being taken over by the welfare state and mass education. This undermined the traditional nuclear family and opened up a space for a greater variety of more equal relationships giving greater freedom to women and men, bearing out one of Marx's predictions about the impact of work on relations between men and women. However, these trends are limited by the realities of capitalist crisis and the continuation of the family as the key institution for the reproduction of labour power.

The current obsession of the ruling class with austerity measures will continue to hit women workers in the public sector but still leave them strategically placed both in the public sector and in the economy overall. Austerity will seriously undermine the very institution, the working class family, the government expect to take over the reins of the welfare state it is dismantling. Millions of people are going to suffer.

But there will be resistance. It will no doubt take many different forms as the student demonstrations over student fees, the SlutWalks, the Occupy movement, the marches over hospital closures and the one-day strikes over pensions, have shown. But women workers are now at the very heart of the working class movement, in unparalleled numbers and levels of union organisation. Women workers need to use their collective strength (alongside men) to fight over pensions, jobs, pay and services and against sexism. Revolutionary socialists have a key role to play in encouraging and participating in resistance whether it is to sexist comments, harassment, the government's austerity measures or bosses' attacks on wages and conditions. Equally, it is of fundamental importance to win the strategic argument with all those in struggle, students, workers and the unemployed alike, that women are both exploited and oppressed in capitalist society and that women must look to their collective strength as workers alongside male workers to bring down a society which both exploits and oppresses women.

117: All the figures are taken from Stephenson, 2011.

References

Alakeson, Vidhya, and Alex Hurrell, 2012, "Counting the cost of childcare", www.resolutionfoundation.org/media/media/downloads/Counting_the_costs_of_childcare_2.pdf

Anonymous, 2012, "At work it's called banter. But there's still a culture a culture of sex harassment in TV", *Observer* (14 October), www.guardian.co.uk/media/2012/oct/14/savile-tv-culture-of-female-harassment

Blackwood, E, 1985, "Sexuality and Gender in Certain Native American Tribes: the Case of Cross-Gender Females", *Signs: Journal of Women in Culture and Society*, volume 10, number 1.

Bradshaw, Jonathan, and Millar, Jane, 1991, "Lone parent families in the UK", Department of Social Security Research Report 6, www.statistics.dwp.gov.uk/asd/asd5/rrep006.pdf

Brenot, Philippe, and Pascal Picq, 2012, *Le Sexe, l'Homme et l'Evolution* (Odile Jacob).

Breugel, Irene, 1976, "Wages for Housework", *International Socialism 89* (first series, June), www.marxists.org/history/etol/newspape/isj/1976/no089/bruegel.htm

Brown, Heather, 2012, *Marx on Gender and the Family* (Brill).

Cliff, Tony, 1974, *State Capitalism in Russia* (Pluto), www.marxists.org/archive/cliff/works/1955/statecap/index.htm

Cliff, Tony, 1984, *Class struggle and Women's Liberation* (Bookmarks).

Cochrane, Kira, 2012, "Rape Crisis is 40—and the need is greater than ever", *Guardian* (18 December) www.guardian.co.uk/society/2012/dec/18/rape-crisis-40-years-on

Dallas, Elana, and Judith Hamilton, 1976, "We came to Bury Housework not to Pay for it", *International Socialism 90* (first series, July/August), www.marxists.org/history/etol/newspape/isj/1976/no090/hamilton.htm.

Daycare Trust, 2013, "Childcare costs surveys", www.daycaretrust.org.UK/pages/childcare-costs-surveys.html

Dorling, Danny, 2011, *So you think you know about Britain* (Constable)

Dorling, Danny, 2012, *The No-Nonsense Guide to Equality* (New Internationalist).

Eisenstein, Hester, 2009, *Feminism Seduced* (Paradigm).

Engels, Frederick, 1847, *The Principles of Communism*, www.marxists.org/archive/marx/works/1847/11/prin-com.htm

Engels, Friederick, 1978 [1884], *The Origin of the Family, Private Property and the State*, (Foreign Languages Press).

Engels, Friedrich, 1993 [1845], *The Condition of the Working Class in England*, (Oxford University Press).

Ennis, Kath, 1974, "Women's Consciousness", *International Socialism 68* (first series, April), www.marxists.org/history/etol/newspape/isj/1974/no068/ennis.htm

Fawcett Society, no date, "Equal Pay", www.fawcettsociety.org.uk/index.asp?PageID=23

Federici, Silvia, 2012, *Revolution at Point Zero* (PM Press).

Fine, Ben, 1992, *Women's Employment and the Capitalist Family*, (Routledge).

German, Lindsey, 1981, "Theories of Patriarchy", *International Socialism 12* (summer), www.isj.org.uk/?id=240.

German, Lindsey, 1989, *Sex, Class and socialism* (Bookmarks).

German, Lindsey, 2007, *Material Girls* (Bookmarks).

Ginn, Jay, and Sue Himmelweit, 2011, "Unkindest Cuts: Analysing the effects by gender and age", www.radstats.org.uk/no104/HimmelweitGinn104.pdf

Gold, Tanya, 2012, "It's not in vogue, but this is a perfect storm of inequality," *Observer* (2 April), www.guardian.co.uk/commentisfree/2012/apr/02/women-work-perfect-storm-inequality

Grant, Linda, Sue Yeandle and Lisa Buckner, 2005, "Working Below Potential:Women and Part-time work", www.sociology.leeds.ac.uk/assets/files/research/circle/wbp-synthesis.pdf

Harman, Chris, 1984, "Revolutionary Socialism and Women's Liberation", *International Socialism 23* (spring), www.marxists.org/archive/harman/1984/xx/women.html

Harman, Chris, 1988, *The Fire Last Time* (Bookmarks).

Harman, Chris, 1994, "Engels and the Origins of Human Society", *International Socialism 65* (winter), www.marxists.de/science/harmeng/index.htm

Harris, Scarlett, 2012, "Women, part-time work and underemployment", http://touchstoneblog.org.uk/2012/05/women-part-time-work-and-underemployment/

Hefez, Serge, 2012, *Le Nouvel Ordre Sexuel* (Kero).

Horrell, Sara, and Jane Humphries, 1992, "Old Questions, New Data, and Alternative Perspectives: Families' Living Standards in the Industrial Revolution", *The Journal of Economic History*, Volume 52, 4.

Humphries, Jane, 1981, "Protective Legislation, the Capitalist State and Working Class Men: The Case of the 1842 Mines Regulation Act", *Feminist Review*, 7.

Land, Hilary, 1980, "The Family Wage", *Feminist Review*, 6.

Lenin, V I, *What is to be Done?*, www.marxists.org/archive/lenin/works/1901/witbd/iii.htm

Luxemburg, Rosa, 1918, "Our Program and the Political Situation", www.marxists.org/archive/luxemburg/1918/12/31.htm

Manning, Alan, and Barbara Petrongolo, 2005/06, "The part-time pay penalty", *CentrePiece* (winter) http://cep.lse.ac.uk/pubs/download/CP194.pdf

Martinson, Jane, 2012, "Women paying the price for Osborne's austerity package", *Guardian* (31 March), www.guardian.co.uk/lifeandstyle/2012/mar/30/women-paying-price-osborne-austerity

Marx, Karl, 1976, *Capital,* volume 1 (Penguin).

Marx, Karl, and Friedrich Engels, 1848, *The Manifesto of the Communist Party*, www.marxists.org/archive/marx/works/1848/communist-manifesto/ch01.htm#007

McGregor, Sheila, 1989, "Rape, Pornography and Capitalism" *International Socialism 45* (winter), www.marxists.de/gender/mcgregor/rapeporn.htm

McVeigh, Tracy, 2012, "Wait till your mother gets home—why full-time dads are invisible men", *Observer* (29 January), www.guardian.co.uk/lifeandstyle/2012/jan/29/stay-at-home-dads-policy

McVeigh, Tracy, 2013, "Childcare costs rise 6 percent in past three months alone, says survey", *Observer* (20 January), www.guardian.co.uk/money/2013/jan/20/childcare-costs-rise-three-months-survey

Molyneux, Maxine, 1979, "Beyond the Domestic Labour Debate", *New Left Review*, I/116 (July-August).

Odih, Pamela, 2007, *Gender and Work in Capitalist Economics* (Open University Press).

Orr, Judith, 2010, "Marxism and feminism today", *International Socialism 127* (summer), www.isj.org.uk/?id=656

Osborne, Hilary, 2012, "Grant Thornton's annual study of divorce in the UK", *Guardian* (31 August), www.guardian,co.uk/money/2011/aug31/divorce-family-finances

Stephenson, Mary-Ann, 2011, "TUC Women and the Cuts Toolkit", www.tuc.org.uk/equality/tuc-20286-f0.cfm

Standing, Guy, 2011, *The Precariat* (Bloomsbury Academic).

Vogel, Lise, 1983, *Marx and the Oppression of Women* (Pluto Press).

Wahl, Asbjorn, 2011, *The Rise and Fall of the Welfare State* (Pluto Press).

Wallop, Harry, 2009, "Death of the traditional family", *Daily Telegraph* (15 April), www.telegraph.co.uk/women/mother-tongue/5160857/Death-of-the-traditional-family.html

Wilkinson, Richard and Kate Pickett, 2012, *The Spirit Level* (Penguin).

Lenin's "Left-Wing" Communism: An Infantile Disorder revisited

John Rose

The proletarian vanguard has been won over ideologically... But that is still quite a long way from victory. Victory cannot be won with a vanguard alone. To throw only the vanguard into the decisive battle...would be... criminal. Propaganda and agitation are not enough for the entire class, the broad masses of working people, those oppressed by capital, to take a stand. For that, the masses must have their own political experience. Such is the fundamental law of all great revolutions.[1]

Lenin's famous pamphlet *"Left-Wing Communism"*: *An Infantile Disorder* (*LWC*), published in April 1920, is far more significant than we realise.[2] It holds the key to unlocking the reasons why the October 1917 Russian Revolution failed to spread to the more advanced industrial countries in Europe: essential for understanding the greatest question of all in the 20th century—why communism failed.

Applied properly this intervention—as it analyses the past—sharpens our ability to understand the present: the impasse inhibiting the revival of a full blown public and global discussion of the need for "real", "genuine"

1: Lenin, 1968, pp75-76. This article is an adaptation and development of talks given on this subject at the *International Socialism* conference in September 2012 and the *Historical Materialism* conference in November 2012.

2: "Rarely has such a short work had so powerful and lasting influence on the labour movement. Its influence could be compared to the *Communist Manifesto*. It was of enormous importance in creatively developing the strategy and tactics of the revolutionary movement"—Cliff, 1979, p24.

communism as an answer to the most profound economic, political and environmental crisis of capitalism in our lifetimes:

> Politics is a science and an art that does not fall from the skies...to overcome the bourgeoisie, the proletariat must train its own proletarian class politicians of a kind in no way inferior to bourgeois politicians.[3]

Lenin here stresses the unique intellectual and theoretical component as essential precondition for the agitational component of the revolutionary party. This is of tremendous significance as I shall argue that the catastrophic failure of political intelligence to implement Lenin's principles finds its response in arguably one of the most misunderstood yet intellectually sophisticated Marxist documents from the last century, Antonio Gramsci's *Prison Notebooks*. We should take the two, admittedly very different, sets of writings together as the basis for a highly dynamic, creative open theoretical and practical model as useful today to understand and hence act on the present, as it is to analyse the past.

Lenin's underlying argument called on revolutionary socialists to work wherever the masses are to be found. Lenin was particularly concerned that the growing wave of emerging young communist parties across Europe and beyond learned simultaneously to relate to the revolutionary minorities and the reformist majorities in the working class movements at the same time. Above all this meant working within the reformist trade unions as well as taking national parliamentary, regional and local elections very seriously. This included standing communist candidates where appropriate. Lenin even called it "obligatory" on the party of the revolutionary proletariat to stand candidates. He repeats the word many times.

Of course, Lenin had no illusions in the parliamentary process but recognised that most workers did have just such illusions and that this "democratic" and very public forum had to be utilised to its maximum potential. He even argued that it "is not possible to bring about the soviets' victory over parliament without getting pro-soviet politicians into parliament, without disintegrating parliamentarianism from within".[4]

This recognition of the tenacity of parliamentarianism, especially in the advanced industrial countries of Western Europe, was partly a bitter reflection on the speed with which the reformist "socialists" of the SPD, the Social Democratic Party of Germany, had undermined the flowering of

---

3:   Lenin, 1968, p63.
4:   Lenin, 1968, p64.

workers' and soldiers' councils in the November 1918 German Revolution. The prospect of rapid advance of socialist revolution from Russia into Western Europe was shattered, symbolised by the assassinations of Rosa Luxemburg and Karl Liebknecht in January 1919. As part of their overall strategy the SPD had very effectively counterposed the national assembly, the German parliament, to the workers' and soldiers' councils.

Although Lenin rarely refers to this period in the pamphlet,[5] it is a silent and menacing presence. All the mistakes which were made at the belated founding conference of the KPD, the German Communist Party, at the end of December 1918, when the German Revolution might still have been rescued, were reproduced by the breakaway ultra-left KAPD, the German Communist Workers Party, in April 1920. It is the KAPD that is the foil for many of Lenin's general arguments.

It cannot be coincidence that Lenin's insistence that you had to be inside parliament to undermine its effectiveness echoes exactly a famous speech by Rosa Luxemburg at the KPD's founding conference:

> We are now in the midst of revolution and the National Assembly is a counter-revolutionary fortress erected against the revolutionary proletariat. Our task is thus to take this fortress by storm and raze it to the ground. In order to mobilise the masses against the National Assembly...we must utilise the elections and the platform of the National Assembly itself... To denounce...all the wily tricks of this worthy assembly, to expose its counter-revolutionary work step by step, and to appeal to the masses to intervene and force a decision—these are the tasks of participation in the National Assembly.[6]

Luxemburg lost the argument in the conference vote. We will return later to the other appalling mistakes made at the KPD conference in December 1918.

Lenin also challenged revolutionaries active in the workers' movement in Britain, like Sylvia Pankhurst and Willie Gallacher, who he hoped would establish a British communist party. His sharp and detailed polemics in *LWC*, whilst praising their furious class hatred of reformist politicians, mocked their unwillingness to make tactical compromises with them. With heavy irony, he implied British prime minister Lloyd George had a better grasp of Marxism! Lenin even "dedicated" the pamphlet to Lloyd George.[7]

5:   It is curious that Lenin never wrote specifically about this period.
6:   Cliff, 1979, pp15-16
7:   Lenin, 1968, p101.

Lenin singled out a speech made by Lloyd George in March 1920 which called for Liberal-Tory unity to face down the growing parliamentary threat of the Labour Party. Lloyd George worried about Labour "Bolshevik" promises on the common ownership of the means of production, a threat to private property that put civilisation itself "in jeopardy".[8] It was Labour's industrial working class supporters that really alarmed Lloyd George: "Four fifths of the country is industrial and commercial...more top heavy than any other country in the world, and if it begins to rock, the crash here...will be greater than in any land".[9]

Lloyd George understood both the importance of unity on his side of the class divide and the power of ideas. Lenin argued that British communists should learn the lesson. There should be temporary electoral unity with Labour leaders like Henderson and Snowden against the Liberal-Tory alliance. If possible communist candidates should be part of an electoral bloc but retaining "complete freedom of agitation, propaganda and political activity".[10]

Though Lenin doesn't use the phrase he is nevertheless recommending nothing less than an electoral united front. The Bolsheviks had had a long experience of these type of political compromises. Earlier in the pamphlet Lenin spells out in some detail a string of political—including electoral—alliances, around an agreed set of demands, that the Bolsheviks forged with the bourgeois liberal Kadets, as well as later with the reformist Mensheviks and the peasant party, the Social Revolutionaries. We "always adhered to this policy", but at the same time "we never stopped our ideological and political struggle against them as opportunists and vehicles of bourgeois influence on the proletariat".[11]

The Bolsheviks were ready for any allies, however surprising. This included Father Gapon, the Christian socialist who led the workers' uprising at the start of the 1905 Revolution. This was despite the fact that Gapon's movement grew out of the police trade unions, the Tsarist state's crude attempts to undermine the independent trade unions.[12] The principle

---

8:   Lenin, 1968, p65.

9:   Lenin, 1968, p65.

10: "Without this condition we can't agree to a block, that would be treachery...need complete freedom to expose the Hendersons and Snowdens"—Lenin, 1968, p69. "I want to support Henderson in the same way as the rope supports the hanging man"—Lenin, 1968, p71. This was one of Tony Cliff's favourite quotes.

11: Lenin, 1968, p55

12: Gapon himself was later exposed as a police spy. Cliff reports Lenin's infatuation with Gapon—Cliff, 1975, p149-158.

was reflected in Lenin's attitude to propaganda. In 1900, developing the revolutionary socialist newspaper *Iskra,* Lenin was ready to invite Peter Struve, future Kadet leader, to write for it, "opening the paper up to polemics with liberals".[13]

Here was the underlying principle: "It is necessary to link the strictest devotion to the ideas of communism with the ability to effect all the necessary practical compromises, tacks, conciliatory manoeuvres, zigzags, retreats...to accelerate the inevitable friction, quarrels, conflicts and complete disintegration".[14]

The principle applied just as much if not more so in the trade unions. In a previous issue of this journal John Riddell provided a detailed account of how it was pioneered in Germany by the transformed mass-based communist party, the much enlarged KPD, following its merger with the left wing of the Independent Social Democrats.[15] An "Open Letter" in January 1921 called on trade union leaders for joint mass action over agreed demands. This had enormous potential, precipitating mass actions as well as winning thousands of reformist minded workers to the revolutionary camp. The March Action in 1921 cut it dead. John Riddell described *LWC* as "the as yet unformulated united front approach".[16]

The "Open Letter" approach, which set a standard for united front initiatives, helped to crystallise and fully formulate the principles of the united front which would become Comintern policy.[17] It can be summed up in the three-prong formula: demands/elections/ideology, as relevant today as they were in Lenin's period.

1) The demands that the party raises—which go way beyond the ranks of the party—are the vital means of reaching out to the wider "non-revolutionary" masses of workers and other potential allies in the class struggle
2) Participation in reformist trade unions and in all elections
3) The centrality of the ideological struggle.

Livorno
Alas, formulated or unformulated, Lenin's argument fell on stony ground. Is it not truly shocking that within just five years of the 1917 October Revolution, the revolutionary movement that took power and held it

13: Cliff, 1975, p73.
14: Lenin, 1968, p78.
15: Riddell, 2011, p119-124.
16: Riddell, 2011, p118.
17: Riddell, 2011, p134.

in Europe was the very opposite of communism—Mussolini's Fascism in Italy in 1922?

And is it not equally shocking that one year earlier, in Germany, where the spread of October was still eagerly anticipated despite the failure of the November 1918 Revolution, its prospects were fatally weakened by the notorious "March Action" of 1921? This was the crazy ultra-left adventure labelled by Chris Harman "the March Madness".[18]

There is a link between the two catastrophic events which helps us make sense of this depressing picture—the Livorno Conference of the PSI, the Italian Socialist Party, very early in 1921. The PSI was unique among the parliamentary socialist parties in Europe. It had opposed Italy's entry in the First World War. It sustained its Marxist credentials to such an extent that it had applied for membership of the Comintern. Yet when it came to the fabled *biennio rosso*, Italy's two "red years" with the Turin factory workers' council movement at its centre, the PSI stood on the sidelines paralysed. The paralysis blocked development of the workers' movement.

The case for splitting the PSI was overwhelming along reformist and revolutionary lines—but on what basis? How to bring about a split which followed Lenin's principles allowing for a distinctive revolutionary socialist current but one which could continue to relate to the working class and peasant majority? One of the most prominent communists in Italy who might have understood how to do this was Antonio Gramsci.

Gramsci and his comrades had turned the PSI Turin workers' newspaper *L'Ordine Nuovo* into "the paper of the factory councils".[19] Gramsci wrote in it how he and his comrades toured Turin's factories winning the argument for transforming the Turin factory council "*biennio rosso*" movement into revolutionary soviet type institutions.

L'Ordine Nuovo had in effect become the paper of a Bolshevik faction inside the Turin PSI. And although Gramsci had been excluded from the PSI delegation to the Second Congress of the Comintern in July 1920, Lenin explicitly singled out *L'Ordine Nuovo* as the key to progress the spread of socialist revolution in Italy.

The 17th clause of the "Theses on the Fundamental Tasks of the Second Congress of the Communist International" very publicly endorsed *L'Ordine Nuovo* criticisms of the PSI's paralysis in the face of the Turin factory council "*biennio rosso*" movement.[20]

18: Harman, 1982, p192-220.
19: Fiori, 1990, p120; Trudell, 2007, p73.
20: Fiori, 1990, p134.

Nevertheless the task of splitting the PSI at the Livorno conference proved daunting and the notorious ultra left communist Amadeo Bordiga, also the subject of criticism in Lenin's *LWC*, unfortunately proved to be a far more capable operator than Gramsci. Now this is not the place to discuss the reasons why Gramsci failed to stand up to Bordiga. But it resulted in Gramsci helping "to create the sort of party he did not want".[21] Bordiga's version of the split proved decisive with the immediate result of *isolating* the new communist party from the mass of workers.

However another factor was at work here—frankly catastrophic Comintern intervention, influenced by the so-called "theory of the offensive".[22] This resulted in the ultra left "March Action" in Germany 1921 which simultaneously destroyed Paul Levi, Rosa Luxemburg's successor as KPD leader, as it almost certainly fatally destroyed prospects for socialist revolution in Germany.[23]

And the point is this: Levi was present at the PSI Livorno conference and opposed the Comintern delegates support for Bordiga. This led to Comintern manoeuvres to drive Levi out of the leadership of the German communist party in preparation for the March Action 1921.

Thus Livorno saw the immunisation of both Gramsci and Levi as potentially corrective influences in the face of an isolationist ultra leftism which would help undermine the revolutionary potential of workers' movements in both Italy and Germany.

Bordiga's ultra leftism proved absolutely appalling and must count as a major factor in the failure to challenge the rise of Mussolini. This is the subject of a brilliant book by the late Tom Behan which details the rise and enormous potential of the wonderfully named *Arditi del Popolo* (ADP, People's Shock Troops),[24] the spontaneously formed mass-based Italian anti fascist movement. It developed a united front perspective with one aim—halting Mussolini's mobilisations, by mass based force if necessary, with maximum involvement across the political spectrum of the left. Alas, although many PSI and PCI activists took part, this was not the official line of these organisations.

By July 1921 at least Gramsci had belatedly realised the serious threat that fascism posed and called for Communists to support the ADP.[25] But Bordiga disagreed. His first major article on the subject published in

---

21: Bambery, 2007, p89.
22: Bambery, 2007, p89, also Broue, 2006, p488-490; Harman, 1982, p207-8.
23: See Zehetmair and Rose, 2013.
24: A rough translation, according to Behan, 2003, p121 fn2.
25: Behan, 2003, p62.

Il Comunista on 14 July argued: "The proletariat's revolutionary military organisation must be on a *party* basis... Communists therefore must not take part in activities organised by other parties, or which in any event arise outside the party".[26] And even Gramsci was not always fully consistent with his support for the ADP.[27]

A year later in July 1922 with Mussolini just three months away from taking power, Bordiga mocked the prospects. He wrote: "So the Fascists want to burn down the parliamentary circus? We'd love to see the day!"[28]

The PCI refused all offers of joint work with the parliamentary socialists as well as with the ADP. As Bordiga had put it in May 1921: "Fascists and social democrats are but two aspects of tomorrow's single enemy".[29] Again Gramsci was ambiguous.

This failure to understand either the threat of fascism or how to confront it affected some of those Comintern leaders who had earlier promoted the theory of the offensive. This remained true even after Mussolini had seized power. Thus Comintern president Zinoviev asked: "Is it a coup or a comedy? Perhaps both at the same time. From a historical point of view it is a comedy. In a few months the situation will turn to the advantage of the working class".[30]

Nevertheless the Comintern had been shifting. Following the disastrous March Action in Germany, the Third Congress of the Comintern in the summer of 1921 adopted the principles of the United Front. Though too late, the Comintern in January 1922, finally issued a stinging rebuke to the Italian communists for failing to respond to the ADP:

Where were the effective leaders of the working masses? Where were the Communists in this period? Were they busy scrutinising the movement with a magnifying glass to see whether it was sufficiently Marxist and in keeping with their programme? We don't believe so. On the contrary—to us it appears that at that moment our young PCI was too weak to be able to dominate this spontaneous movement. The doubt arises that the party's pedantic and formulaic position towards Arditi del Popolo was the cause of this weakness... The PCI should have immediately and energetically joined the Arditi movement, making common cause with workers and therefore turning petty bourgeois elements into their sympathisers. Adventurists should

---

26: Behan, 2003, pp67-68. Emphasis in original.
27: Behan, 2003, p74.
28: Behan, 2003, p92.
29: Behan, 2003, pp92-93.
30: Behan, 2003, p94.

have been denounced and removed from positions of leadership, and trusted elements placed at the head of the movement. The Communist Party is the heart and brain of the working class, and there is no movement in which masses of workers take part which could be too low level and impure for the party... For our movement it is always more advantageous to make mistakes alongside the masses rather than away from them, isolated in a closed circle of party leaders who declare their principled virginity.[31]

The Italian working class would pay a heavy price for this failure by the left, as would its potentially most gifted leader, Antonio Gramsci.

Gramsci's Prison Notebooks and the Modern Prince

The publication of *The Gramscian Moment* by Peter D Thomas has given added weight to the perspective on Gramsci's writings that the late Chris Harman, former editor of this journal, developed over many years.[32] Thomas draws similar conclusions based on his detailed engagement with a wide range of Gramscian scholarship, much of it hostile to such a perspective.[33]

"Running through the notebooks," argued Chris, was a concern with "why was the revolutionary upsurge in Italy unsuccessful, ending with Benito Mussolini coming to power?"[34] Part of the answer was the failure to implement united front principles, which Gramsci had by now fully embraced—not just in relation to opposing Mussolini, but also earlier in relation to the failure of the Turin factory workers' council "*biennio rosso*" movement to lead a society-wide movement of millions towards a revolutionary challenge to the Italian state. This would have meant spelling out the "practical and ideological steps to draw in all workers, the mass of peasants, demobilised soldiers and the discontented layers of the petty

31: Behan, 2003, pp107-108.
32: In *International Socialism 114*, Chris, with the help of several comrades, brought together a lifetime's study of Gramsci under the rubric "Antonio Gramsci's Revolutionary Legacy".
33: While inevitably conceding some of its arcane scholastic language, Thomas pierces much of its pretension. In a note to me about this article, he writes, "Point out that I reference one of Chris's texts on Gramsci...as an antidote to post-Marxist readings... Chris and I also spoke together at an *International Socialism* day school on Gramsci in 2007, and I was pleased to see that we were in agreement on central issues. Regarding your point [that the *Prison Notebooks* are a response to the left's catastrophic defeat in Italy resulting in Mussolini's victory], I think that what you write is generally accurate—however, I would add that the *Prison Notebooks* and the concept of the Modern Prince in particular need to be understood also, and perhaps above all, as a rejection of the "third period" [of Stalinism], and the call for a renewed united front in the 1930s."
34: Harman, 2007, p107.

bourgeoisie".[35] Here Gramsci's most important yet misused concept of hegemony comes into play.

Gramsci came to believe that "the ideological ties binding people to existing states are stronger than they were in Russia because of the existence of dense networks of formal and informal organisations ('civil society'). These influence the lower classes but their leaderships are tied in one way or another into the structures of existing society and serves as a channel which feeds the ideologies into 'subaltern' (ie lower) classes." Thus the "hegemonic struggle is a double battle—to free the working class from the ties that bind it to the existing exploitative order and to bind other sub-altern classes into a 'bloc' with the working class".[36]

But how is this objective to be achieved? Here Chris introduces arguably one of Gramsci's most celebrated passages with its focus on the "active man in the mass":

> The active man in the mass has a practical activity, but has no clear theoretical consciousness of his practical activity, which nonetheless involves understanding the world in so far as it transforms it. His theoretical consciousness can indeed be historically in opposition to his activity. One might almost say that he has two theoretical consciousnesses (or one contradictory consciousness): one which is implicit in his activity and which in reality unites him with all his fellow workers in the practical transformation of the real world; and one, superficially explicit or verbal, which he has inherited from the past and uncritically absorbed.[37]

Contradictory consciousness can paralyse the active man of the mass. She/he has to overcome the numbing ideological inheritance from the past, but cannot do this alone. A revolutionary combat organisation is essential which raises the ideological struggle, as part of the class struggle, to the highest plane. This is the Modern Prince:[38]

> A human mass does not "distinguish" itself, does not become independent in its own right without, in the widest sense, organising itself; and there is no organisation without intellectuals, that is without organisers or leaders,

---

35: Harman, 2007, pp107-108.
36: Harman, 2007, pp108-109.
37: Gramsci quoted in Harman, 2007, p109-110; Thomas, 2010, p378.
38: Why the Modern Prince? See Harman, 2007, p106. Also: "Of all the themes explored in the *Prison Notebooks*, few are as little discussed today as Gramsci's theory of the working class political party as an 'organisation of struggle'"—Thomas, 2010, p437.

in other words, without the theoretical aspect of the theory-practice nexus being distinguished concretely by the existence of a group of people "specialised" in conceptual and philosophical elaboration of ideas.[39]

Thomas adds to this argument by introducing Gramsci's empowering idea of the "democratic philosophy", where the intellectuals are at least as often the "educated" as they are the "educators" and who combine with worker activists, "to construct an intellectual-moral bloc that renders politically possible a mass intellectual progress". They are to be "permanently active persuaders" struggling for proletarian hegemony to form the basis for a new society.[40]

The lost revolution in Germany

We are now in a position to revisit the causes of failure of the German Revolution. At a critical point in his book *The Lost Revolution: Germany 1918-23* Chris Harman opens the way for this intervention by introducing the "active man in the mass" passage from Gramsci.[41] He is describing how SPD pressures undermined the revolution.

The recent publication in English, *All Power to the Councils! A Documentary History of the German Revolution of 1918-1919*, edited and translated by Garbriel Kuhn, allows a unique test of Gramsci's insight here by focusing on one of the key "active men in the mass", Richard Müller. Müller was a leading member of the Executive Committee of the Workers' and Soldiers' Councils in Berlin. The book groups together several speeches and written statements by four of the key leaders of the German Revolution in the crucial months of November and December 1918, Rosa Luxemburg, Karl Liebknecht and the Berlin revolutionary shop stewards and workers' leaders Richard Müller and Ernst Daumig. All four had been in prison for anti-war activities.

One theme dominates every contribution: how the councils must assert their authority over the revolution and resist the SPD's ferocious ideological, strategic and tactical attempt to subordinate the councils to the demand for a national assembly. And yet one of the most obvious conditions—the essential Gramscian theme—for mounting such resistance was spectacularly absent: unity of revolutionary intellectuals and worker

---

39: The intellectuals here are "organic" intellectuals, "a new type, which arise directly out of the masses"—Gramsci, quoted in Harman, 2007, pp110-111.

40: Gramsci, quoted in Thomas, 2010, p436.

41: Harman, 1982, p148.

leaders in a common organisation.[42] This remained true even at the German Communist Party (KPD) foundation conference in late December 1918.

The isolation of Luxemburg and Liebknecht was gratuitously underlined when they were deliberately excluded from the National Congress of Workers' and Soldiers' Councils in mid-December.[43]

Richard Müller was intellectually and political disarmed. His precarious position was exacerbated by the majority of SPD activists on the executive of the Berlin Workers' and Soldiers' Committee. Not that they were all in agreement with each other. All of them, some sincerely, others less so, were enthusiasts for the revolution and its working class majority. And several were genuinely confused by the councils versus assembly debate. Their group, and much more importantly their supporters in the factories, could be split, and indeed mobilised for action, by astute strategy and tactics coming from the revolutionary side. Reflecting critically on his role several years later in an article reproduced in this collection, Richard Müller wrote:

> The first and most important duty of the Executive Council was to give the revolution a programme, and thereby content and direction. Instead the Executive Council got caught up in a thousand things, let the first weeks pass without any initiative, and allowed both opportunists and outright opponents of the revolution to shape public opinion and to announce a date for national assembly elections.[44]

Pierre Broué provides a graphic description of how Müller was outmanoeuvred on the committee by a resolution which superficially supported the councils but in practice anchored them to the national assembly.[45] SPD appeals for "workers' unity", and Müller's susceptibility to seek a compromise too far,[46] made him literally a prisoner of contradictory consciousness.

Müller's absolutely justified if belated recognition of the need for a programme was indeed the way to break out of this impasse. Rosa Luxemburg had developed such a programme, a programme of demands predicated on mass working class action, and in the same article Müller

---

42: A serious weakness with this book is its failure to address this adequately. It should be read alongside the following chapters, "Days of Workers Power" in Harman, 1982, pp52-72, especially the last part, and "The Period of Dual Power", Broué, 2006, pp157-188.

43: Harman 1982, p56; Nettl, 1966, p745.

44: Kuhn, 2012, p61.

45: Broué, 2006, pp177-179.

46: Broué, 2006, p178.

later reports on it.[47] If acted upon, it raised the prospects, in her words, of nothing less than "a united front of the entire German proletariat, bringing together the south and the north, the country and the city, the worker and the soldier".[48] Here was the mechanism to appeal to SPD supporters in the workplaces over the heads of their leaders. Key demands focused on the need to mobilise, and begin the transfer of power at the base:

> Election of shop councils in all workplaces; in collaboration with the workers' councils, the shop councils will be responsible for controlling the inner affairs of the workplace, the labour conditions, the production, and, eventually, management.

The very next demand provided the mechanism for implementation:

> Instalment of a central strike commission that shall, in constant collaboration with the shop councils, give the strike movements emerging across the country a unified leadership and socialist direction, while at the same time securing the highest possible support by the workers' and soldiers' councils.[49]

As Luxemburg explained at the KPD founding conference this was the necessary next step from the political to the "economic revolution and therefore socialist revolution".[50] Her projection, indeed prediction, of "strike movements across the country" was confirmed in the early months of 1919, tragically after the assassinations of both her and Liebknecht. However, because of the abject failure of the KPD conference to adopt policies to fit the situation and recruit worker leaders like Richard Müller and Ernst Däumig, and potentially thousands of others,[51] it failed to build the unified leadership and hence could not properly provide socialist direction for the strike movement.[52] Nevertheless Luxemburg's intervention, in principle even if it could not be carried out in practice, confirms the validity of the united front perspective implicit in Lenin's *LWC*, including Gramsci's refinements.

47: Kuhn, 2012, pp70-71.
48: Kuhn, 2012, p102.
49: Kuhn, 2012, p105.
50: Harman, 1982, p67; Broué, 2006, p219.
51: "Disastrous"—Harman, 1982, p72. See also the sad and infuriating article by Liebknecht, "Negotiations with the Revolutionary Stewards"—Kuhn, 2012, pp119-121. See also Müller's "Revolutionary Gymnastics"—Kuhn, 2012, pp76-78.
52: See also the chapters, "The Months of Civil War", in Harman, 1982, pp96-124, and "The Noske Period" in Broue, 2006, pp261-283.

Her programme of demands was about mobilising the mass of workers to break the paralysis of the revolution and the SPD's assertion that the National Assembly took precedence over the Workers' and Soldiers' Councils. The demands would involve workers experiencing and hence acting directly to bring about a fundamental shift in power at the productive base of society and hence of the revolution itself. These practical steps had to be accompanied by an ideological offensive, very explicit in so much of Luxemburg's writing at the time, which distinguished genuine socialism, based on workers' power from below, from the SPD's elitist version where socialism would be introduced by decree in the National Assembly.[53]

However, Luxemburg never for a moment underestimated the continuing appeal of the SPD version: what a "nice idea to realise socialism the parliamentarian way, by a simple majority vote".[54] This is what made

---

53: However, there is an unresolved puzzle about the section of her programme entitled International Tasks. It called for: "Immediate establishment of regular communication with international socialist parties in order to provide the socialist revolution with an international platform and to administer and secure peace by the fraternisation and the revolutionary uprising of the world proletariat"—Kuhn, 2012, p105. It did not mention the need for solidarity with the successful seizure of power by workers in Russia in October 1917 and the bitter struggle to defend this historic development that had raged throughout Russia in 1918. This is particularly surprising because the ideological showdown between reformists and revolutionaries in November and December 1918 in Germany was especially intense over the wildly differing interpretations of events in Russia. Liebknecht reports that by mid-December a majority of soldiers had been "incited against Bolshevism"—Kuhn, 2012, p107. Richard Müller quotes Kautsky. "The councils...can never legitimise the rule of the masses in the same way [as national assembly elections]. That's why the [Bolshevik] terror became necessary"—Kuhn, 2012, p69. Lenin had warned repeatedly just how dangerous Kautsky was as an ideological opponent. This is why he wrote the pamphlet *The Proletarian Revolution and the Renegade Kautsky*—Broué, 2006, p121. It was a defence of soviet democracy against parliamentary democracy as well as a polemic against Kautsky's attacks on the Bolshevik Revolution. How forcefully did Luxemburg and Liebknecht respond to Kautsky's attacks? The entire German political class, the political spectrum ranging from Kautsky through all the parliamentary parties, left, centre and right, to the crumbling German aristocratic establishment and the military top brass, were lined up against the Bolshevik "virus" spreading to Germany. The propaganda barrage was suffocating. Did Rosa Luxemburg's severe doubts about the Russian Revolution, expressed in her manuscript *The Russian Revolution*, written just before she was released from prison in August September 1918, affect her judgment about how to respond? Paul Levi had visited her in prison and persuaded her not to publish it—Broué, 2006, p123 fn49. See also Cliff's "Rosa Luxemburg's Criticisms of the Bolsheviks in Power" in Cliff, 1959. Of course, we should exercise extreme caution before making superficially plausible hindsight critical judgments on Luxemburg and Liebknecht. Nevertheless this is a legitimate area for investigation. It is a further example of where increasing our capacity to know increases our capacity to act: see the conclusion to this article.
54: Kuhn, 2012, p113.

the other point of the demands/elections/ideology united front formula so essential. To adapt the earlier reported remark of Lenin to the German context, a workers' and soldiers' councils' victory over parliament was not possible without pro-council politicians in parliament, without disintegrating parliamentarianism from within.

Lessons for today

There is an immediate lesson for the one country in the world in the middle of a revolution, Egypt. The question of its future direction, and the prospects for transforming it into a socialist revolution, is a live and vigorous debate among thousands of revolutionary activists. It is a debate stimulated partly by the Revolutionary Socialists (RS).

In early summer last year the Egyptian RS faced a challenge over electoral democracy with uncanny echoes of the arguments facing the German communists in 1918-19. There was a mood among activists to boycott the elections, especially among some of the hardened street fighters who had helped topple Mubarak. The mood affected many members and supporters of the RS. It was compounded by the fact that in the final run-off between presidential contenders the choice was between a supporter of the old regime and a Muslim Brotherhood candidate unambiguously hostile to the left. Enormous crowds in Tahir Square responded by waving their shoes and shouting, "We want neither plague nor cholera."

At the same time, though, the majority of Egyptians enthusiastically welcomed the elections as the most visible prize yet of the revolution itself. Surely one of the great aims of the revolution, democracy, was about to be fulfilled?

A sharp argument blew up within the RS. A statement by their leadership, later made public, made the case against an election boycott. It put into the practical electoral context of Egypt 2012 all the arguments from Lenin explored earlier in this article. From the many passages, perhaps the most fascinating is this one, not least because of the prophetic polemic aimed at Muslim Brotherhood candidate Morsi who, of course, became president:

> The choice between Shafiq and Morsi is not a choice between a revolutionary candidate and a counter-revolutionary candidate... It is rather a choice between a military bourgeois candidate hostile to the revolution and a vacillating bourgeois candidate who wants neither a return to the old order nor the completion of the revolution to its end. This means a choice between two enemies. And the question is who among them do we prefer to struggle against: a general who will send out tanks against the citizens, or

a waffling opportunist Brother subject to pressures from below, who can possibly be exposed before his own base and citizens?[55]

More broadly, there are important lessons also for understanding the failure of the left in the revolutions in the last half of the last century as well as guidance for our practice in this century. We learn that revolutionary crises can throw up spontaneous and very advanced forms of workers' organisations. But we also learn that pressures from the old society will undermine these new structures unless a highly sophisticated revolutionary socialist party, ideologically innovative, rapidly developing a mass base in the revolution, can intervene and give it direction. This includes helping to raise self-confidence among workers to see themselves as the new rulers in a socialist society.

The Bolsheviks, of course, faced just such a crisis. Lenin was completely alone in April 1917 when he called for "All Power to the Soviets". As in Germany the soviets, the workers' councils, were dominated by reformist voices calling for a national assembly. The Bolsheviks were vacillating. Describing this historic moment in his biography of Lenin, Tony Cliff entitled his chapter "Lenin Rearms the Party", the military metaphor underpinning the decisive significance of Lenin's ideological offensive.

The absence of even the serious beginnings of a revolutionary party in Poland, Iran and South Africa in the late 1970s and 1980s made inevitable the complete paralysis and later disintegration of the revolutionary potential of the workers' movements in those countries, despite their decisive role in removing authoritarian regimes.[56]

55: I would like to thank Anne Alexander for the information about the boycott mood in Tahrir Square and for obtaining this statement for me. The full statement can be viewed at www.scribd.com/doc/97156218/To-the-Comrades. See also Sameh Naguib's excellent article in which he explains why the Revolutionary Socialists must themselves be ready to participate in parliament, insisting that parliament must not be left to the Islamists: "We can't pretend to be too pure to get involved"—Naguib, 2013.

56: The political biography of Jacek Kuron, the former revolutionary socialist, who became a leading adviser to the Solidarity-led workers' movement in Poland, and then a reformist labour minister in the new post Stalinist, pro-Solidarity government, serves as a negative or reverse template for the argument developed here. See Zebrowski, 2004. The failure of the left in the workplaces during the Iranian Revolution allowed Khomeini and the Islamists to fill the vacuum. They turned the Lenin and Gramsci arguments inside out. Khomeini launched an ideological barrage against "Marxism" in the workplaces and successfully adapted the shoras' (the embryonic workers' councils) demands to the welfare programme of the "Islamic" revolution, imposing "Islamic" shoras on the existing structures. The failure of the left also gave the revolutionary Islamic electoral democracy legitimacy, with voting to the Iranian parliament in post-revolutionary Iran taken seriously by a majority of the public. See Poya, 1987, pp123-168.

Contributing to the stalling and collapse of the workers' movements in Poland, Iran and South Africa was of course the gathering crisis in the Soviet Union and its satellites which exploded, or rather imploded, in 1989. Official Communism's impending obsolescence had hung over the three struggles. In Poland the workers' revolt was itself aimed at Official Communism. In Iran the ultra-loyal pro-Soviet Tudeh Party was itself virtually obsolete. In South Africa the SACP, the South African Communist Party, capitulated to neoliberalism following the disintegration of the Soviet Union. Never mind reform versus revolution, the SACP was so ideologically disoriented, it wasn't even able to counter the ANC's embrace of market-led policies with aggressive state-led reforms to tackle the grinding black township poverty left over from the apartheid years.

Most of the world, including especially its intellectuals, on the right and most of the left, interpreted this breakdown of official Communism as an irreversible defeat for the principles of communism, as outlined by Marx and Engels in the *Communist Manifesto* of 1848. We are foolish in the extreme if we underestimate the intensity of the cluster of attitudes which have now developed as part of a new "common sense"[57] taking for granted the "truth" of this as a tried and failed project.

Or to put the point in another way, returning to the passage from *LWC* at the beginning of this article, in the aftermath of October 1917 Lenin assumed that the vanguard of the workers' movements in Western Europe had already been, or was about to be, won ideologically to Bolshevism. This was a not an unreasonable assumption as tens, if not hundreds, of thousands of working class activists hailed and identified with the October victory. Lenin and the Comintern rallied these workers and other activists, encouraging the formation of new communist parties as well as pressurising left reformist and anarchist sympathisers with October to join with them.

The Russian Revolution and its subsequent Stalinist degeneration would dominate the vanguards of the workers' movements across the world and throughout most of the 20th century. Activists leading workers' movements in the 21st century carry this memory as a damaging historical burden which has yet to be properly addressed. Worse, it has led to ideological disorientation among activists, a lack of conviction in a socialist alternative where often "socialism" at best means exerting mass pressure on the capitalist state to soften the worst effects of crisis.

It makes the question of the ideological struggle in our period

---

57: For Gramsci "common sense" was ideologically conservative inducing passivity. See Harman, 2007, p109; Thomas, 2010, p16.

fundamentally more important than in Lenin's period. It means we have arrived at what Peter Thomas calls the "Gramscian Moment".[58]

Deepening our understanding of the failure of Communism with a capital "C" in the 20th century increases our capacity to know and therefore act in the struggle for communism with a small "c" in the 21st century. Hopefully this article serves as a modest contribution to this proposition.

References

Bambery, Chris, 2007, "Hegemony and Revolutionary Strategy", *International Socialism 114* (spring), www.isj.org.uk/?id=306

Behan, Tom, 2003, *The Resistible Rise of Benito Mussolini* (Bookmarks).

Broué, Pierre, 2006, *The German Revolution 1917-1923* (Haymarket).

Cliff, Tony, 1959, *Rosa Luxemburg*, www.marxists.org/archive/cliff/works/1959/rosalux/index.htm

Cliff, Tony, 1975, *Lenin, volume 1: Building the Party* (Pluto).

Cliff, Tony, 1979, *Lenin, volume 4: The Bolsheviks and World Revolution* (Pluto).

Fiori, Giuseppe, 1990, *Antonio Gramsci, Life of a Revolutionary* (Verso).

Harman, Chris, 1982, *The Lost Revolution: Germany 1918 to 1923* (Bookmarks).

Harman, Chris, 1996, *Party and Class* (Bookmarks).

Harman, Chris, 2007, "Gramsci, the Prison Notebooks and Philosophy", *International Socialism 114* (spring), www.isj.org.uk/?id=306

Lenin, V I, 1968 [1920], *"Left-Wing" Communism: An Infantile Disorder* (Progressive), www.marxists.org/archive/lenin/works/1920/lwc/ch09.htm

Kuhn, Gabriel (ed), 2012, *All Power to the Councils! A Documentary History of the German Revolution* (Merlin).

Naguib, Sameh, 2013, "Egypt: the Muslim brotherhood under pressure", *Socialist Review* (February), www.socialistreview.org.uk/article.php?articlenumber=12217

Nettl, J P, 1966, *Rosa Luxemburg*, volume 2 (Oxford University Press).

Poya, Maryam (alias Elaheh Rostami Povey), 1987, "Iran 1979: Long live Revolution!...Long live Islam?" in Colin Barker (ed), *Revolutionary Rehearsals* (Bookmarks).

Riddell, John, 2011, "The Origins of the United Front Policy", *International Socialism 130* (spring), www.isj.org.uk/?id=724

Trudell, Megan, 2007, "Gramsci: The Turin Years", *International Socialism 114* (spring), www.isj.org.uk/?id=306

Thomas, Peter D, 2010, *The Gramscian Moment: Philosophy, Hegemony and Marxism* (Haymarket).

Zebrowski, Andy, 2004, "Obituary: Jacek Kuron", *Socialist Review* (July), www.socialistreview.org.uk/article.php?articlenumber=8974

Zehetmair, Sebastian, and John Rose, 2013, "Germany's Lost Bolshevik: Paul Levi Revisited", *International Socialism 137* (winter), www.isj.org.uk/?id=850

58: That "identity of theory and practice" promoted by the revolutionary party that "becomes the critical art of finding, on the one hand, the adequate theoretical form of a practice, capable of increasing its capacity to act, or, on the other hand, the adequate practical form of a theory, capable of increasing its capacity to know", a "revitalisation of a Marxism that strives to become, to quote Gramsci, an 'alternative conception of the world'"—Thomas, 2010, p383; also pp450-453.

Two in one?

Leandros Bolaris

A review of Donny Gluckstein, **A People's History of the Second World War: Resistance Versus Empire** *(Pluto, 2012), £19.99*

The Second World War (1939-1945) was the bloodiest conflict in human history. But for millions it was and still is the example of the "good war", the just war—a war that put an end to Auschwitz, a war fought not only by regular armies but also by mass movements of anti-fascist resistance.

This tradition is still alive. In a country like Greece where the neo-Nazi party of Golden Dawn's thugs got 7 percent in the last general election the memories of the anti-fascist resistance of EAM-ELAS (the National Liberation Front and its military wing) are an inspiration for the anti-racist and anti-fascist movement. Not only that but also the history of that period has become a battlefield between the "revisionist" "new history" which in various ways tries to absolve the right wing collaborators with the Nazi Occupation for their crimes, arguing that objectively nothing distinguishes "black" from "red terror", and the historians who insist on setting the record straight and defending the anti-fascist credentials of the Greek left.

But for revolutionary Marxists then and now the same war is considered an imperialist one, the product of imperialist rivalries tuned to a crescendo by the pressures of the Great Depression of the 1930s. That was Leon Trotsky's analysis and the tiny forces of revolutionaries—concentrated mainly in the ranks of the Fourth International—entered the war and the occupation in many European countries armed with it. For them the alternative to the crisis and to fascism was the proletarian revolution. And they had paid a very heavy price in blood for sticking to their internationalist and revolutionary principles.

Any Marxist interpretation of the Second World War has to integrate convincingly an explanation of the imperialist character of the conflict with the hopes, politics, struggles and views of the millions who had been caught in it. Donny Gluckstein's book, *A People's History of the Second World War*, is an attempt at such a synthesis. One can find interesting information in its pages—the chapters on Poland and Latvia, for example, or the one on India.

Gluckstein is very insistent on the fact that for the governments of the "Allies" the war had very little to do with democracy, anti-fascism, etc, and everything to do with the selfish interests and strategic calculations of the ruling classes. You don't have to search hard to find proof of that: Greece entered the war in October 1940 on the side of the British Empire as a royal-military dictatorship. Ioannis Metaxas's regime had close ideological ties with Fascist Italy and Nazi Germany –the "corporate state", a mandatory National Youth Organisation, the fascist salute in all official ceremonies, etc.

Parallel wars?

But Gluckstein goes further than that. He claims that we can see the Second World War as two parallel wars, an imperialist one and a people's war. This, he writes, "to use the language of dialectics", means that the Second World War "represented a unity of opposites".[1] He argues that:

> There is nothing startling about the idea that different sections of society had varying interests or behaved in different ways; nor that the formal declaration of war did not automatically suspend these differences. What was unique about the Second World War was that these tensions amounted to parallel wars rather than tensions within the same war.[2]

This, he argues, was in contrast to what had happened in the previous world conflagration. "The First World War did not create a people's war *alongside* an imperialist war, but its opposite—people's uprisings to *stop* an imperialist war".[3]

But here the first question arises: if in the Second World War we witness a "unity of opposites" then what was its unifying element? What was its essence? To answer, as Gluckstein does, that the war was both an imperialist conflict and a people's war is like going round in circles. The

---

1: Gluckstein, 2012, p208.
2: Gluckstein, 2012, p209.
3: Gluckstein, 2012, p210, emphasis in the original.

trouble is that through circular arguments like these we can easily end up accepting that the Second World War was an anti-fascist one: after all it was the American bombers and the Russian tanks that smashed the Nazi war machine and the vast majority of the resistance fighters considered their struggles as a contribution to that effort.

The problem with such an analysis goes deeper. Gluckstein devotes the first chapter of his book to the "The Spanish Prelude". His opening words are: "To the extent that the Second World War was truly a fight for democracy against fascism then it did not begin in 1939 in Poland but in Spain three years earlier".[4] And he concludes:

> One possible objection to the concept of the Second World War involving a people's war might be that, in propaganda terms, all modern imperialist wars are presented as "progressive" and "democratic". The Spanish experience shows that the current of people's war that manifested itself during the Second World War had independent origins, and indeed developed in the face of antipathy from Allied governments.[5]

Well, no one disagrees that the motives of the people who fought the Nazis had "independent" origins (and that, of course, applies to a lot of people who fought *for* the Nazis, as Gluckstein makes very clear in the chapter on Latvia, for example). But if we follow his logic to the end, the beginning of the people's war is not in Spain 1936 but in Austria 1934, when the Social Democratic Schutzbund fought the right wing Heimwehr and the federal army in the working class suburbs of Vienna and Linz. And why stop there? We can go further back and hear the first shots of "people's war" fired by the workers' detachments of Arditti del Popolo in Parma in 1922. Furthermore, the "Spanish experience" tell us something very different: that there was an alternative both to fascism and war and that was the workers' revolution. In that sense, the defeat of the Spanish Revolution was more like an "epilogue" than a "prelude".

Reluctant warmongers?

Reading the book sometimes you get the impression that the "democratic" ruling classes didn't really want to fight the war. This is what Gluckstein says about the French ruling class, following a long line of left wing historians and commentators. The argument goes like this: France's rulers

---

4:   Gluckstein, 2012, p15.
5:   Gluckstein, 2012, p21.

were more afraid of the Popular Front than the Germans. The fact that the Popular Front was a corpse long before September 1939 and that the workers' movement had been crushed—the epilogue was the defeat of the General Strike of 30 November 1938—contradicts these explanations.

Not that the French ruling class entered the war with optimism and the will to victory. They did not. They were afraid that a prolonged blood-bath would result in further deterioration of France's status as a great power. That's why the French prime minister, Édouard Daladier, signed the Munich Agreement in September 1938, at the same time as his government started the final attack on the working class gains from the Popular Front period.

The same goes for the "conservative mindset of French generals". Yes, their mindset was very conservative, but the assumption that they thought "in terms of First World War trenches rather than the latest technology [and that] Hitler's forces relied on planes and armoured columns that overcame these obstacles with terrifying ease" is simply wrong.[6] Actually the French generals were planning to wage the decisive battles not in the trenches of northern France but on the open terrain of Belgium and Holland. That's why they had concentrated near the borders all their elite, motorised and tank formations. The Maginot Line was never intended as the main front of the war but as a formidable barrier that could allow the employment of forces in other sectors. And, of course, the Germans' attack when it came did not "overcome these obstacles with terrifying ease" because in the Sedan sector there were very few of them.[7] It was not a Blitzkrieg in the strict sense but the implementation of the classic Napoleonic principle of concentrating overwhelming force at the weakest point of the enemy's order of battle.

French imperialism lost the "Battle of France" and only then did the rulers of its state decide that the best course was to embark on the path of collaboration. The reasons for this defeat are manifold but not the ones Gluckstein implies. As for the workers, their mood in the months leading to the war was one of disorientation, apathy and cynicism, not eagerness to fight a "people's war". Of course, they hated the fascists but they were not willing to go to war to be massacred—for what? Gluckstein quotes the rejection of the Munich Agreement by the French Communist Party (PCF) approvingly, and then goes on to condemn its—no doubt—despicable welcoming of "German imperialism" as a "temporary ally", as if the PCF stance in 1938 was somehow the "good one".[8]

6:    Gluckstein, 2012, p85.
7:    For these details and a very balanced discussion of this subject see Jackson, 2004.
8:    Gluckstein, 2012, p87.

We have to look to Trotsky to find the basis on which we can build our explanation of the defeat:

> The regime of the senile Marshal Pétain represents a senile form of Bonapartism of the epoch of imperialist decline. But this regime too proved possible only after the prolonged radicalisation of the French working class, which led to the explosion of June 1936, had failed to find a revolutionary way out. The Second and Third Internationals, the reactionary charlatanism of the "People's Fronts" deceived and demoralised the working class. After five years of propaganda in favor of an alliance of democracies and of collective security, after Stalin's sudden passage into Hitler's camp, the French working class proved caught unaware. The war provoked a terrible disorientation and the mood of passive defeatism, or to put it more correctly, the indifferentism of an impasse. From this web of circumstances arose first the unprecedented military catastrophe and then the despicable Pétain regime.[9]

A war for global domination

And there's a second question. Gluckstein seems to imply that anti-fascism "from below" had been the driving force of the people's war. That would be a valid point if only the European and to a lesser extent the North American working class movement were involved. As Trotsky wrote shortly before his murder, referring to the US workers, "They bear a sentimental hatred against Hitler mixed with confused class sentiments. They have a hatred against the victorious brigands".[10] But what about the millions who took part in the Quit India movement? Why is there nothing in the book about the complexities of the Chinese Revolution in the 1940s? So why have just two parallel wars? Ernest Mandel has argued that we must grasp the Second World War as a combination of five separate conflicts, one "unjust" and four "just" ones: the unjust being the inter-imperialist war for world domination, and the rest the defensive war of the USSR, the struggle of the Chinese people, the national liberation wars in Asia and the same struggles in occupied Europe.[11] It was a weak argument, but at least had the merit of pointing to the complexity of the conflict. Gluckstein manages to avoid the thorny questions of the USSR and China by giving us a more simplified version of Mandel's account.

9: Trotsky, 1973a, p498.
10: Trotsky, 1973b, p302.
11: Mandel, 2011, p45. For a critique of Mandel's book, see Hallas, 1987.

Claudio Pavone's[12] concept of the Italian Resistance as combining a patriotic war (against German invaders), a civil war (against the Fascist regime) and a class war (against the industrialists and landowners who had supported fascism for two decades) can be very fruitful in exploring the "contradictory consciousness" of the Resistance fighters and the complex ways that different elements in the consciousness of the workers can be combined during a revolutionary challenge to the existing social order. But whatever the ideas and feelings of those fighting in the Resistance, the reality of the imperialist war imposed itself in a very brutal way when the Allies announced in November 1944 that there would be no new operations in the north of Italy for the coming months and that the partisans should stand down and go home. The British and American generals had spoken and the partisans had to suffer the consequences as the Germans went onto the offensive against them.

Here's another example: Marseilles, 25 May 1944. A demonstration by women protesting against food shortages triggers a general strike. The strike collapsed two days later after an Allied bombing raid that left 1,700 dead behind it. When two months later the Communist resistance organisations issued a call for a general strike on 14 July, the city remained silent.[13] This raid did not shake the conviction of the Resistance or the city's population in the justice of the Allied cause. But it did put a heavy obstacle in the way of the "people's war".

Gluckstein claims: "For its part the people's war transmuted into a successful, sometimes violent, struggle for decolonisation plus a movement for the establishment of welfare states and decent living conditions".[14] A successful movement, it must be added:

> It might seem that French imperialism had vanquished the people's war completely, yet the impact of the latter was long-lasting. In the words of a resister, Stephane Hessel, the *CNR [National Council of Resistance] programme of 1944 "set the principles and values that formed the basis of our modern democracy"* with its wide ranging reforms in the economy, welfare and education. In 2010 Hessel suggested that despite the passage of 65 years it required the current economic crisis to threaten the final vestiges of this heritage. *This statement is true for most of Western Europe, where a post-war "social-democratic consensus" prevailed after 1945*, and is today being fought over once more.[15]

12: The account of Pavone's views is based on Behan, 2009, pp56-60.

13: Jackson, 2001, p558.

14: Gluckstein, 2012, 214.

15: Gluckstein, 2012, p96: emphasis added.

Algerians may have a different opinion about the principles on which the Fourth Republic had been based after the war. Stephane Hessel may have an honourable record as a champion of many just causes—Palestinians in Gaza, for example[16]—but for any socialist to accept that the French state of today is somehow the thing that the Communist immigrant workers in the ranks of FTP-MOI [Francs-tireurs et partisans—main-d'œuvre immigrée], the famous urban guerilla unit,[17] fought and died for, is hubris and opens the back door to ideological capitulation.[18]

As for the today legendary but always ill-defined "social democratic consensus" of the long post-war boom, the explanation lies in very different factors than the influence of the "people's war". Social "peace" (a low level of class struggle) and political apathy are not the same as "consensus". The working classes in France and Italy had to endure decades of erosion of their trade union strength, living standards that always lagged behind the economic growth and the political isolation of the Communist parties before having the chance—literally—to strike back in 1968 and after and win some important and tangible gains.

There can be no doubt that the Italian workers in the north in 1943-45 fighting their war against the Fascist Italian Social Republic and the Wehrmacht, the activists and fighters in the National Liberation Front and its armed wing (EAM-ELAS) in occupied Greece, Tito's partisans, a huge portion of French resisters (but not all) had a very different motivation from Churchill, Roosevelt or Stalin—not only motivation but also goals. For many, perhaps the majority, of the Italian workers in the north of Italy the prize of their struggle would be a Red Italy, one with workers in power (that applied to many activists of the Italian Communist Party [PCI]—the party leadership had to fight hard to defuse all these "ultra-left" notions). For EAM-ELAS fighters the goal was "Laokratia" ("people's power"), a regime radically different from the pre-war Greece of stark class inequalities and state oppression. And this does not apply only to wartime Europe. The Huks[19] in

16: But it would be useful to remember that Hessel had been a Gaullist agent of BCRA—the Free French intelligence service.

17: FTP was the armed wing of the Communist Resistance. MOI was the immigrant workers' organisation of the Communist trade union federation CGT-U after the early 1920s.

18: And allows for some very bizarre, to say the least, formulations. The title of the chapter on France is "Imperial Glory versus Resistance Ideology". Is that so simple? Was the "Glory of France" or of the republic something separate from its imperial glory, its colonies and the "civilising" influence of the French culture on them? The Free French were a part of the Resistance and the Gaullist ideological baggage was full of praise for "imperial glory".

19: Hukbalahap—*Hukbo ng Bayan Laban sa Hapon* (People's Army Against Japan), the armed wing of the Communist Party of the Philippines. It is strange that in Gluckstein's book there's not

Philippines fought bravely against the Japanese occupation but also against "their" landlords and then, from 1946 to 1956, the American-backed regime.

But this is not the end of the story. First, the notion of a parallel war is very misleading. The French Resistance acted under the orders of the Allied High Command just before and during the Normandy landings in June 1944. Afterwards its armed forces, the FFI, were incorporated into the regular French Army under the command of officers many of who had nothing to do with the Resistance, even the Gaullist one. ELAS put itself voluntarily under the command of the British Army HQ in the Middle East.

It was not just a "marriage of convenience". For the hegemonic political forces in all these movements, the Communist parties, the "military-technical" cooperation—subordination is more fitting—had been the expression of a political concept; namely that of the "anti-fascist", "patriotic" war. And that concept had a "past" also; the Popular Fronts of class collaboration in the 1930s. The implementation of the Popular Front strategy in Spain, for example, meant the crushing of the revolution and the eventual victory of Franco.

The story of the heroic Italian Resistance is not only the strikes and the partisan struggle, the GAPisti and the insurrection, but also the Svolta di Salerno of April 1944 and the Rome Protocols of December 1944. The "turning point of Salerno" was the decision of PCI to enter the Badoglio government under King Emmanuel II after the return to Italy from Moscow of Palmiro Togliatti, general secretary of the party. The Rome Protocols put the partisans in the North under the command of the Allied HQ and committed the Resistance there to surrender all power to the Allies after the liberation. The story of EAM-ELAS was not just the "People's Power" in the Greek mountains, the impressive general strikes and urban guerrilla warfare in Athens's working class suburbs, but also the "Lebanon" and "Caserta" agreements, in May and September 1944 respectively. After a three day conference in Lebanon the EAM decided to enter the Greek government in exile as a minor partner with only four ministers and its delegation renounced the movement of the soldiers and sailors in the Greek armed forces in Egypt as a criminal act. In the other conference ELAS accepted a British general as a commander of all Greek forces and committed itself not to enter Athens. It was not only the "Red

---

even a mention of the Huks and instead Indonesia gets a full chapter, despite the fact that the national liberation struggle there started after the Japanese defeat and that almost all of its leaders, Sukharno included, had assumed a very ambivalent stance towards Japanese rule.

December" of 1944 in Athens, when ELAS fought the British army, but also the treacherous Varkiza Agreement of February 1945—the surrender of its arms and its disbandment, which laid the basis for defeat at the hands of the royalists and their British and American backers in the Civil War of 1946-9. True, the decisions for all these compromises and sell-outs had been taken by the Communist leaderships and thousands of militants in the base were instinctively critical and wanted to "go further". But where and how? The politics of patriotic anti-fascist war put a limit, blocked and fragmented all the questioning, the objections, even the revolts of the rank and file.

The tragedy of the Greek revolution

There are two European countries where the Resistance clashed militarily with the Allies; Poland and Greece.[20] The Greek case is unique because in contrast to Poland the movement there was not just left-leaning but almost totally dominated by the Communist Party of Greece (KKE). Gluckstein is wrong when he writes that EAM-ELAS had been "less directly tied to communism than the Yugoslav partisans".[21] This point is important because many people have tried to explain the radicalism of the Greek Resistance by claiming either that the Communists did not control it or they were deeply split themselves.

When the Axis forces occupied Greece in the spring of 1941 there were around 2,000 Communists in jails and exile islands and around 200 free, organised in small and mutually hostile groups. In December 1942, at the time of the Second National Conference of the party, the "reconstruction" was complete, and its members were somewhere from 15,000 to 20,000. Then came a spectacular growth and by October 1944 party membership stood at 412,000. Also, there was a qualitative difference from Tito's movement. Gluckstein quotes Milovan Djilas saying that when the partisans liberated Belgrade there was not even one party member in the city. On the eve of the liberation of Athens the KKE had 35,000 members in Athens, a city of around 600,000 inhabitants, and the local edition of the party's paper had a print run of 40,000 to 60,000 copies.[22] EAM in Greece

20: In Belgium the military confrontation had been averted in the last minute in November 1944. See Kolko, 1990, pp97-98.
21: Gluckstein, 2012, p41.
22: D Eudes's numbers are just wrong as is much of his account—Eudes, 1972. My numbers come from Hadzis, 1977, pp52-57, KKE, 2005, pp461-462, and Bartziotas, 1983, pp263-264. Thanasis Hadzis was a candidate member of the party's Central Committee and EAM's general secretary from 1941 to 1944. Vasilis Bartziotas was a member of the politbureau of the party and secretary of its Athens organisation from 1943 to 1946.

included some tiny socialist and left groupings and various liberal politicians or professors but no one had any doubt that the "Party" was in command.

According to Hagen Fleischer the wing of the Agrarian Party that joined EAM by 1942 had become "a crypto-communist organisation". It was a long process that began in 1935.[23] This applies to ELAS as well. Its most famous chief Aris Velouchiotis (his real name was Thanasis Claras) was not "nominally a communist".[24] He had been a party member since the middle 1920s, *Rizospastis* (the party daily) journalist and member of the illegal apparatus of the party. He was "suspect" because of his conduct during his imprisonment under Metaxas's dictatorship but during the occupation years he had been a loyal party member, who "took to the mountains" on the party's orders. Stephanos Sarafis, the ELAS chief of staff, was an ex-Liberal colonel but joined the party in 1944 and remained a member till his death in 1957 (in 1951 he became a candidate member of the party's Central Committee). All military commanders and "kapetanioi" of every big ELAS unit were party members by the end of the occupation.[25]

So the question is why such a tightly controlled movement came to fight the British Army in December 1944 for 33 days in Athens's streets.

This conflict was not predetermined. The British government tried to co-opt EAM-ELAS again and again in various ways. They wanted Greece in their sphere of influence, of course, and the king restored to the throne, but there was nothing in principle to rule out the participation of EAM and KKE. Actually EAM and KKE went out of their way to cooperate, as did the PCF or PCI. Gluckstein refers to PEEA, the Political Committee of National Liberation. Its inauguration in March 1944 was intended as a lever to press the British and the royal government in exile in Cairo to accept EAM's participation on equal terms.[26] But for the base of

---

23: Fleischer, 1995, p146. After its 6th Congress in December 1935 KKE decided to send all party members in the countryside to join the AKE (Agrarian Party) and dissolve the party cells in the villages.

24: Gluckstein, 2012, p40.

25: There are many more factual mistakes in Gluckstein's account. For example, Metaxas was not a general but the prime minister when he and the king imposed their dictatorship on 4 August 1936. KKE leader Nicolaos Zachariadis did not formulate the "theory of the two poles" (a Greece balancing between Britain and Russia but recognising the "legitimate" interests of the British Empire) during the occupation but in June 1945 in the 12th Plenum of the party's Central Committee. General Alexander's talk about the "Rotterdamisation" of Athens was actually an explanation of the slow progress of operations during the December Days, not a part of "Operation Manna". And of course, the British Army did not fire 2,500 shells and cause 13,700 civilian casualties in the first 24 hours of the conflict.

26: This explanation is buried in the notes of the chapter on Greece—Gluckstein, 2012, p230.

the movement, and specially the left organisations of soldiers and sailors in the Greek army in Egypt and Palestine, that was the signal that at last "our power has been established" with the "Government of the Mountains".

There were not just two protagonists in the Greek drama but three: the ruling class and the imperialists, the movement, and the movement's leadership. For the ruling class the problem was that its state had collapsed. That was the case neither in France nor in Italy. There wasn't any state institution which hadn't been delegitimised in the eyes of the majority of the Greek population.

The movement's centre on the other hand was not just the radical-ised peasants—although they were a very important element of it—but a radicalised and very well organised working class. And the third protag-onist, the leadership, had the difficult task of all reformist leaderships in analogous situations in history—to try to balance between the two oppo-site pressures; to try to defuse the radical edge of its base using it at the same time as a bargaining chip. A first sign of how things could get out of control was the Greek army's mutiny in Egypt in 1944. And in the weeks after liberation in October, in the volcanic political and social atmosphere of Athens, the leadership lost control again. It was for a brief moment but enough to trigger the armed conflict and the "Red December".

The movement was strong enough to force this confrontation but too weak politically to take it to the end. And part of this political weakness had been the idea that the war was an anti-fascist/democratic struggle of "our great Allies". There's a small incident in the first days of the "December events" that illustrates this. William Hardy McNeil, second military attaché of the US Embassy in Athens, describes how:

> In the grey light of dawn on 6 December ELAS made its attack. Men clad in civilian clothes, and equipped only with rifles, made their way through the Royal Gardens, climbed the iron fence and started across Kifissia Boulevard, a broad avenue along which lay the Foreign Office, the Ministry of War and other key government buildings. The attack failed. One reason was that it was delivered half-heartedly, and by relatively few men. A more important reason was that when the attackers arrived near their goal they were thrown into confusion by the unexpected presence of British soldiers. Perhaps General Scobie [British commander in Greece] had knowledge of the leftists' intentions. Whether he did or not, a few hours before the attack was started, British sentries were posted in front of all the principal government buildings. ELAS had no instructions to attack the British, and many of its members had no wish to do so. *Consequently, when in the early morning light they saw the figure*

of a lone British soldier in front of each building, they did not know what to do. Some of the more reckless spirits pressed on, regardless; others hung back. The attack was consequently weak and easily repulsed by the police detachments which had been assigned to guard the buildings. The British sentries joined in the battle. Thus for the first time ELAS and British soldiers fired at one another, and began open warfare. [27]

That was the tragedy of the Greek revolution, to use the famous words of Saint-Just: "Whoever half-makes a revolution digs his own grave". This is what happened to Aris Velouchiotis. As a loyal party member he kept his doubts and disagreements to himself during the occupation; he sent two letters to the party Central Committee but nothing further. Then on November 1944 he organised a conference of "kapetanioi" of ELAS's divisions in the town of Lamia. He proposed to move their units closer to Athens despite the Caserta Agreement (under its provisions ELAS heavily armed "mountain" divisions should remain well outside Athens). The conference ended up in confusion when one of the "kapetanioi" asked: "Is the party politbureau informed?"

Later Aris signed the order for ELAS's demobilisation after the Varkiza Agreement but he didn't obey the party's order to go to Athens and become president of the ELAS Veterans' Association. He tried to go to Albania, to "talk to the comrades there". When he found out that the party was not helping him to do this he tried to organise a "New ELAS". But not to fight. He put all his hope in the return of Zachariadis, the KKE "leader" (*archigos*—that had been his official title since the 1930s). Zachariadis returned and immediately denounced the "adventurer", "déclassé" and "suspect" Velouchiotis. Denied any help by party organisations, Velouchiotis committed suicide on 16 June 1945 when he and his small group got surrounded by units of the National Guard.

Gluckstein writes: "What happened in Greece was not a difference of opinion within a single world conflict. It was two types of war clashing to such an extent that bombs, tanks, torture, rape and prisons decided the outcome",[28] and that "the opposition between the two wars here was total and violent".[29] But this again is a description, not an explanation. For that we have to use a different tool of analysis from the concept of the parallel wars. And that is the concept of an imperialist war triggering vast social

---

27: McNeill, 1947, pp145-146.
28: Gluckstein, 2012, p54.
29: Gluckstein, 2012, p213.

upheavals, revolts and revolutions. But nowhere, and that is a real difference from the "Great War", did these revolts end up in a successful workers' revolution as in Russia or in a straightforward challenge to the capitalist social order as in Germany, Italy and Hungary, and nowhere did the radicalisation crystallise into new more or less mass revolutionary parties.

Conclusion

There's no doubt that the Second World War had many differences from the previous one. The ideological factor, the battle against fascism, is not the only one. In contrast to the Great War, for example, it was a really global conflict. Its battles and campaigns raged from the Arctic Circle to the jungles of Burma and from Dakar to the Solomon Islands.[30] Not only the fighting but also its consequences had a really global and devastating character. As Lizzie Collingham writes, "Most westerners have never heard of the famine in the Vietnamese region of Tonkin in 1943-44 which probably killed more peasants than all the years of war which followed".[31]

Both world wars were products of capitalism in its imperialist stage. But the First World War came after a period of capitalist expansion while the Second World War came after the Great Depression of the 1930s, the worst crisis in the history of capitalism.

There are other differences. When the First World War broke out there was a spontaneous wave of enthusiasm in all countries. Huge crowds went to the streets to express their support to "their" governments, expecting a short and glorious campaign. There was no enthusiasm when the war finally came in September 1939. People knew what to expect; death, misery and destruction on a massive scale.

All these bring us back to the old question of the relationship of capitalism, crisis, fascism and war. Gluckstein has written a valuable book about the relationship between the Nazis and capitalism in Germany that every socialist and anti-fascist should read. One of the many strengths of Gluckstein's argument in that book is that it examines German society from "above" and from "below" in order to prove that "Nazism was based on class forces operating within a capitalist framework" but also that it was "the product of a specific combination of circumstances".[32] But in his last book he fails to do such a thing. It is more a thesis about the viability of the concept of

---

30: A J P Taylor in *The Origins of the Second World War* claims that there were two wars, the one in the West and the other in the East "overlapping in time"—Taylor, 1991, Kindle locations 612-616.

31: Collingham, 2011, Kindle locations 181-182.

32: Gluckstein, 1999, p2; p221.

the "people's war" and less a "people's history" of the war. Like the famous "percentage agreement" between Churchill and Stalin, Gluckstein compiles a catalogue in which Greece is 100 percent people's war, Yugoslavia is 90 percent to 10 percent imperialist war, France is 60 percent to 40 percent, Latvia is 100 percent imperialist war, etc. This is not convincing.

The link between the two world wars, especially the second, and capitalism has never been self-evident. But establishing it, not along general lines, but in detailed studies and works of broad synthesis, is necessary for revolutionary Marxists today. In this regard, Trotsky's ideas and analysis are always a good place to start.

References

Bartziotas, Vasilis, 1983, *Ethniki Andistasi kai Dekemvris 1944* [National Resistance and December 1944] (Sychroni Epohi).

Behan, Tom, 2009, *The Italian Resistance, Fascists, Guerrillas and the Allies* (Pluto Press).

Collingham, Lizzie, 2011, *The Taste of War: World War Two and the Battle for Food* (Penguin, Kindle Edition).

Eudes, Dominique, 1972, *The Kapetanios: Partisans and Civil War in Greece, 1943-1949* (Monthly Review Press).

Fleischer, Hagen, 1995, *Stemma kai Swastika, 1* [Crown and Swastika, 1] (Papazisis).

Gluckstein, Donny, 1999, *The Nazis, Capitalism and the Working Class* (Bookmarks).

Gluckstein, Donny, 2012, *A People's History of the Second World War: Resistance versus Empire* (Pluto).

Hadzis, Thanasis, 1977, *I Nikifora Epanastasi pou Hathike Protos Tomos* [A Victorious, Lost Revolution First Volume] (Papazisis).

Jackson, Julian, 2001, *France: The Dark Years (1940-1944)*, (Oxford University Press).

Jackson, Julian, 2004, *The Fall of France* (Oxford University Press).

KKE, Central Committee, 2005, *Dokimio Istorias tou KKE, Protos Tomos, 1918-1949* [Essay on the History of KKE, First Volume, 1918-1949] (Sychroni Epohi).

Kolko, Gabriel, 1990, *The Politics of War* (Pantheon).

Mandel, Ernest, 2011 [1986], *The Meaning of the Second World War* (Verso).

McNeill, William Hardy, 1947, *The Greek Dilemma: War and Aftermath* [Golancz].

Taylor, A J P, 1991, *The Origins of the Second World War* (Penguin, Kindle Edition).

Trotsky, Leon, 1973a [1940], "Bonapartism, Fascism and War", in *Writings 1939-40* (Pathfinder), www.marxists.org/archive/trotsky/1940/08/last-article.htm

Trotsky, Leon, 1973b, [1940]," Discussions with Trotsky", in *Writings 1939-40* (Pathfinder).

Interview: Agriculture, class and capitalism

Henry Bernstein, a professor at the School of Oriental and African Studies (SOAS) in London, has for decades been at the forefront of research into the class structure and political economy of agriculture. He spoke to Joseph Choonara about his work.

Can you start by telling me a little about your background and the formative experiences that shaped your approach to the study of agrarian questions?
I think the most important factor was the new development of agrarian political economy in the 1970s, which was spearheaded by Terry Byres at SOAS. There was a quite extraordinary Peasants Seminar, convened by Terry at the University of London, which ran from 1972 to 1989. All the top Marxists of the day spoke at it, along with many younger people—it was really cross-generational. It was also part of an international intellectual effort of the left.

This helped to rediscover and reinvent a political economy that could be applied to agrarian change. It was stimulated in part by developments in countries in Asia and Africa, partly too by what were regarded as peasant wars in Vietnam and some parts of Africa. It considered both the changes taking place in these societies and the relationship of peasants to revolutionary politics.

There was also great curiosity about China, because many on the European left looked to the communes in China as an alternative to both capitalist development in the countryside and Soviet-style Stalinist collectivisation.[1] Well, of course, that disappeared in time, but it was very much of the moment.

I think that for Marxists the single most important component in the revival of agrarian political economy was the rediscovery of Lenin's *The Development of Capitalism in Russia*.[2] Marx's own writings were important, but Marx's comments on agricultural issues are fairly scattered. In addition, in the 1970s and 1980s we had the first full English translation of Karl Kautsky on *The Agrarian Question*—earlier Jairus Banaji had done a translation of extracts.[3] Another important work was the English translation of a book by Alexander Chayanov, the great Russian agricultural economist, and there was a lot of stuff from the heroic period of the Russian Revolution.[4] All of that fed into the new developments in agrarian political economy.

And that led to the birth of the Journal of Peasant Studies?
It did. The journal came out of the seminars that Byres and others organised. In terms of my own biography, I came back from four years in Tanzania in 1978, during which time I had been working on agrarian questions. So I already knew Terry Byres and I connected very much with what he was doing.

Subsequently there was another journal, the Journal of Agrarian Change, which you have also been associated with. Is it fair to say that this journal carried on the tradition?
Absolutely. For various reasons, we continued and updated the mission of the *Journal of Peasant Studies*. Relations between the two journals are comradely. I would say that *Agrarian Change* is today more centred on political economy and *Peasant Studies* is more focused on political sociology, rural politics and so on.

1:    Agricultural communes, consisting of thousands of households, were formed in China at Mao Zedong's initiative. They were envisaged as a part of Mao's Great Leap Forward that began in 1958, which was supposed to lead to rapid industrialisation, allowing Chinese output to overtake that of Western countries such as Britain. The "leap" in fact ended in disaster, with millions dying in the resulting famines.
2:    This book, published in 1899, helped establish Lenin's reputation as a Marxist theoretician. It can be found on the Marxist Internet Archive and is available in various English translations, such as Lenin, 1987.
3:    This work by Kautsky, then the leading German Marxist theoretician, was also originally published in 1899. The first full English translation, in two volumes, was by Zwan publications in 1987—Kautsky, 1987.
4:    Chayanov was a Russian economist, executed under Stalin in 1937. His major work, *Theory of Peasant Economy*, was first published in German in 1923 and Russian in 1925. The earliest English translation was in 1966. It has been reprinted by Oxford University Press—Chayanov, 1987.

One of your arguments is that the whole concept of a "peasantry" can be misleading. It can encourage us to think of them in the way we would think of feudal peasants. You talk instead about small-scale commodity producers who are integrated into the circuits of capitalism.

That is one of the key questions. I think it is misleading to talk about peasants in today's world because our historical image of peasants was formed in the principal grain-growing areas of pre-capitalist civilisations, especially in Europe and Russia, but also in India, China and elsewhere. The term "peasant" is usually used today in association with populist positions.

Agrarian populism declares the virtues of peasant or family farmers and identifies with their struggles against those who threaten their reproduction and wellbeing, from merchants and banks, capitalist landed property, agrarian capital and agribusiness, to projects of state-led "national development" centered on industrialisation, in all their capitalist, nationalist and socialist variants, of which the Soviet collectivisation of agriculture in the 1930s was the most potent landmark. Modern versions of populism draw on the legacy of Chayanov, himself a victim of Stalin's purges, whose vision of a future "peasant utopia" combined household farming with cooperation to achieve economies of scale. Agrarian populism today champions small farmers, including their ostensible ecological virtues, against large-scale mechanised capitalist agriculture and global agribusiness. Perhaps the best-known agrarian populist movement today is Via Campesina, which means "the peasant way".

The agricultural petty commodity producer within capitalism is a social category that was formed first in transitions to capitalism in Europe and North America, then under colonialism, followed by independence in Asia and Africa, which obviously came earlier in Latin America. My own position is that small farmers today have to be seen and studied as petty commodity producers.

However, the rural masses in many countries, not least India, where they are estimated to be over 60 percent of the population, are not in fact reproducing themselves primarily through their own farming, because they are unable to do so. They are members of classes of labour; they reproduce themselves primarily through wage labour, with an element of subsistence coming from their own farming. So they are not petty commodity producers in the full sense.

Petty commodity producers in the Global South, allowing for all the differences in farming environments and social conditions, are not so different a category from so-called family farmers in the North. They are all in effect small capitalist enterprises, except that those in the North tend to have higher levels of investment and higher labour productivity.

Marx talks about the petty bourgeois under capitalism, for instance the small shop-keeper, being cut into two people: one a capitalist and the other a worker. Effectively they exploit themselves, and sometimes their family unit too. Those living on the land are in a similar position, with the added complication that they can sometimes be divided into three people, a landlord as well as a capitalist and worker if they own their own land. So this social category is obviously quite a complex one.

Indeed, in my little book *Class Dynamics of Agrarian Change* I use Lenin's classic schema for the differentiation of the peasantry.[5] In *Capital* Marx clearly had an enclosure model based on what had happened in England when he discusses primitive accumulation. One of the interesting things about Lenin, whose writings didn't so much contradict as complement Marx's, was that he argued that class differentiation of the peasantry could be another model through which capitalist agriculture could form, rather than enclosure of land by aristocratic landowners, who then, according to Marx, rented it out to capitalist farmers.

In Lenin's scheme, rich peasants are those who accumulate enough land that they have to start employing wage labour beyond their household and they become capitalist farmers. The middle peasantry are those who don't achieve this but who succeed more or less in simple reproduction as petty commodity producers. And the poor peasantry are those who become classes of labour. They become proletarianised in effect, even if not completely.

Marx is sometimes said to have predicted the disappearance of the peasantry, who are supposed to be squeezed out by capital and labour. It's a bit of a myth. Nonetheless many people would expect the peasantry to be eliminated by capitalist development.
There's the famous passage from Lenin's *Development of Capitalism in Russia* where he expresses scepticism about the stereotype that capitalism always requires the free landless labourer. That is confirmed by what we find across large areas of the Global South today.

There has been a big debate within Marxism about why capitalist development has not eliminated small-scale farming, and various reasons have been given. One is that, all else being equal, it can be more difficult for capital to reap the same rate of profit, and to continue to do so through expanded reproduction, in farming compared to industry. In industry you can introduce technologies that raise the productivity of labour virtually indefinitely; it's much more difficult in farming.

It is true of periods in the past and it is certainly true today with glo-balisation that big capital in agriculture is not primarily found in farming

---

5:   Bernstein, 2010. This short book forms an excellent introduction to Bernstein's work.

but in seed companies, chemical companies, machinery companies, and so on, upstream of farming; and also downstream of farming in corporate food processing, distribution and retail.

Another reason, connected to the first one, was put forward by Susan Mann and James Dickinson in the 1970s, in a famous article in the *Journal of Peasant Studies*, about the obstacles to capital in farming.[6] One obstacle is that you have to allow for the natural material processes involved in the maturation of crops and livestock. Capital during that time is tied up, and capital can only appropriate surplus value from labour during the production process. In agriculture a gap, that may be bigger or smaller, opens up between labour time and production time, while crops are ripening or livestock is maturing.

One of the things that modern capitalist technology is trying to do in relation to this is to develop crops that mature ever quicker and livestock pumped full of antibiotics and growth hormones. So capitalism aims to reduce the duration and uncertainty of natural processes.

A third argument, which becomes clear if you abolish the term peasant as anachronistic and accept that we still have many petty commodity producers in farming, is that, some political economists would say, these producers can produce commodities more cheaply. That is because they do not have to pay the various costs associated with the capitalist control and supervision of the labour process. If it is household labour that is used, they have other means of disciplining the workforce.

One more populist argument is that peasants persist because they resist the encroachment of capitalism and the market; they strive for autonomy. I think that's a rather romantic argument. Nonetheless, sometimes there are political struggles against the establishment of large-scale capitalist production, for instance in parts of India where there are densely populated farming areas. Here there might be political barriers to dispossessing people on the land as happened historically in England before and during the time of the Enclosure Acts and even more dramatically in the Soviet Union in the 1930s.

This is beginning to be a big issue in relation to China. China and India still have the largest preponderance of small farmers, and, while it is possible they are being hammered in other ways, they are not generally being dispossessed en masse. When they are displaced it is usually to make the way for infrastructure projects, industry or mining, not to replace them with large-scale farmers.

So you have the resilience of small-scale producers, but most of them are linked to

---

6:    Mann and Dickinson, 1978.

heavily commoditised markets in inputs and outputs.
Yes, because it is more profitable for capital to concentrate upstream or down-stream from farming, and that's where some of the new profit frontiers of capital are: genetically modified organisms (GMOs), biofuels, and so on. That's another thing that's common to the Global North and the South.

One of the factors in the generally poor performance of African agriculture since structural adjustment is that fertiliser use has gone right down.[7] Previously it was subsidised by government rural development pro-grammes; now it's left to the market.

I want to come back to the contemporary developments in agriculture. But when people hear about agrarian change they often think about the rise in productivity during what's called the Green Revolution roughly from the 1960s.
First, it is important not to confuse rising labour productivity with rising productivity of land or rising yields. One of the classic populist arguments is that yields are generally higher in small-scale agriculture, at the cost, Marxists point out, of massive drudgery and excessive hard work because labour productivity is much lower.

One reason it was called the Green Revolution was that it was seen as an alternative to "red revolution", which was very much on the minds of the Americans because of Vietnam. But I think the Green Revolution was in some ways quite impressive, for example, allowing India to become self-sufficient in basic food grain production.

The idea was that it was scale neutral. If you have miracle seeds and fertiliser, plus water, then the idea was that it would have the same impact (growth potential) on a small farm as a big one, but there's a lot of evidence that in India it was bigger farmers who benefited the most.

It has since been heavily criticised, and it seems that the rate of yield increases cannot be sustained in the long term using those technologies. That is perhaps why there has been a shift towards GMOs, because bio-chemically they are different entities. The Green Revolution revolved around high yielding varieties that were bred as hybrids; GMOs are geneti-cally modified in laboratories.

To what extent did the Green Revolution extend beyond India?

7:    Structural adjustment refers to the policies imposed on the Global South by institutions such as the International Monetary Fund and World Bank, especially in the 1980s and 1990s. They involved sweeping privatisation, the removal of state subsidies and the liberalisation of trade and capital flows.

You really need to distinguish it by grains. There are the big three global food grains: wheat, rice and maize. There were varying levels of success among the three grains in particular parts of India. In some regions like the Punjab, where you have good irrigation, both wheat and rice did very well, but that wasn't necessarily true in other areas. There was success with rice in the Philippines and maize in Latin America. In this period maize became internationalised following the US pattern where it is grown mainly as an animal feed crop.

In fact, the original Green Revolution was in the US. There's a wonderful Marxist account by Jack Kloppenburg of how big seed corporations appropriated the results of public research into improved seeds in the US, which led directly to the developments in the Global South, driven largely by the Rockefeller Foundation.[8] There is again a connection between the North and South.

There have been other success stories. Africa has largely been left out, with the partial exception of South Africa and big farms in Zimbabwe, which were of course big settler farms comparable to those in North America or Argentina. According to recent figures I've seen, commercial farming in South Africa, which is still in everything but name white farming, has the highest rate of take-up of GM seeds in the world. There they have retained quite high levels of yields.

But Africa generally presented real material obstacles to the Green Revolution, because you have such a wide variety of microenvironments in sub-Saharan Africa, and very vulnerable farming ecologies in terms of rain and soils. The hopes that were invested at the time of the Green Revolution have not materialised. And of course, the social conditions of many farmers in Africa are completely screwed up by the impact of structural adjustment programmes.

Since the Green Revolution there have been further big changes in agriculture. One obvious change is the level of trade in agricultural products. Farming has been increasingly tightly bound up with global capitalism. One consequence seems to have been to make food security in regions of the Global South extremely fragile.

There are a number of different stories. Some of these loom large in agit-prop literature, the positions of the green non-governmental organisations, and so on, so each of them has to be looked at more carefully.

But there is undoubtedly growing corporate concentration and power in agricultural inputs and technologies, and in processing, the supermarkets, the fast food industry and so on. Something that is very topical is the effort

---

8:   Kloppenburg, 2004.

being made by the big supermarket chains to break into India. There is quite a lot of resistance for various reasons from Indian capital.

Some of the best land in some African countries has been given over to contract farming for Northern supermarkets, which use air freighting of so-called exotic fruit and vegetables so you can buy them all year round in North America and Europe, which can involve diverting resources from food production for domestic markets.

There is another aspect to the land-grab issue, which involves big agribusiness companies working with sovereign wealth funds, for instance from the oil producing countries of the Middle East and from China, acquiring large tracts of land. This takes place especially in Africa, but in other continents too. They set up large-scale production of biofuels, and basic food grains destined for the Gulf States and China, which are designed to help their food security. But it is not a simple story. I recently heard from a Ugandan woman who works for an NGO. She argued that in the area of Uganda where she works, which is a densely populated farming area, the worst land grabs are due to class and gender differentiation at a local level, rather than the work of some large global corporation.

Another important issue is the development of biofuels. Massive profits are being made out of these, partly with the help of subsidies provided by the US government, the EU and so on. Again it's difficult to generalise but there is certainly a danger that land is being diverted from food production.

In addition, with the spike in food prices that took place around the time of the financial crisis of 2007-8, and another spike that seems to be happening now, there's certainly a well-founded argument from the left that as hedge funds and other big financial institutions face problems in the pure money markets they start speculating on agricultural commodity futures. That has been a big part of the food price spikes, which affects people in the South a great deal.

Another interesting story is how countries such as Argentina and Brazil have become major players in agricultural exports on a global scale. China now imports most of its soya from these two countries. Historically, Brazil exported cocoa, coffee and so on, and now you have this really massive scale grain production for export, a lot of it to do with animal feeds or biofuels, with Brazil pioneering the production of sugar to make ethanol as a car fuel. Brazilian corporations are hand in glove with US corporations on this—there is a lot of global cooperation between multinationals.

An interesting point concerns the role of the World Trade Organisation (WTO). Before the WTO was established, the General Agreement on Tariffs and Trade, which preceded it, generally ignored agricultural trade because the Americans did not want to include it. Since the late 19th century the US has been the biggest agricultural exporter, but we have seen the rise of competitors, such as the Cairns Group of big agricultural exporters: Australia, Canada, Brazil, Argentina, South Africa. They are constantly pushing against US and EU subsidies for agriculture. So there is a lot of uncertainty about how far the WTO has got in achieving its objective of free trade in agricultural commodities. Much agricultural trade still tends to take place within particular regional trading blocs such as the North American Free Trade Agreement.

Those are just some of the changes that have taken place recently.

You talk about a series of different factors leading to food insecurity, but you stress how complicated a picture it is. It seems that there is still a very strong regional dynamic and lots of diversity.

Regional differences must not be overlooked. One of the clear exceptions to the idea of globalisation creating similar societies the world over is that the two most populous countries, India and China, are still by and large self-sufficient in food production. And this is either on the basis of incredibly small-scale farming as in China or relatively small-scale farming in India. You might be a relatively strong capitalist farmer in India with five or ten hectares of land in an irrigated area. That is very different from Argentina or Brazil where you are talking about grain farms of tens of thousands of hectares.

So there is a lot of variation. Whether India and China can maintain their broad self-sufficiency in food production for over a third of the world's population is an interesting question. For instance, in China people are eating more meat, so the soy it imports is increasingly destined to go into animal feed.

There are political factors that governments have to consider, even with the rapid pace of capitalist development in India and China generally. India was, for example, one of the first countries to put a ban on food exports when there was the big food price spike.

*In your book **Class Dynamics of Agrarian Change** you give a picture of some of the varieties of struggle in agrarian areas. What are the main flashpoints for struggles today?*

Again it is a complicated question. To take farm workers, they have generally been regarded by the left as harder to organise and therefore more quiescent than other workers. But even here, I've heard that there have been some eruptions of farm workers' struggles in South Africa in the wake of the Marikana miners' struggle.

Your question is important because the major struggles against corporate, industrialised agriculture today, with its high environmental and energy costs, are coming from movements with a strong populist flavour to them. The best known is the Via Campesina movement, which started in Central America and has spread far beyond that. Some of my Marxist colleagues would dismiss these populist movements out of hand, but I think it is more complex. In certain conditions populist movements can have progressive elements. The issue is that they are cross-class alliances centred on ideologies of an inclusive "people of the land". These movements are an important reality of contemporary politics. They are often in the vanguard of struggles against land grabs and corporate agribusiness, so we have to engage with them, albeit critically.

They are not simply a rerun of peasant movements of a previous period, as people such as James Petras have pointed out in the case of Latin America. If they are successful in achieving alliances in the countryside and beyond against corporate capital, how should we position ourselves in relation to them? That is a problem for the left parties in India, for example, where you have very strong rural social movements.

My own feeling is that the politics are highly contradictory. One can identify more progressive tendencies that we can encourage. Some of the more progressive elements are collectivist ideas, in that they argue that there are forms of collectives and cooperatives that are part of the way forward. And then there are some really retrograde tendencies, which look to a myth of a golden past and romanticise the small autonomous producer, harmonious with nature.

One of the issues at stake concerns levels of production and productivity. The size of the world population today, compared to the time in world history when most production was by peasants, is massively expanded. More than 50 percent of the world's population is now urban, so the notion that reconstituted small farmers are the future is one I find difficult to believe, especially if it is the romantic notion that they should use only the most simple tools and avoid modern technologies.

I have no problem with relatively small-scale farming as part of the future, but it would have to use advanced technologies, with high labour productivity, and it would have to be integrated in certain kinds of social arrangements and not simply take place as individualised petty production.

The kind of thing I am advocating would include trying to appropriate technologies developed by capitalism. I am not against GMOs in principle; the problem is that they are mostly developed and controlled by the big chemical corporations.

There are ways of developing the forces of production in agriculture on different scales, in a manner that is not destructive in the way that capitalist farming is today.

To go back to Lenin, part of his point in his identification of the different elements within the peasantry was to try to work out which of them the urban proletariat could ally itself with in revolutionary struggle. What are the prospects for urban-rural alliances? In many contexts, people have one foot in the countryside and one foot in the city.

I agree that one of the most important aspects of the reproduction of labour in the countryside is that it is combined with elements of wage labour and of migration, with strong urban-rural links developing. How you then move beyond that, as a given of existence, towards some kind of programmatic position, which could form the basis for organisation, is rather difficult. There are few recent powerful examples to draw on. All we can say is that almost everyone who is a worker, or part of the reserve army of labour or an informal labourer, does share a common interest. Even in the countryside many people are net buyers of food produced by others.

There are problems though. Organised urban workers will always push for lower food prices, which would probably be against the interest of small farmers and petty commodity producers who are producing food for the market.

People point to possible examples of unity between the classes of labour. Some would say that the Movimento dos Trabalhadores Rurais Sem Terra (MST, the Landless Labourers' Movement) in Brazil was an example because it has a lot of support from the Workers' Party and the radical wing of the Catholic church, which was involved in founding the MST. But we have to ask difficult questions. What would be the aims or demands of that kind of alliance? People have suggested things such as workers running urban food cooperatives, of the kind that existed under Salvador Allende in Chile in the late 1960s and early 1970s, in which there are direct links of supply between smaller farmers and urban working class consumers. It stimulates the imagination but it's hard to think what it would look like scaled up to a society such as Brazil with a population of almost 200 million.

In India you have the Karnataka farmers' movement, which the best informed sources tell me is really a rich farmers' movement, yet it has a big international reputation on the left because they have opposed GM seeds, so they are seen as being the good guys. But one of their major campaigning issues is for bigger subsidies for fertilisers and I'm told some of their leading supporters are among the most vicious in how they treat their farm workers.

Lots of people think that the class differentiation in the countryside is less important than the fact that these populist movements are challenging globalisation and industrialisation. That position is problematic for Marxists who have to investigate and assess class formations and forces in the countryside, which includes their linkages with urban and industrial social dynamics.

For those interested in finding out more, can you recommend some reading on the themes you've discussed?
In general the *Journal of Peasant Studies* and *Journal of Agrarian Change*, and the other works we've discussed, are a useful starting point. A recent issue of the *Journal of Agrarian Change* contained a piece by Jason Moore, entitled "The End of the Road? Agricultural Revolutions in the Capitalist World-Ecology, 1450–2010".[9] Some recent collections on agrarian issues include *Peasants and Globalisation, and Transnational Agrarian Movements Confronting Globalisations.*[10] There are also Weis's *The Global Food Economy* and a collection that I helped edit entitled *The Food Question.*[11]

References

Akram-Lodhi, A Haroom and Cristóbal Kay (eds), 2009, *Peasants and Globalisation, Political Economy, Rural Transformation and the Agrarian Question* (Routledge).

Bernstein, Henry, 2010, *Class Dynamics of Agrarian Change* (Kumarian Press).

Bernstein, Henry, Ben Crow, Maureen Mackintosh and Charlotte Martin (eds), 1990, *The Food Question: Profits Versus People?* (Monthly Review Press).

Borras, Saturnino M, Marc Edelman and Cristóbal Kay (eds), 2008, *Transnational Agrarian Movements Confronting Globalisation* (Wiley-Blackwell).

Chayanov, Alexander, 1987 [1923], *Theory of Peasant Economy* (Oxford University).

Kautsky, Karl, 1987 [1899], *The Agrarian Question*, in two volumes (Zwan).

Kloppenburg, Jack, 2004, *First the Seed: The Political Economy of Plant Biotechnology* (University of Wisconsin).

Lenin, VI, 1987 [1899], *The Development of Capitalism in Russia*, in *Collected Works, volume 3*, (Lawrence and Wishart), www.marxists.org/archive/lenin/works/1899/devel/index.htm

Mann, Susan, and James Dickinson, 1978, "Obstacles to the Development of a Capitalist Agriculture", *Journal of Peasant Studies*, volume 5, number 4.

Moore, Jason W, 2010, "The End of the Road? Agricultural Revolutions in the Capitalist World-Ecology, 1450–2010", *Journal of Agrarian Change*, volume 10, number 3.

Weis, Anthony, 2007, *The Global Food Economy: The Battle for the Future of Farming* (Zed).

9:   Moore, 2010.

10: Akram-Lodhi, Haroom and Kay, 2009; Borras, Edelman and Kay, 2008.

11: Weis, 2007; Bernstein, Crow, Mackintosh and Martin, 1990.

Greece, politics and Marxist strategy

Thanasis Kampagiannis

In *International Socialism 136*, Richard Seymour and Panos Garganas gave two different assessments of the political strategy the left should adopt in Greece.[1] It is an important debate for revolutionaries in Greece and elsewhere. Panos puts forward an argument that the anti-capitalist left should intervene in the ongoing social and political struggle through Antarsya (the Front of the Anticapitalist Left), outside the political formation Syriza (the Coalition of the Radical Left). Richard, on the other hand, proposes a strategy of a "critical support" to Syriza, and "wholehearted" support for the slogan a "government of the left". Furthermore, Richard criticises the conception of "left reformism" that Alex Callinicos has argued in his discussions of Syriza,[2] saying that this term might "gloss over some important details". I think the stress on concrete details is correct. The purpose of this note is to provide some of the details that need to be taken into consideration if international comrades are to make informed assessments on the Greek situation.

Some correction should be made to some information provided by Richard in particular. Richard refers to the "student rebellions in 2009" in error. There were student rebellions against education reforms

1:   Seymour, 2012a and Garganas, 2012. This article was first published on the Left Flank blog. Thanks to its editors Tad Tietze and Elizabeth Humphrys—http://left-flank.org/
2:   Callinicos, 2012a and 2012b.

in 2006 and 2007—and most famously the large youth rebellion of December 2008—but nothing of the kind in 2009. He also refers to Synaspismos (which is the party that constitutes the biggest component of Syriza) joining the Greek Social Forum in 2006, which is again incorrect. The Greek Social Forum was an umbrella organisation *created* by Synaspismos in 2004 to hegemonise the anti-capitalist movement, so clearly Synaspismos didn't join something it had initiated. The Greek Social Forum participated in the organising of the European Social Forum in Athens in 2006, which many comrades from the UK and Europe will recall. But these are minor errors, and it is more important to consider the larger and more important ones.

In order to successfully argue for what he calls elsewhere the "atypical" reformism of Syriza,[3] Richard points to the existence of revolutionary left organisations inside the formation. He implies that these organisations, working alongside the Synaspismos left, can significantly determine Syriza's politics. Richard complains that Alex's treatment of this question "does the subject injustice". However, we need to be more concrete here. The existence of these organisations and a left current in Synaspismos are not enough for us to determine that they will impact on the party's policy-making. For example, in the 1980s the British Labour Party included a strong left wing, as well as organised revolutionary groups, inside it—and yet the left was subordinate in policy making. In addition, the relation of forces between the left and the right was different at different points during the course of the decade. So where are we now?

The left of Syriza
The far left of Syriza participated in the 2012 elections after the most important political challenge it had ever mounted against the leadership of Synaspismos (and consequently Syriza) had suffered a major defeat. The challenge was the formation, back in 2010, of the Front of Solidarity and Rupture (MAA), led by the ex-president of Synaspismos, Alekos Alavanos, and supported by the two organisations that Richard refers to, the Maoist KOE (Communist Organisation of Greece) and the Trotskyist DEA (Workers Internationalist Left). MAA made some interesting interventions, highlighting the moderate trajectory of the Syriza leadership and its pro-European Union (EU) and pro-euro line. But mostly it looked for allies inside Synaspismos, especially the Left Current and its leader Panayiotis Lafazanis. Not unexpectedly, Lafazanis never left the party to join MAA in

---

3:   Seymour, 2012b.

a new formation (although disappointingly for people who made the centre of their political strategy the assumption that Lafazanis would do so).

After it became evident that MAA had failed to create a mass base for a break with Syriza, the organisations that supported MAA decided to dump it and roll back to supporting Syriza, although from a much weaker and more conservative political position. KOE suffered a split during this sharp turn (half its leadership left the organisation, once famous for its old Communist jargon against the EU and the euro but now arguing that "the EU and the euro are not the main issue"). The current political line of KOE can hardly be characterised as being to the left of Synaspismos: its emphasis is on creating a "national" anti-memorandum front, in cooperation with even the right wing anti-memorandum parties (like the party of the Independent Greeks, led by a nationalist anti-Turkish ex-Tory MP, Panos Kammenos, the equivalent of Nigel Farage). Synaspismos (and Syriza) has thankfully until now rejected this proposal (it has said, though, that it might agree to a government with the "critical support" of this right wing party).

But what about the other organisation that Richard refers to: DEA? Well, the 2008 article by Antonis Davanellos that Richard cites (for some reason he gives two references for the same article) is quite telling.[4] Davanellos ends the piece by saying:

> The main topic of the discussion was the proposal made by Alekos Alavanos, the president of Synaspismos, for a "left wing government with a programme based on opposition to neoliberalism and capitalism". DEA, along with many other groups, disagreed with such a proposal, proposing that Syriza position itself as an electoral opposition aiming to reverse neoliberal policy. The topic has not been decided and was left open to discussion for the future.

But why did DEA disagree with the proposal of then Syriza leader Alekos Alavanos back in 2008 while supporting it under current leader Alexis Tsipras in 2012? Certainly, the reason was not a turn to the left by the new leadership of Synaspismos: even its most partisan member will admit that Alavanos is to the left of Tsipras. In reality, the left of Syriza (and the organisations of the revolutionary left within it) was pulled by the Syriza leadership's strategy, of calling for a "government of the left".

In the months after the 2012 elections, this description of the relation of forces was vindicated by events, contrary to the abstract references to a "powerful" left wing. At the last Syriza conference the leadership of

---

4:    Davanellos, 2008 and 2012.

the formation pulled the whole party in a more moderate direction: the emphasis was now placed on a renegotiation of the loan treaties with the EU and IMF by a "national salvation" government that will not "unilaterally" make any radical decisions. The left in the conference presented a "Left Platform" (KOE, which Richard refers to, sided with the leadership) and polled 25 percent, less than the usual figure that the Left Current polls inside Synaspismos. It is now widely accepted that the left of the party has little influence on its political trajectory, while it would be accurate to say that in Syriza's economic think-tank the left's influence is nil.

The main task of the party is now to prove its "ability to govern", a strategy that has been pursued through trips by Tsipras to Latin America to meet with Lula (Brazil) and Kirchner (Argentina), a meeting with German finance minister Wolfgang Schäuble and most recently a trip to the US to court the IMF and liberal think-tanks (including the Brookings Institution). Tsipras startled even his most dedicated supporters, delivering a speech to praise Greece's most important conservative politician Konstantinos Karamanlis (the uncle of the ex-PM Kostas Karamanlis) for his "moderation", a "hegemonic" strategy that will supposedly draw votes to the left from the right. If the left inside Syriza is not capable of determining its trajectory now that the party is in opposition, it is not unsafe to predict what will be the case when the party will be in office, ie under the huge pressures of the state, bourgeois legality and the ruling class.

The euro: the key link

For left activists observing these developments, the immediate question is: Does this always need to happen? Is it historically determined that when a party of the left approaches power it will automatically water down its radicalism? The answer to this is thankfully not found in Robert Michels' "iron law of oligarchy", but is rather a political question of strategy. When I say strategy, I don't simply mean the more eternal question the workers' movement needs to address—reform or revolution—but the way that question is made concrete at a particular conjuncture. Here the issue of the euro is key.

There is an analogy between the question of the euro and the left's approach to the First World War. The decision to break with the war effort—and, even more, to break with it unilaterally—became central to the realignment of the left. This does not mean that everyone who was in favour of peace was a Marxist. The same goes today: not everyone in favour of breaking with the euro is a revolutionary socialist. For example, Costas Lapavitsas's proposed "Grexit" programme, which Richard refers to, is a radical anti-neoliberal programme for restoring Greek capitalism's competitiveness outside the straitjacket of the euro through depreciation of a national currency. Nevertheless, there can be no doubt that breaking with the euro is the necessary step for any anti-capitalist politics that wants to end austerity and start imposing a pro working class agenda.

The pro-euro line of the Syriza leadership has been a lever used by the ruling class to tame the radicalism of the movements in Greece and direct them onto a more moderate path. Contrary to what Richard asserts, the debate around the euro has not been an ideological diversion put forward by the revolutionary left in order to justify rejecting an electoral proposal from Syriza. Nor has Syriza's pro-euro line been a mere tactical decision by its leadership, based on an estimate of the current level of consciousness of the working class.

Rather the defence of the euro has been a political and ideological blackmail deployed by the ruling class against a movement that was delegitimising the debt narrative being pushed by business and politicians. Hence it is a question that needs a bold answer. Syriza's own pro-euro position is a result of its long held pro-EU strategy, ie the old Eurocommunist belief that the EU institutions are a somehow internationalist and progressive transcendence of the nation-state. Accepting the limitations that the euro places on dealing with the Greek economic crisis means parroting the arguments of the US Republican right for "slashing deficits" and "budget surpluses"—and this is what the leading Syriza economists are increasingly doing. The anti-capitalist left in Antarsya, on the other hand, is putting forward a programme that will cancel the debt and the memoranda, nationalise the banks and take control of investments. All of these demands mean a break with the euro.

Government = politics?

The central question is: Who will implement the anti-capitalist programme necessary to resolve the crisis? Richard praises the strategy of a "government of the left" as a "valuable step" since, as he repeatedly says, there are no soviets in place. One of the most striking developments in the argument has been a return to the Comintern's discussions in its Fourth Congress in 1922, particularly by people on the left who usually suggest Leninist politics are obsolete. My dedication to the revolutionary lessons of the early Comintern remains staunch, but in considering the strategy put forward by Syriza it seems that a return to the experience of the 1970s rather than that of the 1920s is much more relevant. What we are dealing with is a rebadging of the old Eurocommunist position of the French Communist Party (PCF), for a "government of the left" (let's note though that the PCF was much more rooted in the working class than Syriza is today). My view is that a "government of the left" *can* be part of a "pedagogical process" for the movement and can render gains to the working class—with one major precondition: that the vanguard of the workers' movement is politically independent from the government, whose rise is the result of the activity of the movement itself.[5] This is not a negation of politics; it is a different kind of politics to the "realism" of a governmental perspective. Moreover, this is not about revolutionary romanticism: the emphasis the revolutionary left places on workers' struggles today builds the subjectivity that will be crucial for the implementation of any radical programme tomorrow. It is crucial not only for the fight against any reactionary backlash by the ruling class, but a subjectivity that will, in the end, be able to acquire power through its own organs.

Unfortunately, the debate around the "government of the left" within the revolutionary left has revealed a misconception of what politics actually is on the part of some. Stathis Kouvelakis, in a speech on Greece, exemplifies this line of argument:

> What is really striking about the Greek situation is that 24 general strikes, occupations by hundreds of thousands of people of the main squares of the country for weeks in spring 2011, all that has been unable to obtain a single significant success. None of the memorandums—or not a single measure, actually, of those absolutely barbarian and draconian austerity packages—was retreated. It became thus absolutely clear that, for all those who wanted to stop and reverse these types of policies, what was needed was a political alternative.[6]

This is a distorted notion of the political, that does not flow from the movement's activity, but is actually a substitute for dealing with the movement's limitations. The same misconception can be found in views that misuse the Gramscian notion of the "integral state" and understand politics solely as a struggle inside and for the state. The state is a crucial condensation of the political, but they should not be equated.

The experience of fighting the rise of Golden Dawn is a good example of how the movement—and the revolutionary left inside it—does politics, even if it doesn't embrace the agenda of entering a "left government". The successful demonstration of 19 January this year, and the rise of the anti-fascist movement more generally, is a significant political move orchestrated by the Greek anti-capitalist left and with the Socialist Workers Party (SEK) playing a leading role inside it. These factors can have a decisive

---

5:   For an elaboration of this line of thought, see Harman and Potter, 1977.
6:   Kouvelakis, 2012.

impact on the political landscape, much more than Syriza's abstention while waiting for the next electoral battle. Smashing Golden Dawn is now a necessary step in the fight against the government of Samaras, and the stakes are even higher since a new wave of youth radicalisation is mobilising against the fascists and state repression. For those interested in the political unity of the left, we should remind ourselves of the need to forge social unity between the working class and radicalised youth. The abstention of Syriza from the anti-fascist front risks a strategic split, but one the forces of the anti-capitalist left are thankfully fighting to avoid.

In defence of the revolutionary left

This brings me to a final point. The capitalist crisis has a profound effect in destabilising social and political alliances of the past. The tempo of the crisis is not the same everywhere; nevertheless this is a worldwide process. For older generations of activists, essentially for the working class, this has meant breaking with right wing social democracy and has been expressed by a rise of left reformist formations. In most cases these formations have been led by "old men of the left" relaunching themselves as tribunes of the people: this is what happened with Die Linke and Oskar Lafontaine, Rifondazione and Fausto Bertinotti, Respect and George Galloway, the Front de Gauche and Jean-Luc Mélenchon, and Syriza and Alexis Tsipras (while he is the youngest leader he has the oldest party behind him)—and we can expand this list with emerging "people's" politicians rising on the back of the Arab Spring. For newer generations of activists, essentially the youth, this is expressed in an attraction to street politics, student movement eruptions, autonomist ideas, new radical anti-oppression movements and so on.[7] The revolutionary left has precious ideological capital to offer within these evolving processes, but it has a difficult and patient task in order to deliver on that potential.

The revolutionary left needs to embrace the radicalising youth and shape its politics beyond an apolitical movementism, which is still the dominant politics in youth circles. In order to do that, we need to have a theory and a practice far more radical than that of the conventional parties of the reformist left—even of its *most* left wing versions. At the same time, revolutionaries will need to bring these new radical layers into contact with the disaffected working class in order to break its old allegiances and offer a real option to the left. This will definitely mean persistently relating to the left reformist formations (whatever form this might take), but it must be done

---

7:    Panos Garganas had spotted this "richer mix" back in his debate with Alex Callinicos and Francois Sabado in this journal—Garganas, 2009.

without tailing their strategy. Our experience in Greece is that in engaging in these struggles the revolutionary left needs to maintain ideological and organisational independence. This is not a fetishisation of these questions, but the hard-learned lessons from witnessing and participating in struggle over the last few turbulent years.

The destabilisation of the old politics will mean that new political formations arise. But it will also mean that old strategies and ideological currents will reappear and be put to the test. Apart from the Second International and Third International in the 1920s, there was also the "Two and a Half International"—a current that sought to manoeuvre "between reformist minimum programmes and revolutionary maximalism", to use Richard's words . The debate regarding the strategy of the Greek left suggests that a similar current will be present internationally in the months and years ahead. For those who unashamedly situate ourselves in the revolutionary Marxist tradition, the building of revolutionary left organisations, such as SEK in Greece or the SWP in Britain, is the key strategic task if we want a world without the catastrophes of capitalism.

References

Callinicos, Alex, 2012a, "The Politics of Europe's Rising Left", *Socialist Worker* (19 May), www.socialistworker.co.uk/art.php?id=28461

Callinicos, Alex, 2012b, "The Second Coming of the Radical Left", *International Socialism 135* (summer), www.isj.org.uk/?id=819

Davanellos, Antonis, 2008, "Greek Workers Move Left", *International Socialist Review*, 59 (May-June), www.isreview.org/issues/59/rep-greece.shtml

Davanellos, Antonis, 2012, "Where Did Syriza Come From?", *Socialist Worker* (US) (17 May), http://socialistworker.org/2012/05/17/where-did-Syriza-come-from

Garganas, Panos, 2009, "The Radical Left: A Richer Mix", *International Socialism 121* (winter), http://www.isj.org.uk/?id=513

Garganas, Panos, 2012, "Greece After the Election", *International Socialism 136* (autumn), www.isj.org.uk/?id=855

Harman, Chris and Tim Potter, 1977, "The Workers' Government", *SWP International Discussion Bulletin*, number 4, www.isj.org.uk/?id=295

Kouvelakis, Stathis, 2012, "Greece: Stathis Kouvelakis on tasks facing Syriza following its electoral breakthrough", *Links—International Journal of Socialist Renewal*, speech delivered on 07/12/2012, http://links.org.au/node/3145

Seymour, Richard, 2012a, "A Comment on Greece and Syriza", *International Socialism 136* (autumn), www.isj.org.uk/?id=854&issue=136

Seymour, Richard, 2012b, "The Challenge of Syriza", www.leninology.com/2012/06/challenge-of-Syriza.html

Characterising the period or caricaturing capitalism?
A reply to Nigel Harris
Adrian Budd

In a recent issue of *International Socialism* Nigel Harris provided a perspective on "characterising the period". As one of its former editors and author of important articles and books, Nigel has made a significant contribution to the elaboration of some of the fundamental ideas associated with this journal. In particular, he highlighted earlier than most the emergence of the trend towards economic internationalisation that would later be dubbed "globalisation".[1] There was, however, a suspicion that, as with many trail blazers, the openness to new trends accompanied a tendency to downplay contradictory evidence and continuities with the past. His recent contribution reinforces that suspicion and betrays a tendency towards one-sidedness, which means that the perspective that he presents fails to appreciate fully the contradictory and complex nature of contemporary global capitalism. This is particularly true in two areas of great significance for a Marxist understanding of contemporary capitalism—the relation between global capitalism and the nation-state and, secondly, imperialism.[2]

1: See in particular Harris, 1983 and 1986.
2: For a fuller analysis in these areas see Budd, 2013, part two.

Contemporary capitalism and the nation-state

The core of Nigel's perspective comprises the following interconnected arguments.[3]

1) In the era of "economic globalisation" of recent decades, national economies have become increasingly integrated into "a single world economy", a "single economic system". This is driven by global markets such that the global economy is "organised by global markets, not as hitherto believed (rightly or wrongly), by national states".[4]

2) The state has become "an agent" of external forces, "enforcing global imperatives on the domestic population rather than representing it to the world at large (let alone defending it against external threats)". State powers are weakened or relinquished, including "any ambition to shape the domestic economy", the state "restricting itself to managing efficiently the accommodation of global forces".[5] Central bank independence of political authorities illustrates this tendency.

3) Under pressure from globalisation there has been an erosion of social solidarity and the social contract between state and society. Nigel argues that "we are now within sight of the reversal of many of the major historical efforts to tame the destructive power of markets—from the New Deal and Great Society legislation in the US (even the right to collective bargaining) to the welfare state and the provision of social and educational services in Europe".[6]

4) A global ruling class has emerged alongside, and potentially transcending, national ruling classes, albeit that Nigel notes the movement between the

---

3: I focus here on Nigel's perspective on structural aspects of the world system. I ignore his rather uncritical view of globalisation and his suggestion that capitalism can solve the problem of world poverty, including the claim that "the reduction in world poverty since 1980 is a staggering record", poverty perhaps having "halved since 1990...in all regions of the world"—Harris, 2012, p143. UN figures show that the number living in extreme poverty in the developing world has fallen: "the proportion of people living on less than $1.25 a day fell from 47 percent in 1990 to 24 percent in 2008—a reduction from over 2 billion to less than 1.4 billion"—United Nations, 2012, p4. But is the headline attainment of the UN's Millennium Development Goals sufficient? Is $1.25 a day an adequate threshold for extreme poverty? Isn't the figure of 1.4 billion in extreme poverty even on the (arbitrary) basis of $1.25 a shocking indictment of capitalism? And, has there not been a colossal widening of inequality in the last two decades as the very poorest have earned a few additional cents a day? Failure to explore behind the UN's headlines means that we risk becoming trumpeters for neoliberal globalisation.

4: Harris, 2012, p138.

5: Harris, 2012, p142, p140.

6: Harris, 2012, pp139-140.

two. For the global ruling class "nationality is a mere contingency, not a matter of overriding loyalty".[7] The ideology of this transnational class, neo-liberalism, is ascendant and dominates policy-making globally.

Nigel and similar writers are clearly grappling with developments of real significance. Part of his argument is consistent with the traditions of this journal and in particular its critique of state capitalism in the Soviet Union. Trotsky argued that "Marxism takes its point of departure from world economy, not as a sum of national parts, but as a mighty and independent reality which has been created by the international division of labour and the world market, and which in our epoch imperiously dominates the national markets".[8] But if Trotsky was demonstrating the impossibility of Stalin's socialism in one country here, elsewhere he emphasised the une-venness of global capitalist transformation and how its impact was shaped by pre-existing social and political relations. National ruling classes and their states have never been passive bearers of global capitalism's impera-tive and logic. As that logic unfolded in the late-19th century, capitalism both dismantled and began to re-erect state-built protective barriers around national economies. Capitalism transformed the world's societies and states, but states now shaped particular national forms of capitalism.[9]

Rosa Luxemburg captured the emerging statisation of capitalism: "Capitalist development modifies essentially the nature of the state, widening its sphere of action, constantly imposing on it new functions...making more and more necessary its intervention and control in society".[10] Reflecting on the relationship between national and international relations three decades later, Gramsci wrote that they interpenetrate and "intertwine" to produce:

a combination which is "original" and (in a certain sense) unique: these relations must be understood and conceived in their originality and uniqueness if one wishes to dominate them and direct them. To be sure, the line of development is towards internationalism, but the point of departure is

---

7:   Harris, 2012, p142. For similar arguments see Robinson, 2004, and Sklair, 2001.
8:   Trotsky, 1929.
9:   Michael Löwy rightly criticised the *Communist Manifesto* for "a certain economism and a surprising amount of Free Tradist optimism" when it argued that capitalism's expansionary dynamic "batters down all Chinese Walls", and that "national differences and antagonisms between peoples are daily more and more vanishing"—Löwy, 1976, p82; Marx and Engels 1942, pp209, 225.
10: Luxemburg, 1989, p43.

"national"—and it is from this point of departure that one must begin. Yet the perspective is international and cannot be otherwise.[11]

There is no essential contradiction between Trotsky's "world economy" and Gramsci's "national" points of departure. Trotsky reminds us that Marxism understands the capitalist world system as a totality that impacts on all its parts, while Gramsci emphasises Marxism's practical revolutionary side, the differentiation and fragmentation of that totality, and the way that the parts impact on the whole. One powerful attempt to grasp the dialectical relation between the national and the international in the 20th century was Bukharin's *Imperialism and World Economy*. Noting capitalism's tendency towards internationalisation, Bukharin wrote that "there grows an extremely flexible economic structure of world capitalism, all parts of which are mutually interdependent. The slightest change in one part is immediately reflected in all".[12] But, as interdependence deepened so international competition intensified: late developers such as Germany, Russia and Japan faced up to Britain's global leadership by pursuing state-orchestrated social and economic change to facilitate rapid capital accumulation while, more generally, capitals enlisted the help of their national states to defend their interests, including via geopolitical strategies of power projection. Internationalisation thus provoked "a reverse tendency towards the nationalisation of capitalist interests".[13] There followed an entire epoch of state capitalism and, as economic and military competition dovetailed, militarised inter-imperialism.

Harris's arguments are similar to those of the Marxist transnationalist theorist William Robinson, for whom the reversal of the trend towards state capitalism has been so powerful that the very idea of a national economy must be questioned. He asks, "What is a 'national economy'? Is it a country with a closed market? Protected territorially-based production circuits? The predominance of national capitals? An insulated national financial system?" He rightly answers that "no capitalist country in the world fits this description".[14] Werner Bonefeld is also sceptical, regarding "national economy" as "a regressive concept that lends itself, at best, to ideas of national developmental methods…or, at worst, to the reactionary and romantic ideas and practices of nationalism".[15] Robinson and Bonefeld alert us to real dangers, but while its critics should acknowledge the reality of some of the changes that underlie

11:   Gramsci, 1971, p240.
12:   Bukharin, 1987, p36.
13:   Bukharin, 1987, p62.
14:   Robinson, 2009, p69.
15:   Bonefeld, 2006, p52.

the transnationalisation perspective, so transnationalists themselves should recognise some vital continuities in capitalism's global political economy.

Emphasising only one part of what the Marxist international relations writer Hannes Lacher calls the national/global dialectic locates transformative powers almost entirely within the global economy, denies the continuing reality of state power and reduces states to the role of mere agents of global forces, operating to adjust national economies to world economy imperatives.[16] This is certainly part of what states do, but leaving matters there, as Philip McMichael wrote about Robinson's approach, "suspends the dialectic".[17] The balance between the two may change over time, and three decades of neoliberal transformation have certainly reversed important aspects of the trend towards state capitalism, including nationalised industry and capital controls, for instance. But we should beware a one-sided focus on transnational economic processes that can produce an unexamined economism, whereby the transnationalisation of capital automatically transnationalises capitalist states and the entire capitalist system. Nation-states have not been fundamentally or irreversibly weakened by globalisation, and global capitalism continues to be shaped by both the major capitals and the most powerful of the world's states, within whose jurisdictions those capitals are largely based.

Global expansion is, of course, in capital's DNA, but it cannot be abstracted from capitalism as a contradictory living reality. Gramsci's argument about the intertwining of national and international social relations captures a geographical dimension of this reality, but he also highlighted capitalism's historical construction and contradictions:

> every real historical phase leaves traces of itself in succeeding phases, which then become in a sense the best document of its existence. The process of historical development is a unity in time through which the present contains the whole of the past and in the present is realised that part of the past which is "essential".[18]

Geographical intertwining—producing Gramsci's unique combinations of social relations—itself intertwines with the historical sedimentation of essentials, with continuities from the past that limit and shape the

---

16: Lacher, 2003. The neo-Gramscian Robert Cox, for instance, argues that the nation-state once provided a "bulwark defending domestic welfare from external disturbances" but is now "a transmission belt from the global to the national economy"—Cox, 1992, p31.

17: McMichael, 2001, p201.

18: Gramsci, 1971, p409.

dynamic of change. In the short-to-medium term at least, all that is solid does not melt into air. Thus even "globalised" capitalism comprises an interweaving of particular local, national and regional patterns of social relations. As Sam Ashman puts it, "local conditions mediate the impact of capitalism's 'laws of development'".[19] This allows us to continue to use the concept of national economy, not as the hermetically sealed entity suggested by Robinson but in the more limited sense captured by Alex Callinicos of "capitalist economic networks that remain nationally constituted even if their reach may be global".[20]

In a recent issue of this journal Jane Hardy demonstrated empirically that states continue to promote the competitive advantage of nationally-based capitals. Agricultural protectionism by the US and EU has been widely criticised, but Jane shows how these two champions of neoliberal globalisation use a variety of measures across industrial sectors—including films, cars, semiconductors and bio-technology—to enhance capital accumulation of domestic firms and firms based in these territories. Other empirical material (conspicuously absent from Nigel's article) illustrates the nation-state's abiding significance. First, economic activity remains heavily concentrated at national and regional levels. Thus, for instance, the average contribution of exports to annual national income remains only around 10 percent for the most advanced countries.[21] Secondly, the United Nations Conference on Trade and Development (UNCTAD) calculates a "transnationality index" for firms and countries in some of the issues of its

---

19: Ashman, 2006, p90. Henk Overbeek make a similar point: "transnational neo-liberalism manifests itself at the national level not as a simple distillate of external determinants, but rather as a set of intricate mediations between the 'logic' of global capital and the historical reality of national political and social relations"—Overbeek, 1993, pxi.

20: Callinicos, 2004, p432.

21: Figures for exports as a percentage of national income present problems. The value of exports does not accurately measure their contribution to national income. Because of the re-export of imports we need a measure of value added embodied in exports: the data for a country importing a car wheel for $200, adding a domestically-produced tyre for $50, and then exporting a combined product for $250 shows an export of $250, five times the export's contribution to national income. Jonathan Anderson of UBS investigated this and distinguished between "headline" export/GDP ratios for Asia—sometimes a statistically accurate but absurd 100 percent-plus figure—and a much lower "true" figure for export shares. "The average share of GDP for larger Asian countries is in the single digits, and for smaller regional economies the figure is more like 20% to 25%." The figure of 30 to 35 percent for Hong Kong or Singapore makes much more sense than what may be a 200 percent headline figure. By Anderson's calculations China's exposure to exports was slightly below 10 percent of GDP, slightly more than Japan or India—Anderson, 2007, p3. These figures broadly agree with those in Hirst and Thompson, 1996, p112.

annual *World Investment Report*. The index for countries is constructed from four sets of data: FDI inflows as a percentage of gross fixed capital formation; FDI inward stocks as a percentage of GDP; value added of foreign affiliates as a percentage of GDP; and employment of foreign affiliates as a percentage of total employment. Small countries, such as Denmark, Sweden and the Netherlands, have a relatively high transnationality index of around 30 percent. With larger countries, however, we see a significant decline: Britain and France have indices of around 20 percent, Germany and Italy around 10 percent, the US 6 percent and Japan only 1 percent.[22]

Thirdly, UNCTAD also qualified the transnationalisation thesis when its assessment of FDI data for 1990 to 2003 led it to conclude that FDI accounted for only "8 percent of world domestic investment" and "only complements domestic investment".[23] Even with the subsequent deepening of globalisation this conclusion remains valid—UNCTAD's most recent data shows that inward FDI as a percentage of gross fixed capital formation between 2004 and 2010 averaged 10.6 percent for the developed countries and 11.4 percent for the world as a whole.[24] The world is undoubtedly becoming increasingly integrated at the level of production as FDI growth continues to outpace that of global output or trade, but UNCTAD's data suggest that we should exercise caution about what seem to be rather flat-earth claims of a "single global economy". As Ellen Wood argues, "the national organisation of capitalist economies has remained stubbornly persistent".[25]

Exploring beneath the label of "transnational corporations" reinforces the need for caution. A number of empirical studies have highlighted that even the most internationalised firms concentrate the majority of their high value added and strategically important activities within their home states or regions, with the possible exception of TNCs based in smaller advanced economies.[26] Where capitals do restructure internationally it is generally within relatively narrow geographical limits: world FDI and trade are heavily concentrated within a triad of advanced regions—the EU, Japan and its neighbours, and North America. UNCTAD notes that the concentration of FDI within this triad "remained high between 1985 and 2002

22: UNCTAD, 2008, p12.
23: UNCTAD, 2004, p3.
24: My calculations based on UnctadStat table "Inward and outward foreign direct investment flows, annual, 1970-2011, as percentage of gross fixed capital formation" at http://unctadstat.unctad.org/TableViewer/tableView.aspx.
25: Wood, 2003, p23
26: Ruigrok and van Tulder, 1995, and Rugman and Verbeke, 2004

(at around 80 percent of the world's outward stock and 50 to 60 percent for the world's inward stock".[27] What explains the continued attraction of home bases and advanced, usually high-cost, countries as FDI destinations?

Capitalism's chase across the globe has never conformed to bourgeois economists' ideas of free markets and comparative advantage. Political, juridical, military, etc relations are necessarily interwoven with economic relations as permanent features of capitalism and cut from the same cloth as competitive accumulation.[28] Capitals are themselves alienable commodities that share the twin aspects of value of all commodities, being both abstract exchange values and concrete use values. Conceived abstractly, capital has no spatial bounds and is driven by the pressure of capital accumulation to search for markets and sources of surplus value wherever they may be found. As one of its executives once famously declared, General Motors is not in the business of making cars but making profits. It can only do so, however, by making and selling cars, or some other use value, which have specific characteristics, are made from particular raw materials, and embody particular labour skills and components. These concrete aspects of capitalist production mean that the "footloose" quality sometimes ascribed to capital by globalisation theorists, and implied by many transnationalists, is quite limited.[29] Without in the least negating the fundamental relations of competitive accumulation, the production of use values requires considerable cooperation between capitals, commodities being produced and sold within complex networks of production (including supply networks), finance and distribution. These networks remain densest at the national level and capital remains in a relation of what Harman calls "structural interdependence" with states, producing what David Coates has called distinct national "models of capitalism" and business cultures.[30]

An important essay by Peter Gowan highlights the significance of nation-states' efforts to enhance economies of, and returns to, scale on behalf of the capitals based within their jurisdictions. States' efforts are geared towards:

> constructing secure market bases for their companies, training workforces, supplying transport and communication infrastructures—and, of course,

---

27: UNCTAD, 2003, p23.
28: Barker, 1990, p6.
29: Productive capital's relative geographical immobility parallels a frequent immobility between industrial sectors. Car producers have seen average profit rates fall from 20 percent in the 1920s to 10 percent in the 1960s and 5 percent today, yet remain committed to the sector in which their fixed investments are sunk—*Economist*, 2004, p56.
30: Harman, 1991; Coates, 2000

the exercise of geopolitical influence to open and protect overseas markets. Much of the huge expansion of state resources in the 20th century has, indeed, been devoted precisely to activities in this area.[31]

An area of permanent state concern and activity are the relations between capital and labour. Transnationalists are often silent on class struggle and present an image of all-powerful capitalist forces and of transnational restructuring as a relatively automatic process in which post-war class compromises were seamlessly dismantled in conformity with a new consensus on the rules of the global economy. In reality, the defeat of labour movements in major national struggles—the 1984-5 miners' strike in Britain, the 1980 FIAT strike in Italy, etc—was crucial in establishing the conditions for global neoliberal capitalist restructuring. Marxism understands capital not as a thing but as a social relation with living labour and so the confidence, organisation and combativity of labour movements must be central to the analysis of capital's powers of agency. In the aftermath of labour's defeats capital was emboldened to begin to restructure welfare states, attack union rights and increasingly impose market discipline on society, thereby moving the boundary between the public sphere and individual responsibility. But those defeats were not the product of purely economic or industrial relations factors, but were crucially dependent on the mobilisation of state force. Neoliberalism does not straightforwardly weaken states but divests them of some of their existing social obligations and thereby strengthens their capacity to arrive at authoritative decisions in the interests of capital, attracting global financial resources and the political support of the world's dominant states.[32] The class offensive required to achieve this is rendered all but invisible by the idea of an autonomous economic-technical process of economic globalisation that dominates much globalisation theory and which Nigel's article does little to correct.

Emphasising the capital-labour relation also allows us to correct another one-sided judgement—that neoliberal restructuring entails dismantling the welfare state. Under globally intensified competition, ruling classes in the advanced countries make contradictory demands on their states: they demand both reductions in corporate taxation and in welfare support for subordinate classes and, conversely, that states provide them with healthy, educated and motivated workers and social stability. This contradiction is not unmanageable

---

31: Gowan, 2009, p135

32: Pierre Bourdieu also questioned whether neoliberalism weakens states. The "left hand of the state" (reflecting past social struggles) may have been weakened but its capital-friendly "right hand" (the treasury, etc) remained strong—Bourdieu, 1998, p2.

if, for instance, taxation can be shifted from capital onto workers, as has happened to a considerable extent in the wealthy countries. But recent empirical studies demonstrate that, contrary to conventional wisdom, state spending on welfare grew consistently throughout the neoliberal era, at least until the onset of capitalism's most recent crisis in 2007-8. In Britain, part of the neoliberal vanguard, state spending on the National Health Service rose in real terms every year between 1980 and 2008.[33] The detailed analysis of state spending in the OECD countries between 1980 and 2005 by Francis Castles and his collaborators reinforces the challenge to conventional wisdom: after 1980 social expenditure as a proportion of GDP rose quite markedly on average, including by 21 percent between 1980 and 2001.[34] When we look at the evidence, we find strong empirical grounds for, as Gowan put it, contesting "the sweeping claims of the economic globalisation discourse".[35]

Contesting globalisation theory's wilder claims is not to deny the reality of neoliberal restructuring, changes in the capital-labour relation, or welfare state retrenchment. Nor is it to claim that there can be a national solution to capitalist crisis. But it is to recognise the importance of the state in these processes and its role in mediating global pressures and translating them into national policy frameworks. Even in the EU, where six decades of integration have ensured that the transnationalisation of capital is deeper than elsewhere in the world, the interpenetration of the national and the international persists and few issue areas are not subject to intense national disagreement and bargaining. Transnational pressure compels national states to pursue strategies of national economic restructuring, but the pace, scale and shape of restructuring reflect specifically national factors. This is captured in Benno Teschke and Christian Heine's comments that:

> the uneven spread of crisis, non-synchronous national and sectoral business cycles, nationally diverging balances of class forces, and historically different institutional contexts of industrial relations, [have] translated into palpable divergences in political management strategies that do not follow an exclusive economic rationality.[36]

33: Emmerson and Frayne, 2005, p15.
34: Castles, 2007, p21. Today's savage austerity cuts change the picture somewhat, but pre-2008 data suggests no simple correlation between globalisation and the retreat of the state. When the cover of the *Economist* raises the bogey of the revival of state capitalism and suggests that it may be "the emerging world's new model", the interpenetration of capitalist politics and economics may again be revealing itself—*Economist*, 2012.
35: Gowan 2009, p144.
36: Teschke and Heine, 2002, p180.

States remain Janus-faced: as they attempt to manage the national ruling class's common affairs (which may overlap with those of other ruling classes) they simultaneously project into the world system to advance the interests of nationally-based capitals and introject pressures and processes from it. The balance between states' internal and external aspects is not fixed, but the relation between the national and the international is a permanent concern of all states. When state capitalism reached its fullest development the major capitals and their states continued to seek ways to transcend national limits, including by expansion or the consolidation of existing overseas possessions. Today, even as internationalisation has again become the dominant trend, states continue to provide the essential framework within which global capitalism operates—what Ellen Wood calls "the extra-economic conditions of capital's self-reproduction".[37] There is no evidence that capital favours a stateless global neoliberalism over institutionalised interdependence with home states, supplemented by new interdependencies with other, usually neighbouring, states. Rather, as Immanuel Wallerstein has argued, the additional risks involved in the extension of a transnational capital's operations demand "strong state structures" which are "their guarantee, their lifeblood, and the crucial element in the creation of large profits".[38] That capitals are prepared to take these risks tells us something about the competitive pressures compelling them to seek their share of global streams of value. It also encourages us to reflect on Nigel's comments on imperialism.

Imperialism

Related to his argument that the global ruling class has no national attachment, Nigel argues that since the global economy is "outside of the control of any one national authority" and dominates all states, the concept of imperialism has become "threadbare" and "theoretically inadequate".[39] It over-states Washington's power, he argues, and in any case this power is not mobilised in "pursuit of empire" but in "a misguided attempt to fill the vacuum created by the lack of world government in a global economy",

---

37: Wood, 2002, p36. Ruling class efforts to secure the identification of subordinate classes with "their own" nation-states may not always be successful and may contradict the immediate interests of capital in securing, for instance, imported supplies of cheap labour in times of skills shortages. But ruling classes see good reasons for continuing to promote nationalism while simultaneously attempting to inhibit the development of other collective identities. Emphasising the abiding importance of nation-states and nationalism, Neil Davidson rightly argues for "putting the nation back in the international"—Davidson, 2009.
38: Wallerstein, 1998, p47.
39: Harris, 2012, p138, p137, p144.

within which corporations have become "free-floating...with little or no reference to Washington".[40]

We will see shortly that I believe Nigel's arguments are, again, over-stated and one-sided, but he does alert us to an important change. A century ago internationalisation produced a counter-trend towards state capitalism, but in recent decades internationalisation has partially eroded state capitalism. What has happened in the intervening period to explain this? As we have seen, Nigel explains it by reference to the decline in national identity and a new cosmopolitanism among sections of capital.[41] There is undoubtedly some evidence to support this, particularly as far as finance capital is concerned. But capital's relative geographical fixity and dependence on political and juridical state power, discussed above, alongside the general condition of anarchic competitive accumulation, place limits on such cosmopolitanism. The imperialist organisation of the capitalist world provides a better place to look for an explanation.

Beyond a broad agreement on its roots in underlying processes of competitive capital accumulation and monopolisation, Marxist theories of imperialism have divided along three main paths. First, the perspective of inter-imperialist rivalry associated with Lenin and with Bukharin's analysis of the inter-penetration of internationalisation and nationalisation outlined above. This has been the perspective of most contributors on imperialism to this journal. Secondly, Karl Kautsky's perspective of 'ultra-imperialism', which argues that the world's imperialist powers form "a federation of the strongest, who renounce their arms race" and replace rivalry "by a holy alliance of the imperialists".[42] This argument was sometimes used to explain the West's cohesion during the Cold War and is today expressed in William Robinson's transnationalist argument that "the US state has attempted to play a leadership role on behalf of transnational capitalist interests".[43] Nigel's arguments are closest to this perspective. A third perspective, super-imperialism, emphasises the

---

40: Harris, 2012, p145. Cox argues similarly that there is no longer an identifiable "regime of dominance" at the top of the contemporary world order—Cox, 1999, p12.

41: See also Harris, 2003.

42: Kautsky, 1970, p46.

43: Robinson, 2009, p77. Robinson himself rejects the "ultra-imperialism" label, arguing that it suggests collusion between nationally organised capitals whereas he emphasises competition between increasingly transnational capitals. The conclusion Robinson draws, however, that as the transnational capitalist class develops so "competition takes on new forms in the age of globalisation not necessarily expressed as national rivalry" has affinities with the logic of ultra-imperialism—Robinson, 2009, p69.

capacity of a single imperialist power—today the United States—to dominate weaker imperialisms and act as the "organiser of world capitalism".[44] The super-imperialism perspective can be used to imply the transcendence of inter-imperialist rivalry, but an alternative understanding has considerable explanatory power.

Just as monopolisation modifies competition but on the basis of the very competition from which it develops (and may intensify it internationally—think of Airbus versus Boeing), so super-imperialism should be seen as a consequence of inter-imperialist rivalry that then modifies its form without destroying its essence.[45] The super-power rivalry of the Cold War, itself a form of inter-imperial conflict, shaped the relations between the US and the older but now weaker imperialisms of Western Europe. US economic and military predominance over its Western allies allowed it to challenge their global influence but also ensured that economic rivalry did not develop into military rivalry. Although the "loss" of Eastern Europe and, after 1949, China placed limits on the geographical extension of US power, the Cold War served to intensify it within what became a global US-led security zone (Rio Pact, NATO, SEATO, CENTO, etc). As a consequence of the establishment of this security zone the economies of its allies became increasingly interdependent: this was particularly true of Western Europe but there is a striking correspondence between Asian post-war development (led by Japan and then the "tigers") and US security guarantees. Interdependence was reinforced by the long post-war boom, itself a consequence of Cold War military spending. Yet, despite the cementing effect of the "Soviet threat", transatlantic and wider Western interdependence never fully overcame inter-imperialist rivalries.[46] Facing a barrage of West European criticism—concerning its conduct in Vietnam, the international role of the dollar, the power of US multinationals, etc—as well as relative economic decline as a result of its huge arms spending, US Secretary of State Kissinger complained in 1974 that the US's major overseas problems were with its allies rather than its enemies.[47] The US's aggressive unilateral economic statecraft to arrest relative decline under Nixon and, especially, Reagan demonstrates that competitive accumulation and rivalry continued to structure the capitalist world system even under US hegemony.

44: Rowthorn, 1971, p31.

45: The logic of this argument is similar to that of Tony Cliff when he wrote that "monopoly capitalism means a partial negation of the Marxian law of value but on the basis of the law of value itself"—Cliff, 1988, p212.

46: Budd, 1993.

47: See Halliday, 1986, p18.

In the post Cold War era the world's ruling classes continue to jockey for position within a system still fundamentally anarchic and conflict ridden. Nevertheless, there is a second way that US super-imperialism conditions inter-imperialist rivalry. While US military power and economic statecraft serve primarily US interests its ruling class is increasingly aware of a wider interest and responsibility. As Doug Stokes puts it, the US is subject to "dual national and transnational logics" and promotes its own interests while simultaneously seeking to secure a world order safe for capitalism as a whole.[48] These twin logics ensure that conflict within the advanced core of the world system is, at present, unlikely to assume a military form, but geopolitical competition—defined by Alex Callinicos as "all conflicts among states over security, territory, resources and influence"—persists.[49] Indeed, it is not at all clear how Nigel reconciles his belief that the concept of imperialism is threadbare with the fact that the US has been almost permanently at war in one form or another since the end of the Cold War. The contemporary world order is very far from a transnationalised one in which clashes of interest within the advanced core have been transcended but is instead an inter-imperialist order modified by the relative supremacy of a single super-imperialism.

Conclusion

Marxism can only develop realistic perspectives by constantly testing and revising theory in interaction with the novel phenomena and emergent trends of an evolving social reality. It must "historicise theory".[50] This is a perennial strength of this journal and Nigel contributes to this tradition by his willingness to recognise powerful contemporary currents in the global economy. In doing so he dispels any lingering notions that real social change can be built in national isolation. But Nigel's iconoclasm shares with the wider transnationalist perspective a tendency to overlook the contradictory and many-sided nature of reality to produce a partial, one-sided perspective of limited value.

Although they may be formally separate and occupy distinct institutional spheres under capitalism, there is a necessary and unavoidable interpenetration of politics and economics, of relations of non-exchange

---

48: Stokes, 2005, p230. Peter Gowan makes a similar argument: "The US state has not just been pursuing its own interests at the expense of all its rivals, but securing the general conditions for the expansion of capital as a system, in which they have an interest too"—Gowan, 2002, p65.
49: Callinicos, 2009, p74.
50: McMichael, 2001, p202.

with exchange relations. Failure adequately to appreciate the significance of this leads to Nigel's astonishing conclusion that today, as we contemplate "the final phases of the completion of the bourgeois revolution (now on a world scale)", capital "is obliged to step into the limelight, unprotected by political power".[51] Nigel qualifies this by recognising that a prolonged and severe crisis may encourage states to attempt to reverse globalisation and recover lost state powers, including by intensifying nationalism and xenophobia, but he nevertheless argues that economic globalisation is "inexorable".[52] Anything that hinders this comes across as a relic of a disappearing past. This includes the Arab Spring which Nigel comments upon with a faintly dismissive tone: although the "revolutions" may spread, unless they succeed in "breaking the global order…this merely reiterates the same order of competing states which is itself at the core of the problem".[53] This may be abstractly true but it lacks any sense of a living perspective, of real engagement with social forces in movement.

The danger of this abstract internationalism was spelled out by Gramsci. He argued that the working class, which he sometimes referred to as "the international class", must work with less internationalist forces (intellectuals and peasants, for instance) and so "'nationalise' itself in a certain sense". Failure to fully engage in concrete national circumstances and struggles produces the absurdity of "passivity and inertia" where:

> nobody believed that they ought to make a start—that is to say, they believed that by making a start they would find themselves isolated; they waited for everyone to move together, and nobody in the meantime moved or organised the movement.[54]

Without an appreciation of the fundamental role of states in capitalism, even in extended periods of internationalisation, this is the unwitting conclusion that can be drawn from Nigel's perspective. It is one that we should be very careful to avoid.

51: Harris, 2012, p145.
52: Harris, 2012, p138.
53: Harris, 2012, p144.
54: Gramsci, 1971, p241.

References

Anderson, Jonathan, 2007, "Is China export-led?" (UBS Investment Research, Asian Focus), www.allroadsleadtochina.com/reports/prc_270907.pdf

Anievas, Alex (ed), 2009, *Marxism and World Politics* (Routledge).

Ashman, Sam, 2006, "From World Market to World Economy", in Bill Dunn and Hugo Radice (eds), *100 Years of Permanent Revolution—Results and Prospects* (Pluto).

Barker, Colin, 1990, *Beyond Exchange: the Force of Value* (unpublished notes).

Bonefeld, Werner, 2006, "Human Progress and Capitalist Development", in Andreas Bieler, Werner Bonefeld, Peter Burnham and Adam Morton (eds), *Global Restructuring, State, Capital and Labour: Contesting Neo-Gramscian Perspectives* (Palgrave).

Bourdieu, Pierre, 1998, *Acts of Resistance. Against the Myths of our Time* (Polity).

Budd, Adrian, 1993, *The EC and Foreign and Security Policy* (University of North London Press).

Budd, Adrian, 2007, "Transnational Marxism: a Critique", *Contemporary Politics*, volume 13, number 4.

Budd, Adrian, 2013, *Class, States and International Relations: A Critical Appraisal of Robert Cox and Neo-Gramscian Theory* (Routledge).

Bukharin, Nikolai, 1987 [1917], *Imperialism and World Economy* (Merlin Press).

Callinicos, Alex, 2004, "Marxism and the International", *British Journal of Politics and International Relations*, volume 6, issue 3.

Callinicos, Alex, 2009, *Imperialism and Global Political Economy* (Polity).

Castles, Francis (ed), 2007, *The Disappearing State? Retrenchment Realities in an Age of Globalisation* (Edward Elgar).

Cliff, Tony, 1988, *State Capitalism in Russia* (Bookmarks), www.marxists.org/archive/cliff/works/1955/statecap/index.htm

Coates, David, 2000, *Models of Capitalism: Growth and Stagnation in the Modern Era* (Polity).

Cox, Robert, 1992, "Global Perestroika", in Ralph Miliband and Leo Panitch (eds), *Socialist Register: New World Order?* (Merlin).

Cox, Robert, 1999, "Civil Society at the Turn of the Millennium: Prospects for an Alternative World Order", *Review of International Studies*, volume 25, number 1.

Davidson, Neil, 2009, "Putting the Nation Back into 'the International'", *Cambridge Review of International Affairs*, volume 22, number 1.

Economist, 2004, "Perpetual Motion" (4 September), www.economist.com/node/3127302

Economist, 2012, "The Rise of State Capitalism: The Emerging World's New Model" (21 January), www.economist.com/printedition/2012-01-21

Emmerson, Carl, and Christine Frayne, 2005, *Public Spending—Election Briefing 2005* (Institute of Fiscal Studies), www.ifs.org.uk/bns/05ebn2.pdf.

Gowan, Peter, 2002, "A Calculus of Power", *New Left Review*, II/16.

Gowan, Peter, 2009, "Industrial Development and International Political Conflict in Contemporary Capitalism", in A Anievas (ed), 2009.

Gramsci, Antonio, 1971, *Selections from the Prison Notebooks* (Lawrence and Wishart).

Halliday, Fred, 1986, *The Making of the Second Cold War*, second edition (Verso).

Hardy, Jane, 2013, "New Divisions of Labour in the Global Economy", *International Socialism* 137 (winter), www.isj.org.uk/?id=868

Harman, Chris, 1991, "The State and Capitalism Today'" *International Socialism* 51 (summer), www.isj.org.uk/?id=234

Harris, Nigel, 1983, *Of Bread and Guns: The World Economy in Crisis* (Penguin).

Harris, Nigel, 1986, *The End of the Third World: Newly Industrializing Countries and the End of an Ideology* (IB Tauris).

Harris, Nigel, 2003, *The Return of Cosmopolitan Capital: Globalization, the State and War* (I.B. Tauris).

Harris, Nigel, 2012, "Characterising the Period", *International Socialism* 135 (summer), www.isj.org.uk/?id=826

Hirst, Paul, and Graeme Thompson, 1996, *Globalisation in Question* (Polity).

IMF, 2012, *World Economic Outlook Database*, www.imf.org/external/pubs/ft/weo/2012/01/weodata/weorept.aspx

Kautsky, Karl, 1970 [1914], "Ultra-Imperialism", *New Left Review*, 59, www.marxists.org/archive/kautsky/1914/09/ultra-imp.htm

Lacher, Hannes, 2003 "Putting the State in its Place: The Critique of State-Centrism and its Limits", *Review of International Studies*, volume 29, number 4.

Löwy, Michael, 1976, "Marxism and the National Question", *New Left Review*, 96.

Luxemburg, Rosa, 1989 [1898/1899], *Reform or Revolution* (Bookmarks).

Marx, Karl, and Frederick Engels, 1942 [1848], "Manifesto of the Communist Party", in *Karl Marx: Selected Works*, volume 1 (Lawrence and Wishart).

McMichael, Philip, 2001, "Revisiting the Question of the Transnational State: A Comment on William Robinson's 'Social Theory and Globalisation'", *Theory and Society*, 30.

Overbeek, Henk (ed), 1993, *Restructuring Hegemony in the Global Political Economy. The Rise of Transnational Neo-liberalism in the 1980s* (Routledge).

Robinson, William, 2004, *A Theory of Global Capitalism: Production, Class, and State in a Transnational World* (The John Hopkins University Press)

Robinson, William, 2009, "Beyond the Theory of Imperialism: Global Capitalism and the Transnational State", in Alex Anievas (ed), *Marxism and World Politics* (Routledge).

Rowthorn, Bob, 1971, "Imperialism in the Seventies—Unity or Rivalry?", *New Left Review*, 69.

Rugman, Alan, and Alain Verbeke, 2004, "A Perspective on Regional and Global Strategies of Multinational Enterprises", *Journal of International Business Studies*, volume 35, number 1.

Ruigrok, Winfried, and Rob van Tulder, 1995, *The Logic of International Restructuring* (Routledge).

Sklair, Lesley, 2001, *The Transnational Capitalist Class* (Blackwell).

Stokes, Doug, 2005, "The Heart of Empire? Theorising US Empire in an Era of Transnational Capitalism", *Third World Quarterly*, volume 26, number 2.

Teschke, Benno, and Christian Heine, 2002, "The Dialectic of Globalisation: A Critique of Social Constructivism", in Mark Rupert and Hazel Smith (eds), *Historical Materialism and Globalization* (Routledge).

Trotsky, Leon, 1929, *The Permanent Revolution*, www.marxists.org/archive/trotsky/1931/tpr/

UNCTAD, 2003, *World Investment Report 2003: FDI Policies for Development; National and International Perspectives* (United Nations).

UNCTAD, 2004, *World Investment Report 2004: The Shift Towards Services* (United Nations).

UNCTAD, 2008, *World Investment Report 2008: Transnational Corporations and the Infrastructure Challenge* (United Nations).

United Nations, 2012, *The Millennium Development Goals Report 2012* (United Nations).

Wallerstein, Immanuel, 1998, *Utopistics: or, Historical Choices of the Twenty-first Century* (The New Press).

Wood, Ellen, 2002, "Global Capital, National States", in Mark Rupert and Hazel Smith (eds), *Historical Materialism and Globalization* (Routledge).

Wood, Ellen, 2003, *Empire of Capital* (Verso).

Marikana: A View from the Mountain and a Case to Answer

Peter Alexander, Thapelo Lekowa,
Botsang Mmope, Luke Sinwell and
Bongani Xezwi, £7.99

MARIKANA
A View from the Mountain
and a Case to Answer

Peter Alexander
Luke Sinwell
Thapelo Lekgowa
Botsang Mmope
and
Bongani Xezwi

On 16 August 2012 near Marikana, South Africa, striking miners from the Lonmin company were fired on by police, resulting in 34 deaths. The heart of this book is a series of interviews with strikers, most of them recorded on "the mountain" close to where their comrades were killed.

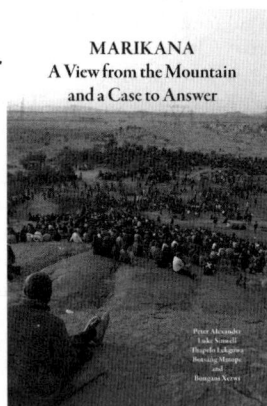

"The book provides a bottom-up account of the Marikana story, to correct an imbalance in many official and media accounts that privilege the viewpoints of governments and business, at the expense of workers." Professor Jane Duncan, chair of Media and Information Studies at Rhodes University

"Well written, extremely scrupulous in its research and forceful in its argument." Professor John Saul, Canadian political scientist, one of the world's top experts on liberation struggle in Southern Africa

"The Marikana massacre marked a watershed in the history of South Africa since the end of apartheid. In what may prove a classic work of engaged scholarship, this book helps the strikers themselves speak and be heard." Alex Callinicos, Professor of European Studies, King's College London

Available now in bookshops nationwide.

Bookmarks the socialist bookshop
1 Bloomsbury Street, London WC1B 3QE
020 7637 1848 www.bookmarksbookshop.co.uk
publications@bookmarks.uk.com

BOOKMARKS
PUBLICATIONS

Being right is not enough: Some thoughts on Paul Levi

Ian Birchall

John Rose and Sebastian Zehetmair[1] are quite right to welcome the publication of David Fernbach's collection of Paul Levi's writings.[2] There is still much to be learnt from the early years of the Communist International.

For far too long the Trotskyist tradition remained defensive, contrasting a Leninist "golden age" to the subsequent Stalinist degeneration. So Tony Cliff's *Lenin*—notably volume four,[3] drawing on the work of Lenin's contemporaries Victor Serge and Alfred Rosmer—helped to open up a new period of historical writing which, while recognising the basically positive role of the Comintern, was also aware of the weaknesses that existed from the very outset. This argument was taken further by Pierre Broué's history of the Comintern,[4] and by the work of scholars such as John Riddell, Jean-François Fayet, Reiner Tosstorff and others.[5] It is on the basis of this work, and in the spirit of openly critical support, that we should look at the case of Paul Levi.

As many of us know, factional disputes can produce enormous bitterness

1: Zehetmair and Rose, 2012.

2: Fernbach, 2011.

3: Cliff, 1979. Cliff's biography originally appeared in four volumes. The 1986 reprint combined the third and fourth into a single volume.

4: See Broué, 1997; also Birchall 1999.

5: Thus Cliff's work is in some senses now dated. It contains enormously valuable insights, but these should be checked against more recent studies.

and personal antagonism. This was even more the case in the aftermath of the Russian Revolution when the stakes were so high. It is not surprising that Levi felt betrayed by those he had regarded as his comrades, nor that his former comrades bitterly resented his public break with the German Communist Party (KPD). Ninety years on there is no point taking sides; but we can learn lessons from Levi's life, and my view is that some of those lessons are rather more negative than John and Sebastian acknowledge.

Paul Levi was a man of penetrating intelligence and personal courage; he did not aspire to leadership of the KPD, but was thrust into it by the murder of Luxemburg and Liebknecht. His promotion of the united front strategy was of great value. After his break with the KPD he remained firmly committed to the self-emancipation of the working class. As part of a stable leadership team Levi could have contributed much; but because the KPD had been formed so recently there was no such team.

In criticising Levi one should of course remember that his generation lived through difficult times. Choices had to be made which were quite literally a matter of life and death, and they had to be made quickly, for revolutionary opportunity was running out. Those of us who have the leisure of retrospective analysis should not judge harshly. But the whole point of studying history is to do better next time, so we should learn from our predecessors' mistakes.

Sebastian notes Levi's lack of tact. Indeed many who knew him noted personality defects. This in itself was not decisive; not all revolutionaries are nice people. But alongside his merits Levi had one very serious weakness. He had a fierce hatred of ultra-leftism and he did not know how to handle ultra-lefts. Now this is a fundamental problem for any revolutionary leader. In any revolutionary situation, indeed in any period of rising struggle, ultra-leftism will make an appearance. Newly radicalised people, especially the young, who have not experienced isolation and defeat, expect quick results. And they have a quite justifiable distrust of parliamentarism and the trade union bureaucracy.

Now ultra-leftism can be a serious problem for revolutionary organisation; it certainly was in the period following the Russian Revolution. John Rose commends Lenin's little book *"Left-Wing" Communism*.[6] This

---

6:    John is unwise to quote Tony Cliff on this point. Cliff's writings contain many valuable observations and repay study. But he also tended to make overstatements for the sake of effect ("bending the stick"). His comparison of *"Left-Wing" Communism* with the *Communist Manifesto* is, to say the least, unhelpful. Moreover John misquotes Cliff. Cliff did not claim that *"Left-Wing" Communism* was as *important* as the *Communist Manifesto* (which contains the first outline of the

contains some fundamental arguments, but it must be set in context.[7] Lenin saw the dangers of ultra-leftism, but he wanted to persuade the ultra-lefts, not push them away.

In particular John cites Lenin on the importance of participating in parliamentary elections. Certainly electoral campaigns may be useful for socialist purposes. But we can hardly win the argument by quoting Lenin, since so much has changed in 90 years. In 1920 many workers—in particular women—were voting for the first time, and there was little experience of reformist parties in power. Lenin stressed that "the masses must have their own political experience".[8] But it was precisely such experience that led to abstention rates of nearly 75 percent in the Middlesbrough and Croydon North by-elections in November 2012.

Levi's own failures with regard to ultra-leftism can be seen in three episodes: first, his conduct of the Heidelberg Congress of the KPD in 1919, which led to the exclusion of around half the party membership. There is a detailed analysis of this congress by Marcel Bois and Florian Wilde. They argue, convincingly, that the methods used by Levi and the party leadership had nothing in common with the later methods of Stalinism. The issues at stake—participation in parliamentary elections and work in the existing trade unions—were fundamental. They examine accusations of undemocratic practices, and show the difficulties caused by the fact that the party was working in illegal conditions. The disputed questions were debated in at least some regional conferences. They also note that the split with the ultra-lefts was a "necessary condition" for the fusion with the Independent Socialist (USPD) left achieved in 1920. The leftists were also intransigent, demanding expulsion of any members who participated in bourgeois parliaments. Bois and Wilde also claim that the Levi leadership tried to build bridges in order to win back some of those excluded.

However, they also note that the Comintern Executive accused the KPD leadership of "driving workers into the arms of the anarcho-syndicalist ranters", and they conclude that the actions of the Levi leadership were "from the point of view of inner-party democracy undoubtedly

---

whole of historical materialism), but said that its *influence* was as great—Cliff, 1979, p24. It is a bizarre comparison, since the influence of the *Communist Manifesto*, though enormous over the following century, was very slow for some decades—there were few Marxists in the Paris Commune.

7:    See Rosmer, 1987, and especially Rosmer, 1971. I develop some of these arguments in Birchall 2010.

8:    Cited in Cliff, 1979, p28. For the full text of Lenin's book see Lenin, 1920.

problematic".[9] The point is not to blame (or commend) a long-dead leader, but to ask whether things might have been handled differently.

Nonetheless it is possible to imagine an alternative scenario. The ultra-lefts were not homogeneous. The new party they founded—the KAPD—flew apart within three years.[10] As Chris Harman noted, it might have been possible to use "salami tactics":

> The party leadership would have done better to have pushed through its own policies at the congress and then taken on and removed the most irreconcilable opposition figures in the localities one at a time—especially since in the months that followed it became clear that different forms of impatience were driving the different oppositionists in completely different directions.[11]

Certainly Lenin regarded the outcome of the Heidelberg congress as little less than a disaster:

> My impression is that they are very gifted propagandists, inexperienced and young, like our own Left Communists ("Left" due to lack of experience and youth) of 1918. Given agreement *on the basic issue* (for Soviet rule, against bourgeois parliamentarism), unity, in my opinion, is possible and necessary, just as a split is necessary with the Kautskyites. If the split was inevitable, efforts should be made not to deepen it, but to approach the Executive Committee of the Third International for mediation and to make the "Lefts" formulate their differences in theses and in a pamphlet.[12]

Levi's role at the Second Congress of the Communist International in 1920 was equally questionable. The Russian Revolution had inspired enormous hopes in the world working class, but it was isolated and under threat. Delegates had been invited from a broad range of political positions, including syndicalists and anarchists who rejected the need for a revolutionary party; many had got to Russia with great difficulty and at some risk. Levi proceeded to lecture them, telling them that "the majority of the western European working class" had resolved the questions "decades ago".[13] Among those who attended the congress Victor Serge noted

---

9: Bois and Wilde, 2007.
10: Reichenbach, 1969.
11: Harman, 1982, p153.
12: Lenin, 1965a, pp87-88.
13: Riddell, 1991, volume I, p166.

Levi's "Marxist insensitivity",[14] while Alfred Rosmer recalled that he was "obsessed" with the leftists excluded at Heidelberg and that "the conflict took on the appearance of a personal quarrel".[15] By contrast, Lenin and Trotsky went out of their way to minimise the differences between Bolsheviks and syndicalists.

It is easy to agree with Sebastian that the March Action was a disaster.[16] The party that Levi had tried to build seemed to be disintegrating. But while his furious response is understandable emotionally, it nonetheless deserves serious criticism.

Fernbach's collection gives us the full text of Levi's pamphlet, *Our Path*.[17] Levi's main line of argument is indeed correct, but various aspects are open to criticism. Firstly, Levi issued this publicly, making it available to the party's enemies at a time of massive repression.[18] Indeed the whole style of the pamphlet set Levi apart from the party—as Lenin noted: "Paul Levi's entirely negative criticism, which lacked that 'feeling of oneness' with the party, and embittered the comrades rather more by its tone than by its content, diverted attention from most important aspects of the problem".[19]

As Lenin pointed out, Levi's style actually played into the hands of the defenders of the "theory of the offensive": "a feeling arose—it also extended to non-German comrades—in which the dispute concerning the pamphlet, and concerning Levi himself, became the sole subject of this contention, instead of the false theory and bad practice of the 'offensive theory' and the leftists: They have to thank Paul Levi that up to the present they have come out so well, much too well. Paul Levi is his own worst enemy".[20]

Secondly, Levi's characterisation of the March Action as a putsch was misleading. Thousands of Communist workers took part, many with enthusiasm, often former Independent Socialist Party members who had joined the KPD hoping for rapid action.[21] The best estimate of those participating was over 200,000 workers on strike, plus unemployed and youth

---

14: Serge, 2012, p121.
15: Rosmer, 1987, p35.
16: Broué, 2005, pp491-525.
17: Fernbach, 2011, pp119-165. Cliff does not seem to have consulted this text, since he quotes it via extracts published in an article in *Survey*—Cliff, 1979, p111.
18: Does John think the SWP should have issued a—well-deserved—public denunciation of the Class War grouping's ultra-left tactics in the immediate aftermath of the 1990 Poll Tax riot?
19: Zetkin, 1934. John cites this at second hand, but fails to draw out the importance of Lenin's analysis of Levi developed in his conversations with Zetkin.
20: Zetkin, 1934.
21: Morgan, 1975, p397.

who took part in demonstrations: far too few for a bid for power, but rather a lot for a "putsch".[22] This was not simply something imposed by the Comintern (though the ECCI's role was certainly questionable), but an expression of a real ultra-left current in the party. As Sebastian notes, the KAPD had exercised an influence on KPD members. There are no organisational solutions to political problems; the ultra-lefts had not vaporised simply because they had been expelled. (The Bolsheviks had had a similar problem in the "July Days" in 1917, but because they had a more stable and well-established leadership disaster was averted.)

But John and Sebastian's main complaint seems to be the alleged "cover-up" of the Levi affair and the March Action by the Third Congress of the Comintern. In this they closely follow Tony Cliff, who devoted a whole chapter of his *Lenin* to "The Great Cover-Up".[23] Cliff at this point seems to have been concerned to stress the fallibility of the Comintern. While his primary intention in *Lenin* was to defend the Leninist tradition, he did not want to encourage an uncritical use of the Comintern as a model. So here he was "bending the stick" back in the opposite direction—perhaps a little too far.

We do not yet have John Riddell's edition of the proceedings of the Third Congress, which may cast additional light on the whole question. The minutes[24] show that, out of the congress's 21 days, five sessions over three days (21 hours of debate) were devoted to Radek's report on tactics, to which the March Action was central. Speakers included Lenin,[25] Trotsky, Bukharin, Georg Lukács and representatives of the KAPD; Clara Zetkin, who defended Levi, was given (at Zinoviev's proposal) an extra 15 minutes. She insisted that the "mistakes" of the March Action were "organically founded in the erroneous theory of the offensive".[26] Earlier in the congress Zetkin had delivered a speech of around two hours (greeted with "vigorous approval and applause") in defence of Levi.[27] This is not what most people would describe as a "cover-up".

The problem is that the final resolution did not make an unambiguous condemnation of the March Action, but described it as a "step forward", while noting that the KPD "made a number of mistakes, of

---

22: Koch-Baumgarten, 1986, pp228, etc.
23: Cliff, 1979, pp110-121.
24: *Protokoll*, 1921.
25: Lenin's speech is at Lenin, 1965b, pp468-477.
26: *Protokoll*, 1921, pp431-671.
27: *Protokoll*, 1921, pp278-300.

which the most important was that it did not emphasise the defensive character of the struggle".[28]

The Third Congress took place in the aftermath of Kronstadt and the introduction of the New Economic Policy. It was no time to force a split at the very top of the leadership of the Russian Party and the Comintern. Even if one accepts Serge's judgement that Zinoviev was "Lenin's biggest mistake", pushing the point would have meant a confrontation with Bukharin and Radek—again we have Serge's testimony that Lenin, Trotsky, Bukharin and Radek were "the brains of the revolution" who understood each other so well that "they seemed to think collectively".[29] Moreover the theory of the offensive had many thousands of supporters in the KPD and other sections of the Comintern.

If John and Sebastian think there should have been a confrontation with Zinoviev and his allies, this raises the question of who should have replaced him. There were scarcely any able but underemployed comrades hanging around looking for a job.

Revolutionary leadership requires both unity and clarity. Sometimes the two conflict and getting the balance right is not easy. As Lenin pointed out, revolutionary leadership is an art as well as a science.[30]

Sebastian refers to Clara Zetkin's[31] record of her conversations with Lenin during the Third Congress. Unfortunately he does not examine or quote from this remarkable document,[32] which shows Lenin at his best.

Lenin condemned the "theory of the offensive", dismissing it as "an illusion...romanticism, sheer romanticism". But he put forward the need for compromise. It was necessary to defeat the ultra-lefts without humiliating them, in order to keep them within the movement:

> If the tactics to be decided upon by the congress are agreed upon as quickly as possible, and with no great friction, becoming the guiding principle for the activity of the Communist Parties, our dear leftists will go back not too mortified and not too embittered. We must also—and indeed first and before all—consider the feelings of the real revolutionary workers both within and outside the party.

28: Degras, 1971, p252.
29: Serge, 2012, pp207, 158.
30: Cited in Cliff, 1979, p30.
31: Zetkin is the one who comes out best from this episode. She backed Levi's position, but stayed to fight inside the party. It is intended to produce an issue of *Revolutionary History* devoted to her writings.
32: Zetkin, 1934.

Well, we shan't deal roughly with the leftists; we shall put some balm on their wounds instead. Then they will soon be working happily and energetically with you in carrying out the policy of the Third Congress of our International. For that means rallying large sections of workers to your policy, mobilising them under Communist leadership and bringing them into the struggle against the bourgeoisie and for the seizure of power.[33]

He urged Zetkin to stay in the party and work patiently for unity: "Your duty now is to keep the party together. I make you personally responsible for seeing that there is no split, or at the most, only a small splitting off. You must be strict with the young comrades who are still without any deep theoretical knowledge or practical experience, and at the same time you must be very patient with them".[34]

Finally, two more general observations on the implications of the Levi affair. Lenin observed to Zetkin that he wished to keep Levi because there was a shortage of able comrades: "We must not lose Levi. For his own sake and for our cause. We are not over-blessed with talent and must keep as much of what we have as we can".[35] Levi himself noted that the Russians could not commit their "best forces" to the Comintern, as they were irreplaceable at home.[36] The collapse of the Second International had meant the loss of most of the cadre accumulated by the international socialist movement over the preceding decades. Hence the Comintern often had to rely on relatively inexperienced comrades and on people who were not up to the job. The fact that major responsibilities were given to Zinoviev, despite his appalling behaviour in 1917, and to Bela Kun (whose stupidity Lenin condemned) was a symptom of this lack of cadre.[37]

Secondly, John and Sebastian are quite right to point to the centrality of the united front with reformist workers, and Levi is to be wholly commended for his role in instigating and promoting this. But the united front takes many forms. What Lenin and Trotsky—but few others—seem to have wanted was a united front with the reformists on the one hand, but on the other hand an alliance with the various ultra-lefts (especially syndicalists) who had some real base in the European labour movement. The besieged revolution needed allies in every quarter.

33: Zetkin, 1934.
34: Zetkin, 1934.
35: Zetkin, 1934.
36: Fernbach, 2011, p161.
37: Cliff discusses this problem of shortage of cadre in Russia and in the Comintern—Cliff, 1978, pp6-7, Cliff, 1979, pp59-65. For a development of the argument see Birchall, 2000.

Could such a "triple alliance"—revolutionaries, reformists, ultra-lefts—have been created to defend and spread the revolution?[38] There would have been many contradictions, much friction. But as I recall Tony Cliff once asking a district aggregate: "Did you think it would be easy?"

38: I leave readers to consider possible parallels with the present day.

References

Birchall, Ian, 1999, "Review of Broué's History of the Communist International", *Revolutionary History*, 7/2, www.marxists.org/history/etol/writers/birchall/1999/xx/broue.html

Birchall, Ian, 2000, "The Success and Failure of the Comintern", in K Flett and D Renton (eds), *The Twentieth Century* (Rivers Oram).

Birchall, Ian, 2010, "Another Side of Anarchism", *International Socialism* 127 (summer), www.isj.org.uk/?id=663

Birchall, Ian, 2011, *Tony Cliff: a Marxist For His Time* (Bookmarks).

Bois, Marcel and Florian Wilde, 2007, "Modell für den künftigen Umgang mit innerparteilicher Diskussion? Der Heidelberger Parteitag der KPD 1919", www.workerscontrol.net/de/authors/%E2%80%9Cmodell-fuer-den-kuenftigen-umgang-mit-innerparteilicher-diskussion%E2%80%9C

Broué, Pierre, 1997, *Histoire de l'Internationale Communiste* (Fayard).

Broué, Pierre, 2005, *The German Revolution 1917-1923* (Brill).

Cliff, Tony, 1978, *Lenin*, volume 3 (Pluto).

Cliff, Tony, 1979, *Lenin*, volume 4 (Pluto).

Degras, Jane, 1971, *The Communist International*, volume I (Frank Cass).

Fernbach, David (ed), 2011, *In the steps of Rosa Luxemburg: Selected Writings by Paul Levi* (Brill).

Harman, Chris, 1982, *The Lost Revolution* (Bookmarks).

Koch-Baumgarten, Sigrid, 1986, *Aufstand der Avantgarde* (Campus Verlag).

Lenin, Vladimir, 1920, *"Left-Wing" Communism: an Infantile Disorder*, www.marxists.org/archive/lenin/works/1920/lwc/index.htm

Lenin, Vladimir, 1965a, *Collected Works*, volume 30 (Progress).

Lenin, Vladimir, 1965b, *Collected Works*, volume 32 (Progress).

Morgan, David W, 1975, *The Socialist Left and the German Revolution* (Cornell University Press).

Protokoll des III. Kongresses der Kommunistischen Internationale, 1921 (Verlag der Kommunistischen Internationale).

Reichenbach, Bernhard, 1969, "The KAPD in Retrospect", www.marxists.org/archive/reichenbach/1969/retrospect.htm

Riddell, John (ed), 1991, *Workers of the World and Oppressed Peoples, Unite!* (Pathfinder).

Rosmer, Alfred, 1971, "Two Books by Lenin", *International Socialism 46* (first series, February-March), www.marxists.org/archive/rosmer/1953/moscow/lenin.htm

Rosmer, Alfred, 1987, *Lenin's Moscow* (Bookmarks).

Serge, Victor, 2012, *Memoirs of a Revolutionary* (New York Review Books).

Zehetmair, Sebastian, and John Rose, 2012, "Germany's Lost Bolshevik: Paul Levi Revisited", *International Socialism 136* (winter), www.isj.org.uk/?id=850

Zetkin, Clara, 1934, *Reminiscences of Lenin* (International Publishers), www.marxists.org/archive/zetkin/1924/reminiscences-of-lenin.htm

Book reviews

Beyond the western world
Ben Selwyn

Kevin B Anderson, **Marx at the Margins** *(University of Chicago Press, 2010),* £15.00

Frederick Engels used to remark that the struggle for socialism occurs on the political, economic and ideological plains. *Marx at the Margins* is a valuable contribution to the latter. Ever since Marx began his ruthless critique of capitalism and advocacy of a socialist alternative, he has been attacked and distorted in almost equal measure by opponents and so-called supporters of socialism. Those coming across him for the first time are subjected to a bewildering array of claims about him— that he supported European colonisation of the non-capitalist world as a means of bringing "development" to it, that his historical materialist method represented an economic determinism, where law-like economic processes determined social and historical development, that he singled out the European proletariat as the only possible leaders of the struggle for worldwide socialism, and that he ignored other forms of oppression such as racism. Such conceptions of Marx's historical materialism were already being made by many of his followers during his lifetime, so much so that he once quipped that "all I know is that I am not a Marxist". An example of the ways in which Marx's historical materialism has been distorted is gleaned from an official (1963) Soviet text, *Fundamentals*

of Marxism-Leninism, which stated that "all peoples travel what is basically the same path... The development of society proceeds through the consecutive replacement, according to definite laws, of one socio-economic function by another."

More recently academics relatively friendly to Marxism have also criticised Marx along these lines. In his *Orientalism* the late Edward Said criticised Marx's early writings on India, arguing that "every writer on the Orient [including Marx] saw [it] as a locale requiring Western attention, reconstruction and even redemption". Said's critique is important because he has influenced the popular school of "post-colonial studies", which emphasises the recovery, past and present, of the voices and agency of populations of the Global South, as part of an emancipatory project to combat Western racism and imperialism. Many post-colonial studies adopt a rather caricatured version of Marx, in the vein of Said's critique.

Socialists should be the natural allies of the this emancipatory project. However, if Marx is deemed to be part of the problem, such alliances will be weakened: Socialists would be excluded, and struggles against imperialism and racism will be denied a firm class analysis. They will often be led by actors who do not conceive of capitalism as their main enemy, and seek to make alliance with "progressive" capitalists. There is a long history of such anti-imperialist movements and their disappointing outcomes, in the second half of the 20th century. The last notable one was the South African case, where, junking their prior anti-capitalist principles in favour of alliances with domestic and international capital, the leading sections of the anti-apartheid movement now preside over a hierarchical, deeply unequal nation. That is why this book is so important.

In a wide-ranging survey Anderson reveals a fundamentally different Marx to the caricature described above. His main thesis is that the young Marx, of the *Communist Manifesto* and other early journalistic writings, was sometimes guilty of the accusations levelled at him by writers such as Said. However, as Marx matured, his views on non-Western societies changed, and, contrary to Said's claims, he became an active supporter and champion of their struggles against Western domination. Anderson argues that whilst in the 1840s Marx held "to an implicitly unilinear perspective, sometimes tinged with ethnocentrism...over time, his perspective evolved towards one that was more multilinear, leaving the future development of these societies as an open question" (p2). Perhaps most importantly, and certainly controversially, Anderson argues that while Marx is often understood as privileging the Western working class as agents of socialist transformation, his writings on non-Western societies demonstrate that he viewed the latter as partners, as catalysts, and eventually as potential leaders of the struggle for worldwide socialist transformation. Moreover, Anderson reveals a Marx who was concerned with and drew analytical and political connections between race, class and national liberation.

In his chapter on "Colonial Encounters in the 1850s" Anderson addresses head-on criticism from writers like Said, who claim that Marx adopted a Eurocentric understanding of "The Orient". Said's argument rests on Marx's statements, in newspaper articles such as "The Future Results of the British Rule in India" (1853) to the effect that "England has to fulfil a double mission in India: one destructive, the other regenerating." If this was all Marx wrote on India, Said's criticism would be well founded. But Anderson shows, with painstaking detail, how Marx's views on India changed rapidly. By 1857 Marx was exposing the divide and rule techniques of British rule in India where "the vital principle of British supremacy" was playing off "the antagonism of the various races, tribes, castes, creeds and sovereignties". A year later, during the huge Sepoy uprising which threatened British rule, Marx propounded a thoroughgoing anti-imperialism, noting in a letter to Engels that "India is now our best ally".

In the chapter on "Race, Class and Slavery". Anderson shows how Marx's analysis of capitalism, while focusing on English industrialisation, was located in a global context, exposing the particular racial and ethnic dimensions of capital accumulation. Marx describes how:

"English modern industry, in general, relied upon two pivots equally monstrous. The one was the potato as the only means of feeding Ireland and a great part of the English working class... The second... was the slave-grown cotton of the United States... As long as the English cotton manufacturers depended on slave-grown cotton, it could be truthfully asserted that they rested on a twofold slavery, the indirect slavery of the white man in England and the direct slavery of the black man on the other side of the Atlantic".*

Marx then describes how where workers are divided they help cement the rule of capital, but how when united they are able to change the course of world history. For

---

* www.marxists.org/archive/marx/works/1861/10/14.htm

example, in his discussion of working class politics Marx noted how the division of the working class in England into ethnically English and Irish sections represented a significant block on the development of a more radical and militant politics. So "every movement in England itself is crippled by the dissension with the Irish, who form a very important section of the working class in England itself". In a similar vein, in his analysis of the utility of racism for capital in the US, he noted that "labour in a white skin cannot emancipate itself where it is branded in a black skin".

Marx also argued, however, that the First International in Britain could potentially play a central role in fostering unity within the working class: "The special task of the [First International's] council in London is to awaken the consciousness of the English working class to the notion that, for them, the national emancipation of Ireland is not a question of abstract justice or humanitarian sentiment, but the first condition of their own social emancipation." He also understood the potential of an Irish revolution and its impacts upon the working class of England. In 1869 he wrote:

"For a long time, I believed it would be possible to overthrow the Irish regime by English working class ascendancy... Deeper study has now convinced me of the opposite. The English working class will never accomplish anything before it has got rid of Ireland. The lever must be applied in Ireland."

For Anderson this and other writings reveal a "broader shift in his thinking, toward the notion that struggles on the periphery of capitalism could become sparks that might very well go off in advance of workers' revolutions in the industrially developed societies" (p151).

In his analysis of the American Civil War, Anderson highlights Marx's drawing together of the fight against slavery in North America to European class struggles. Marx was merciless in his criticism of the European heads of state that supported the Confederates and the maintenance of slavery. In his inaugural address to the First International in 1864, however, Marx stated: "It was not the wisdom of the ruling classes, but the heroic resistance to their criminal folly by the working classes of England that saved the West of Europe from plunging headlong into an infamous crusade for the perpetuation of slavery on the other side of the Atlantic." Marx conceptualised international solidarity, between European industrial workers and North American slaves, as representing a foreign policy of the nascent working class.

In the final chapter Anderson documents how, after the 1872 publication of a Russian edition of *Capital*, volume I, and its popular reception in Russia, Marx took a particularly close interest in the country's system of agrarian village communes. While many of Marx's followers in Russia were already adhering to an economic determinist and linear conception of history, where Russian development was supposedly destined to follow England's, other non-Marxists in Russia (the agrarian "populists") argued that the commune potentially represented a basis for an alternative path of human development. Marx learned Russian and studied the Russian commune in great depth. He concluded, against his orthodox followers, that the commune potentially provided the basis for a non-capitalist development path. However, against the populists, he also argued that if such a path could occur, it would have to do so based on a twin revolution, in Russia against state and capital and internationally as part of a worldwide socialist revolution. Here Marx viewed the agricultural Russian commune as the potential vanguard of the world revolution.

Anderson's study is meticulous, written in a clear and accessible language, and provides readers with a valuable account of the evolution of Marx's thought. It counters the lazy caricatures of Marx put about by his enemies and supporters alike and undercuts arguments that he held to a Eurocentric, unilinear and economic determinist conception of human development.

While *Marx at the Margins* is a necessary and important book, it could, arguably, be even better. The main reason for this is that it resembles a text in the tradition of Marxology, which is concerned to establish what Marx said, when, how and why. Such issues are important, in particular when engaging in ideological struggles over Marx's legacy, but focusing almost exclusively upon them runs the risk of side lining broader theoretical issues. For example, what stands out in the above mentioned discussion of Marx's writings on the Russian commune is that his argument, that the commune could act as the catalyst for and beginning of a worldwide socialist revolution, resembles in some respects the case made by Leon Trotsky some two and a half decades later, during the 1905 Russian Revolution. Trotsky formulated his theory of permanent revolution to explain how economically backward Russia, which had still not experienced a bourgeois revolution, could skip economic and political stages, through a socialist revolution, without waiting for further economic development or following the path already established by advanced European states.

Whilst Lenin and much of the Bolshevik Party embraced the theory of permanent revolution in 1917, with the rise of the Stalinist bureaucracy from the mid-1920s, the theory became heretical within the Marxist mainstream. Rather the "orthodox" conceptions of stagist/unilinear development, and the possibilities of socialism in one country became the official doctrine of Marxism, as reflected in the quote at the start of this review. In many respects then, Marx's writings on the Russian agrarian commune predated Trotsky's conception of permanent revolution. Of course, there was a major difference between the two. Where Marx viewed the Russian peasantry as potential revolutionary subjects, Trotsky identified the burgeoning industrial working class as the revolutionary vanguard. This is an important difference, explained in part at least by the transformations in Russia between the 1880s and the early 20th century—during which Russia underwent a massive industrialisation drive in order to attempt to "catch-up" with the advanced Western powers, and in the process created a new, militant industrial working class.

A second area where Anderson could have expanded his discussion is in his analysis of Marx's 1864 Inaugural Address to the First International.* When Anderson discusses this important text he draws our attention to Marx's statements about the necessity of the (British) working class developing its own foreign policy in its support for the North in the American Civil War, as a means of generating international proletarian solidarity. In his *Beyond Capital*, Michael Lebowitz, drawing on the same document, conceptualises such a foreign policy as part of a broader "political economy of the working class"—a distinct and oppositional political economy to that of the capitalist class. Lebowitz, gives other examples of the political economy of the working class, including

---

* www.marxists.org/archive/marx/works/1864/10/27.htm

the struggle for limits to the working day, and workers' control of industrial cooperatives. Lebowitz demonstrates how class struggle is constitutive of human development more broadly (a key theme in Anderson's book), but also of the form and content of capitalist development (for example, wage rates, forms of exploitation, the extent of workers' rights). Because Anderson is concerned with demonstrating Marx's evolving thinking on non-western societies, he does not delve deeper into Marx's analysis of capitalism in the core of the world system, and how, here too, Marx identified myriad class formations, forms and outcomes of class struggle. The works of Jairus Banaji and Marcel van der Linden are particularly interesting in these respects.

The above comments are less criticisms of Anderson's book than encouragements for future work. In the context of world economic crisis, reaction and revolution, Marx's analyses of the myriad forms that class struggles take are indispensable. Anderson highlights a Marx who participated actively in debates about how to overcome divisions between ethnically stratified sections of the working class, of how to generate international solidarity between predominantly white industrial working classes in advanced capitalist countries and black slaves in relatively backward agrarian economies. He also shows how Marx laboured throughout his life to understand how new conjunctures in world history might kindle revolutionary possibilities, leading to worldwide transition away from capitalism to socialism. For all of these reasons, Anderson's book is a very significant contribution to our understanding of, and ability to draw on Marx in our attempts to transform the this crisis-ridden system.

Is bad Pharma just bad science?
Sophie Williams

Ben Goldacre, **Bad Pharma** *(Fourth Estate, 2012), £13.99*

The threat to our NHS is something we all know about, but *Bad Pharma* exposes another crisis in medicine: the power of the pharmaceutical industry, "Pharma", to protect its private interests. Ben Goldacre is a practising doctor and journalist, author of *Bad Science* (2009) and the same titled *Guardian* column, which has run since 2003. He is interested in "unpicking bad science" as "the best way to explain good science" and is committed to making such debates accessible to a wide audience. *Bad Pharma*, subtitled "How Drug Companies Mislead Doctors and Harm Patients", exposes bad regulation and bad science, but also offers insights into the mechanisms of Pharma's grip on the practice of medicine.

Goldacre explains how Pharma bypasses legislation to retain profitability and how regulatory bodies are more concerned with commercial protectionism than standards of healthcare. The EU's bureaucratic bodies, created to regulate Pharma, are affiliated with industrial rather than health departments, and conflicts of interest surrounding regulator's funding and individual's lobbying potential are concealed and unchallenged. The structures in clinical research reflect wider neoliberal economic policies. The deregulation of clinical trials has resulted in the creation of independent Clinical Trials Organisations (CTOs) which provide trial services at competitive rates. They are able to "undercut" trials conducted in countries with more protective or complete legislation concerning ethics and clinical research. In a sample of clinical trials conducted across developing countries that CTOs are expanding into, less than half required an ethics review board, a basic requirement of clinical trials.

Changes in US legislation in 2008, designed to bring more trials back home, saw the removal of ethical considerations in favour of procedural ones. There is also a trend towards greater drug approval rates. During the Reagan years the rate of drug approval in the last month of the financial year increased significantly relative to other months, indicating a pressure to release new drugs without the strength of evidence being the principal factor.

Commercial interest is allowed to play such an important role, Goldacre argues, because the scientific evidence is manipulated by medical trial design, statistical analysis and publication practice. The lack of pressure on Pharma to provide accurate data, for Goldacre, results from the inability of doctors and the scientific community to confront and undermine inadequate evidence for the safety and effectiveness of new drugs over existing—and often cheaper—alternatives. However, Goldacre limits his argument to suggesting that changing the code of conduct towards better science would be sufficient to undermine Pharma's power. This is made clear in his chapter on "Better Trials", where the war against "Bad Pharma" is played out in the ideological battleground between "better" and "bad trials".

Pharma has turned towards bad science because of the nature of scientific method under neoliberalism. Capitalism has always put profits first, but increasingly Pharma has found it harder to squeeze profits from making useful drugs. The requirement for novel, "high impact" science sidelines criticism and positive results become the primary interest. Many scientific disciplines rely on quantitative rankings for novelty and therefore funding, and, for Pharma, profits depend upon and reinforce this trend. Goldacre shows that the bias towards positive results is higher by a factor of almost two thirds in research funded by industry. This is consistent with the requirement for positive results to illustrate clinical benefit, giving the best chance for a market and maximised profit. At the same time, the loss of investment from research and development and injection into marketing means that, more often than not, a new drug is nothing of the sort. The interest in marketing "me-too" and "me-again" drugs illustrates the changing nature of the value-form, the detachment from the production of better drugs in favour of bigger profits.

Goldacre goes further to show that Pharma tampers with data, albeit short of outright fabrication, to show positive results. Trial data goes unpublished or missing, and statistical mishaps appear which give greater weighting to potentially random conclusions. When this gives rise to a positive result, it is published. When it doesn't, it is deleted. Such tampered evidence harms patients, not only during trials themselves, but more generally through limiting the ability of doctors and patients to make informed decisions.

There are interesting discussions about how academic publications, educational materials and the intervention into the media by Pharma distort cultural attitudes towards certain diseases, both lay and professional. Herceptin, a breast cancer drug costing tens of thousands for each treatment, became a headline test-case for modernisation in centralised healthcare. Two thirds of reports about Herceptin used individual miracle recoveries to illustrate the effectiveness of the drug, even when these women were sourced from PR companies paid by Roche, the manufacturer. The side-effects were rarely mentioned.

The distortion of the benefits of a drug through marketing is paralleled in the marketing of symptoms and diseases themselves. Over-diagnosis and the creation of new forms of disease are particularly relevant to the design and marketing of depression medications.

Goldacre is deeply critical of the political and economic interests that have allowed the industry to go practically unregulated, but it is only by reading between the lines that we see inequality and exploitation at the hands of the pharmaceutical industry to be as crucial as statistical malpractice in boosting profits. His in-depth investigation into the interests of private medicine foreshadows, although never mentions, how privatisation and deregulation in the NHS will affect the industry's practice, and therefore patients in the UK. Similarly, the statistical bias introduced by class, for example mistaking the benefits of hormone therapy treatment for those of a privileged lifestyle, is critiqued as a statistical anomaly but not developed into an analysis of the inequality of the provision of medicine more generally.

Goldacre identifies the responsibility due at every level: governments, regulators, academics, doctors and even patient groups. His message, again aimed at policy makers and patients alike, is to ensure that profit is kept at the margin when drugs are approved for use. Whether this approach will undermine the power of Pharma, I'm not sure.

Bread and circuses
Nick Evans

Review of Peter Brown (2012) **Through the Eye of a Needle: Wealth, the Fall of Rome, and the Making of the Christian West: 350-550** *(Princeton University Press, 2012), £27.95*

How did Christians come to be intensely relaxed about people being filthy rich? Peter Brown, a historian who has transformed ideas of the period once called the "Dark Ages", uses this question to illuminate a world in crisis. This book may not yield the rich social history from below, or detailed economic history, that its opening section seems to promise. But through his presentation of the ideas of major late Roman writers and church leaders in relation to the changing world in which they lived, Peter Brown offers brilliant insights into the emergence of institutions and ideologies we think of as characteristic of the medieval west, and which continue to have major influence in our own time.

The title comes from a line attributed to Jesus: "It is easier for a camel to pass through the eye of a needle than for a rich man to enter the kingdom of heaven." The Marxist historian Geoffrey de Ste Croix once drew attention to how this line, which appears in the gospels of Matthew, Mark and Luke, came to be read by the figures who dominate this book. In only one version, that of Matthew, the line "if you would be perfect" is added in. This qualification, however, was taken up by all the commentators on the incident. Peter Brown's focus on how figures such as Augustine of Hippo helped to take the sting out of Christian critiques of the rich leads him to present familiar texts and disputes in a startlingly new light.

Augustine's dispute with the ascetic preacher Pelagius over the question of humans were inherently evil (Augustine supported the concept of "original sin", which Pelagius challenged), was constantly revisited over the following centuries and became a major issue during the Reformation. Brown shows how the original discussion was all about wealth. Pelagius was no radical on this: he wrote to the notoriously rich Anicii family to reassure them that their wealth derived from their own virtues. This was conventional Roman wisdom on the subject, but Augustine argued wealth came from God alone. This may have been a less flattering message for late Roman aristocrats, but it had the useful effect of treating the origins of wealth as beyond discussion. Brown points out that it also enabled a "no questions asked" approach to donations to the church.

This happened precisely at a time when some Christians were beginning to enquire into the origins of ruling class wealth. An anonymous pamphlet called *On Riches* by a writer influenced by Pelagius put it simply: "If you take away the rich, you won't find any poor" (p313). In the context of the weakening of Roman power in the early 5th century, the writer of the pamphlet pointed not only to the abuses of individual landowners, but to the whole fiscal and administrative system which underpinned their power. This contrasts with the preaching of the otherwise uncompromising figure of Ambrose of Milan, just a few decades earlier, whose criticisms of the rich remained confined to individual behaviour. By the mid-5th century Salvian of Gaul was squarely blaming the burdens of Roman taxation for the victories of the "barbarian" armies.

Alongside the critique of wealth is the question of giving. The Roman aristocracy had long traditions of self-promoting dona-tions to their cities, from public building works to putting on lavish games. But their generosity was only directed to those with the privilege of citizenship. When some rich Romans started giving money to non-citizens Peter Brown reveals the contradictory motivations lying behind such donations. By giving to people to whom they felt they had no social obligations, their gift giving was, in a sense, simply the mirror image of the "ideal" commodity exchange: treating the poor as "others", rather than "brothers", in Brown's words.

The absence of any feeling of obligation to the ordinary people from whom their wealth was derived is starkly revealed by Brown's depiction of the behaviour of super-rich aristocrats Melania and Pinanius during the siege of Rome in 408 CE. The hagiography of Melania tells us that she was reminded of Jesus's warning about the eye of a needle in a dream. So, just at the point when the Gothic armies stood outside the City of Rome, Melania and Pinanius suddenly informed 8,000 of their slaves that they had been emancipated, and thereby abandoned to their fate. It was, as Brown puts it, a context in which, "through renunciation, absentee lords became something worse than absent" (p296).

There are notable absences and imbalances in this book. It begins by responding to recent scholarship indicating late Roman urban civilisation as characterised by a sizeable population of people who belonged neither to the super-rich nor to the poor, and shows churches developing in such a milieu in the 4th century. But the rest of the book concentrates on a small number of exceptional writers largely drawn from higher social circles. Perhaps more surprisingly, it virtually doesn't discuss slaves at all. Much of the economic evidence is dependent on material from Egypt, despite an opening promise to focus on regional diversity.

However, by presenting the ideological conflicts over wealth in the period in such an original fashion, Brown has made a crucial contribution to understanding how the relationship between Western aristocrats and the church in the post-Roman period developed in the way it did.

Lessons from Botswana
Andy Wynne

Motsomi Ndala Marobela, **Political Economy of Botswana Public Sector Management: From Imperialism to Neoliberalism** *(VDM Verlag Dr. Muller, 2010), £68*

Motsomi Marobela provides a comprehensive review of the suite of reforms that have dominated the public sector in sub-Saharan Africa as well as Europe over the last three decades. As such, this book deepens our understanding of this process and so provides valuable lessons on how these reforms can be fought. The major public sector strike in Botswana in 2011 and the ongoing public sector disputes in Britain demonstrate the continuing relevance of the issues raised. Motsomi writes: "The central thesis of this book is that public service transformation has become another area for capitalist accumulation and this forms part of the core capitalist strategy of imperialism, now unfolding under neoliberal globalisation of liberalism and privatisation. Hence the public services in Botswana are adopting private sector management practices such as public private partnership, contracting and outsourcing, as ways of improving efficiency and delivery."

Motsomi connects particular public sector reforms in selected organisations (the Botswana police), through the specific activities of the relevant national and international bodies in advancing the reform agenda set by the global institutions such as the World Bank. It also uses our tradition of Marxist political economy to assert that the labour process is governed (but not determined) by wider political economic forces.

He proceeds from the general to the particular with the first chapter considering the philosophy, critical realism, that is needed for this type of research to be effective. But Motsomi develops this to form a new perspective based on dialectical materialism.

The second chapter situates the history of Botswana within the more general history of capitalism. "This global picture and trajectory is essential for the understanding of profound changes in labour process in Botswana generally and the restructuring of the public sector specifically."

Across most of sub-Saharan Africa neoliberal reforms were forced on heavily indebted governments through the structural adjustment programmes of the 1980s. Botswana was different as the revenue from diamond exports allowed its government to avoid the build-up of public debt. As a result, the strategy for implementing the neoliberal policies of privatisation, competitive tendering, contracting out and pay and employment flexibility in Botswana was different. It was more dependent on winning at least a section of public sector senior managers and leaders to the necessity of implementing such reforms.

Senior civil servants were co-opted to support the reform process through the provision of training, seminars and the use of international consultants. The reforms were further promoted through the inter-relationships between global institutions (the World Bank), international bodies (United Nations Development Programme, Commonwealth Secretariat) and national organisations (Directorate of Public Service Management, Botswana Institute of Development Policy Analysis). One challenge was the need to gain acceptance that fundamental reforms were necessary, even in a country with a successful economic history and a public administration which has been widely accepted as being one of the best in Africa. This was made easier by the benefits that the local elites gained from such reforms and the fact that they were simultaneously being implemented in the neighbouring countries.

Thames Valley Police worked with the British government's Department for International Development, the Adam Smith Institute and the local Central Police Training and Development Authority to reform the organisation and management of the Botswana police. However, these reforms were "contestable and therefore complex to implement because long held values of managing public service cannot be simply transposed with those of the private sector". Resistance was likely, as "these neoliberal reforms...cause more harm than benefit to the majority of workers, for instance, job losses and work speed up". While senior management were persuaded and gained from higher salaries, "ordinary workers have to feel that they too have a role to shape such change to meet their needs".

This was not widely achieved. As a result, there was a wave of strikes by primary school teachers in the 1980s organised as the Job-Evaluation-Unsatisfied Teachers. In 2002 it was the turn of the secondary teachers and local government workers.

Their mass strikes were based on concerns over a job evaluation exercise. Even within the police there has been resistance, as manual workers refused to be outsourced and demonstrated against privatisation in 2000.

Since the publication of this book discontent by public sector workers in Botswana erupted with an eight-week strike from April to June 2011 of up to 100,000 workers. This was the first legal public sector strike in Botswana. Although they won a pay increase of only 3 percent, the implications have been far fetched. In June 2012 the mass dismissals were judged illegal by the High Court and all the affected workers were ordered to be reinstated.

In places Motsomi may uncritically accept the dominant terminology, for example, considering Botswana a "peripheral" country. In reality, the centre-periphery relationship operates on many geographically complex levels. Parts of London are certainly not central to global capitalist accumulation. In contrast the Johannesburg-Pretoria axis of South Africa plays a key role across Southern Africa and beyond. Gaborone, the capital of Botswana, could be considered to be a suburb of this regional centre of capital accumulation.

However, as public sector strikes reappear in Britain, this detailed analysis of the specific approach to public sector reform in Botswana contains important lessons for public sector workers here. It also highlights the common challenges that public sector workers face in both countries.

Theory of a black planet

Christian Høgsbjerg

Minkah Makalani, **In the Cause of Freedom: Radical Black Internationalism from Harlem to London, 1917-1939** (University of North Carolina Press, 2011), £34.50

This work is a very useful if perhaps overly ambitious introduction to what Minkah Makalani calls "the history of inter-war radical black internationalism", a story that "travels from the heights of 1920s Harlem radicalism to the summit of anticolonial activism and black international organising in 1930s London, encompassing the ideas, activities, organisations, and networks of the black radicals who made this history". Taking inspiration from the work of Brent Hayes Edwards—author of *The Practice of Diaspora*—who has been at the forefront of the recent turn in black studies towards a concern with "black internationalism", he has assiduously worked his way through much of the secondary literature and has undertaken a quite staggering amount of archival research internationally over many years—and the result is generally impressive, given Makalani's literary flair and eye for the telling quote or story.

The main original focus on Makalani's research was the African Blood Brotherhood (ABB)—an organisation of up to 8,000 members at its height—that coalesced in 1919 in particular in Harlem around a number of impressive Caribbean intellectuals inspired by the blows the Russian Revolution had struck against racism and imperialism, and critical of the failings of the Socialist Party of America to take race and black self-organisation seriously.

Makalani begins with the ABB, though his method is less to offer us a purely institutional history of organisations such as the ABB and their often strained relationship with what he (problematically) calls "white left" organisations, but more to illuminate such organisational history in a more lively and accessible manner by focusing attention on the political and intellectual evolution of critical black radical activists. I found the resulting account of the rise and fall of the ABB to be a most informative and enlightening read, bringing to life still distinctly neglected figures in radical history such as Hubert Harrison, Cyril V Briggs and Lovett Fort-Whiteman.

Makalani then moves on to the failures and limitations of American Communists with respect to work around race in the 1920s, highlighting the sectarianism that stopped the American Negro Labour Congress fulfilling anything like its potential, and the decision of the Communist International to form the International Trade Union Committee of Negro Workers in 1930. He then turns to international Communism's most famous black leader, the Trinidadian George Padmore, and his break with orthodox Communism in 1933 and the role he subsequently played in London during the 1930s alongside the likes of Amy Ashwood Garvey, CLR James and ITA Wallace-Johnson in forming militant Pan-Africanist organisations like the International African Friends of Ethiopia and the International African Service Bureau (IASB). Makalani concludes by noting that when James met Leon Trotsky in Mexico in 1939 to discuss the strategy and tactics for black liberation in the United States, he rightly suggested that establishing an American branch of the IASB could be a model way for black revolutionaries to organise alongside other campaigners against institutional racism in the US and against colonial oppression internationally.

The strengths of Makalani's work lie in his ability to explore the difficulties faced by those fighting for international black self-organisation and what he calls "inter-colonial" unity in the inter-war period, and how these difficulties (not only due to the short-sighted vision and sectarianism of the "white left" but also rivalries around leadership between Caribbean migrants and "native" black American activists in the context of the US and Caribbean migrants and African migrants in the context of Britain) were not really to any meaningful extent overcome effectively until the formation of the IASB in 1937. The work contains generally accurate and insightful biographical portraits of a whole host of black radicals, many of whose achievements deserve far greater recognition, and though his focus is on "radical black internationalism", Makalani does not overlook the important contribution made by, for example, Indian and Chinese nationalists. His account of the changing visual imagery used by anti-racist and anti-colonial activists was also fascinating.

However, I felt the work was limited somewhat by a failure to effectively contextualise this narrative adequately with respect to the story of what Makalani (again problematically) calls "organised Marxism" and in particular to the internal degeneration of the Russian Revolution during the 1920s followed by the Stalinist counter-revolution of the 1930s—and the consequences of this for international Communism. So when Makalani has Padmore in 1933 outlining "his notion of double revolution: a sequence by which anti-colonial liberation movements would first produce national revolutions against white imperialists, which would then allow colonial proletarian revolutions to emerge against the indigenous bourgeoisie", the idea was not, as Makalani claims "a rather classic Leninist formation". Rather it was a new-fangled concept introduced by the Stalinist bureaucracy in the late 1920s that was a complete break with Lenin's understanding of the strategy and tactics necessary for national liberation. This focused on the importance of independent working class organisation, even in the most economically under-developed countries.

The failure to understand this means that Makalani can't make sense of the real differences over strategy and tactics that did exist between Padmore—who still held to many orthodox Communist perspectives after his break with the Communist International—and the Trotskyist James. Indeed, Makalani's account of James's anti-capitalist and anti-colonialist activism in the 1930s is a little unfair in places, and undermined somewhat by his limited understanding of James's revolutionary Marxist politics, together with an overreliance on the rather sectarian account of James's work in the 1930s by the British Trotskyist John Archer.

More generally speaking, Makalani's categories of "organised Marxism" and "white left" miss out something of the complexity of the relationship of early classical Marxist thought with respect to race, class and colonialism. As Kevin B Anderson has demonstrated in his recent work *Marx at the Margins*, Marx himself—certainly after 1848—was very far from being a "Eurocentric" thinker, while the likes of Lenin and Trotsky were actually remarkably sophisticated and profound "post-colonial" thinkers in many ways, not that it will ever be fashionable in academic circles to say so.

Overall, Makalani has written an important work that brings to light a wealth of information from scattered archives and usefully complements the growing literature on militant anti-colonialism in the inter-war period, seen in recent works by Susan Pennybacker, Carol Polsgrove and Jonathan Derrick. His account of organisations from the ABB and IASB will serve as useful introductions for those who have not previously studied them, while even scholars of these groups will doubtless learn much as well about certain individuals within them that they had not previously known.

Though one might have hoped that Makalani would demonstrate a more nuanced and sophisticated understanding of the left and labour movement (talk of "the leftist conceit of class struggle" seems a little out of place in such a work, particularly given that many of the activists discussed were fervent "class struggle Pan-Africanists"), in general his analysis relating to the struggle by black radical activists to find forms of organisation that were fit for purpose for their heroic fight against white supremacy is most convincing, and will give readers much to ponder for the struggles against the powerful hierarchies of race, class and gender today.

Cultural revelations
Sally Kincaid

Paul Clark, **Youth Culture in China**
(Cambridge University Press, 2012),
£18.99

Paul Clark is a professor in Modern Chinese Popular Culture at the University of Auckland, so there is no doubt this book will end up on the essential reading list for university courses in Chinese culture in the future. This is an extremely well researched book—the notes and bibliography alone take up 30 percent of the entire publication. So this itself will provide a useful starting point for any further studies in modern Chinese culture

Clark sets out to investigate youth culture in China over the last five decades. He focuses on three key years: 1968, 1988 and 2008.

Clark starts by briefly describing the beginning of the Cultural Revolution in 1966 where young people were told to "sweep away the forces of evil". However he gives a far more detailed description of the events of 1968, when Mao needed to restore order, in the cities.

The youth were told to leave the cities and not just to spread the word to the peasants but also to learn from them. This period of the Cultural Revolution allowed youngsters to leave their parental home and travel.

Over 10 million left their families and followed Mao's call to go "up to the mountains and down to the villages". Clark describes the hardship many of these youngsters faced, but also how there was a cultural explosion as these school and college students entertained not only themselves but their peasant hosts. They wrote and performed plays, operas and songs, even setting up cinema screens in the villages.

I found the most interesting section was the way young people are using the internet to try and reduce their alienation from society. Just like in the West there is parallel language developing via text, instant messaging such as QQ or MSN, some of which, Clark points out, does have a political twist. So to invite friends to eat and drink was referred to as *fan fubai* (oppose corruption), as in "let's go and oppose corruption!" He further explains that this is a crafty commentary against the Communist Party's abuse of power at all levels. I was disappointed that Clark did not develop this more, as there are many examples of the way online language is constantly being adapted to get round repressive online censorship.

I was also disappointed with this book as I kept thinking there is more to tell. The historic events in 1989 were almost mentioned as an afterthought.

Clark describes how young people in China are far more likely to watch entertainment programmes on television than news but doesn't explain why there is a lack of interest or trust in the official news in China.

It is not because young people in China are not interested in politics: millions were communicating via Weibo (the Chinese equivalent of Twitter) about the recent US election. They were quoted as saying it was far more interesting than the Chinese election two days before as at least the outcome was uncertain.

Finally, those of you who have ever had the misfortune of having to sit thought *Britain's Got Talent* or *X Factor* on a Saturday night will be pleased to know that there is a Chinese equivalent—*Supergirl*, which 10 percent of the television owning population watch each week. However, unlike Clark, who believes this show adds to the youth culture in China I feel it is the equivalent of suggesting that the introduction of McDonald's and other Western fast food chains has improved their diets.

Pick of the quarter

A masterly analysis of the American presidential election by Mike Davis dominates the excellent new issue of *New Left Review* (II/79).* The article combines a grasp of the complex demographic and sociological trends behind Barack Obama's victory with an eye for the detail of the intense political and ideological struggles on the Republican right (among which is this excellent summary of the brutal essence of politics by one crazed former senior Republican, Dick Armey: "sometimes you're the windshield and sometimes you're the bug"). Davis is clear eyed about Obama—who, he says, regards the Democratic Party "the way a vampire regards its lunch" and "arguably saved Wall Street and General Motors". But the trouble for American capitalism is that the sharp ideological turn to the right by the Republicans shows "the merely wealthy stop[ping] obeying orders from the very rich". Davis's prediction that the Republicans, secure in their gerrymandered stronghold in the House of Representatives, will continue to wage ideological war against Obama has already been confirmed by the failure of the two sides to reach a compromise over reducing the budget deficit.

Other noteworthy articles include an interesting piece on South Korea's political culture by Kevin Gray (who is perhaps overly influenced by the country's left nationalist currents), Adam Tooze's telling review of the final two volumes of Michael Mann's historical sociology of power (which takes him to task for failing properly to integrate the role of imperialism), a generous response to David Graeber's *Debt* by Robin Blackburn,† and Jiwei Xiao's thoughtful reassessment of Michelangelo Antonioni's documentary on China during the Cultural Revolution.

The current *Irish Marxist Review* (volume 2, number 5) contains a number of interesting articles on the history of the Irish workers' movement and the struggle for independence. Paul O'Brien looks back at the Great Lock Out of 1913 in Dublin, while Conor Costick examines the Bureau of Military History, a collection of over 1,700 statements and interviews about struggles in Ireland between 1913 and 1921. Meanwhile, Colm Bryce analyses dissident republicanism and Goretti Horgan reports on the state of loyalism today.‡

The January and February issues of *Monthly Review* contain a couple of interesting pieces on capitalism and ecology. In the January issue, Fred Magdoff unpicks debates about population and natural resource depletion to show how arguments about "overpopulation" obscure the massively skewed global consumption of resources (the richest 10 percent of the world's population account for 59 percent of consumption). While Magdoff makes too many concessions to positions

---

* http://newleftreview.org/II/79/mike-davis-the-last-white-election

† http://newleftreview.org/II/79/robin-blackburn-finance-for-anarchists
‡ All these articles are free to access at www.irishmarxistreview.net/index.php/imr/issue/view/5/showToc

that emphasise sacrifice ("modest living standards"), he nonetheless is clear that it is the systemic imperative of competitive accumulation that is responsible for the degradation of the environment, a problem which can only be solved "with economic and political decisions resolved democratically according to principles consistent with substantive equality among people and a healthy biosphere for all the earth's inhabitants".[*] In the February issue, John Bellamy Foster critically assesses Nasa scientist James Hansen's "exit strategy" from climate change, arguing that "no gradual exit is possible".[†]

The most recent *Historical Materialism* (20.4) was published just as this journal went to press and will be covered in our next issue.

Finally, the Marxists Internet Archive recently added a number of articles originally published in this journal in the mid-1980s, in which John Molyneux,[‡] Sheila McGregor[§] and Lindsey German[¶] debated whether or not working class men benefitted from women's oppression. These were very important debates for the tradition in which this journal stands. We hope their availability online will open them up to a much wider audience involved in contemporary debates around oppression, emancipation and privilege theory.

AC & JJ

---

[*] http://monthlyreview.org/2013/01/01/global-resource-depletion

[†] http://monthlyreview.org/2013/02/01/james-hansen-and-the-climate-change-exit-strategy

[‡] www.marxists.org/history/etol/writers/molyneux/1984/xx/benefits.html and http://www.marxists.org/history/etol/writers/molyneux/1986/xx/benefits.html

[§] www.marxists.org/history/etol/newspape/isj2/1985/no2-030/mcgregor.html

[¶] www.marxists.org/history/etol/writers/german/1986/xx/benefits.html